M000191358

Freedom & Responsibility

Readings for Writers

Edited by Justus Ballard

with additional contributions from Allison Tobey, Jon Boisvert, Alissa Hattman, Laura Scott, Layli Liss, Sam Schwartz, Magdalen Powers, and Tammy Jabin

Freedom & Responsibility

ISBN: 978-1-943536-14-6

© 2016 by Chemeketa Community College. All rights reserved.

Chemeketa Press

Chemeketa Press is a nonprofit publishing endeavor at Chemeketa Community College that works in partnership with the faculty, staff, and students to develop and publish affordable and effective alternatives to commercial textbooks. All proceeds from the sale of this book will be used to develop new textbooks.

Publisher: Tim Rogers
Managing Editor: Steve Richardson
Production Editor: Brian Mosher
Design Manager: Kristen MacDonald
Cover Design: Cierra Maher
Cover Photo: © 2014 by Cierra Maher. Used by permission.

Additional contributions to the design and publication of this textbook came from students in the Visual Communications program at Chemeketa Community College.

Text Acknowledgments

Susan B. Anthony, "Is It a Crime for a Citizen of the United States to Vote?"
Excerpted from the 1898 edition of *The Life and Work of Susan B. Anthony including Public Addresses, Her Own Letters, and Many from Her Contemporaries During Fifty Years (Vol. 2): A Story of the Evolution of the Status of Woman* (Indianapolis: The Hollenbeck Press) by Ida Husted Harper. The transcript of this speech is in the public domain because it was published before 1923.

Marcus Aurelius, "On Getting Out of Bed"
Excerpted and adapted from Book 5 of the 1890 edition of *The Meditations of the Emperor Marcus Aurelius Antoninus* (New York and London: The Chesterfield Society), translated by George Long. This text is in the public domain because both it and its translation were published before 1923.

Additional text acknowledgments appear on pages 317 to 322 and constitute an extension of the copyright page.

Contents

Is It a Crime for a Citizen of the United States to Vote?

by Susan B. Anthony

Susan Brownell Anthony (1820–1906) was an abolitionist, an educational reformer, a labor activist, and a temperance worker, but she is best known for her work promoting women's rights. After her arrest for voting illegally in the 1872 federal election, Anthony undertook a speaking tour in which she delivered this speech more than two dozen times.

Friends and Fellow-citizens:

I stand before you tonight, under indictment for the alleged crime of having voted at the last presidential election, without having a lawful right to vote. It shall be my work this evening to prove to you that in thus voting, I not only committed no crime, but, instead, simply exercised my citizen's right, guaranteed to me and all United States citizens by the national constitution, beyond the power of any state to deny.

Our democratic-republican government is based on the idea of the natural right of every individual member thereof to a voice and a vote in making and executing the laws. We assert the province of government to be to secure the people in the enjoyment of their unalienable rights. We throw to the winds the old dogma that governments can give rights. Before governments were organized, no one denies that each individual possessed the right to protect his own life, liberty, and property. And when 100 or 1,000,000 people enter into a free government, they do not barter away their natural rights; they simply pledge themselves to protect each other in the enjoyment of them, through prescribed judicial and legislative tribunals. They agree to abandon the methods of brute force in the adjustment of their differences, and adopt those of civilization.

Nor can you find a word in any of the grand documents left us by the fathers that assumes for government the power to create or to confer rights. The Declaration of Independence, the United States Constitution, the constitutions of the several states and the organic laws of the territories, all alike propose to protect the people in the exercise of their God-given rights. Not one of them pretends to bestow rights:

> All men are created equal, and endowed by their Creator with certain unalienable rights. Among these are life, liberty and the pursuit of happiness. That to secure these, governments are instituted among men, deriving their just powers from the consent of the governed.

5 Here is no shadow of government authority over rights, nor exclusion of any from their full and equal enjoyment. Here is pronounced the right of all men — and "consequently," as the Quaker preacher said, "of all women" — to a voice in the government. And here, in this very first paragraph of the Declaration, is the assertion of the natural right of all to the ballot; for, how can "the consent of the governed" be given, if the right to vote be denied? Again:

> That whenever any form of government becomes destructive of these ends, it is the right of the people to alter or abolish it, and to institute a new government, laying its foundations on such principles, and organizing its powers in such forms as to them shall seem most likely to effect their safety and happiness.

Surely, the right of the whole people to vote is here clearly implied. For however destructive in their happiness this government might become, a disfranchised class could neither alter nor abolish it, nor institute a new one, except by the old brute force method of insurrection and rebellion. One-half of the people of this nation today are utterly powerless to blot from the statute books an unjust law, or to write there a new and a just one. The women, dissatisfied as they are with this form of government, that enforces taxation without representation, that compels them to obey laws to which they have never given their consent, that imprisons and hangs them without a trial by a jury of their peers, that robs them, in marriage, of the custody of their own persons, wages and children — are this half of the people left wholly at the mercy of the other half, in direct violation of the spirit and letter of the declarations of the framers of this government, every one of which was based on the immutable principle of equal rights to all? By those declarations, kings, priests, popes, aristocrats, were all alike dethroned and placed on a common level politically with the lowliest born subject or serf. By them, too, we, as such, were deprived of their divine right to rule, and placed on a political level with women. By the practice of those declarations all class and caste distinction will be abolished; and slave, serf, plebeian, wife, woman, all alike, bound from their subject position to the proud platform of equality.

The preamble of the federal Constitution says:

> We, the people of the United States, in order to form a more perfect union, establish justice, insure domestic tranquility, provide for the common defense, promote the general welfare and secure the blessings of liberty to ourselves and our posterity, do ordain and established this constitution for the United States of America.

It was we, the people, not we, the white male citizens, nor yet we, the male citizens, but we, the whole people, who formed this Union. And we formed it, not to give the blessings of liberty, but to secure them; not to the half of ourselves and the half of our posterity, but to the whole people — women as well as men. And it is downright mockery to talk to women of their enjoyment of the blessings of liberty while they are denied the use of the only means of securing them provided by this democratic-republican government — the ballot. . . .

For any State to make sex a qualification that must ever result in the disfranchisement of one entire half of the people, is to pass a bill of attainder, or an *ex post facto* law, and is therefore a violation of the supreme law of the land. By it, the blessings of liberty are forever withheld from women and their female posterity. To them, this government has no just powers derived from the consent of the governed. To them this government is not a democracy. It is not a republic. It is an odious aristocracy, a hateful oligarchy of sex. The most hateful aristocracy ever established on the face of the globe. An oligarchy of wealth, where the rich govern the poor; an oligarchy of learning, where the educated govern the ignorant; or even an oligarchy of race, where the Saxon rules the African, might be endured; but this oligarchy of sex, which makes father, brothers, husband, sons, the oligarchs over the mother and sisters, the wife and daughters of every household; which ordains all men sovereigns, all women subjects, carries dissension, discord and rebellion into every home of the nation. And this most odious aristocracy exists, too, in the face of Section 4, of Article 4, which says: "The United States shall guarantee to every State in the Union a republican form of government."

10 What, I ask you, is the distinctive difference between the inhabitants of a monarchical and those of a republican form of government, save that in the monarchical the people are subjects, helpless, powerless, bound to obey laws made by superiors — while in the republican, the people are citizens, individual sovereigns, all clothed with equal power, to make and unmake both their laws and law makers? The moment

you deprive a person of his right to a voice in the government, you degrade him from the status of a citizen of the republic to that of a subject, and it matters very little to him whether his monarch be an individual tyrant, as is the Czar of Russia, or a 15,000,000 headed monster, as here in the United States; he is a powerless subject, serf or slave; not a free and independent citizen in any sense.

But, is urged, the use of the masculine pronouns "he," "his," and "him," in all the constitutions and laws, is proof that only men were meant to be included in their provisions. If you insist on this version of the letter of the law, we shall insist that you be consistent, and accept the other horn of the dilemma, which would compel you to exempt women from taxation for the support of the government, and from penalties for the violation of laws. . . .

In all the penalties and burdens of the government (except the military), women are reckoned as citizens, equally with men. Also, in all privileges and immunities, save those of the jury box and ballot box, the two fundamental privileges on which rest all the others. The United States government not only taxes, fines, imprisons and hangs women, but it allows them to pre-empt lands, register ships, and take out passport and naturalization papers. Not only does the law permit single women and widows to the right of naturalization, but Section 2 says: "A married woman may be naturalized without the concurrence of her husband." (I wonder the fathers were not afraid of creating discord in the families of foreigners); and again: "When an alien, having complied with the law, and declared his intention to become a citizen, dies before he is actually naturalized, his widow and children shall be considered citizens, entitled to all rights and privileges as such, on taking the required oath." If a foreign born woman by becoming a naturalized citizen, is entitled to all the rights and privileges of citizenship, is not a native born woman, by her national citizenship, possessed of equal rights and privileges?. . .

Though the words persons, people, inhabitants, electors, citizens, are all used indiscriminately in the national and state constitutions, there was always a conflict of opinion, prior to the war, as to whether they were synonymous terms, as for instance:

> No person shall be a representative who shall not have been seven years a citizen, and who shall not, when elected, be an inhabitant of that state in which he is chosen. No person shall be a senator who shall not have been a citizen of the United States, and an inhabitant of that state in which he is chosen.

But, whatever there was for a doubt, under the old regime, the adoption of the Fourteenth Amendment settled that question forever, in its first sentence: "All persons born or naturalized in the United States and subject to the jurisdiction thereof, are citizens of the United States and of the state wherein they reside."

15 And the second settles the equal status of all persons — all citizens:

> No states shall make or enforce any law which shall abridge the privileges or immunities of citizens; nor shall any state deprive any person of life, liberty or property, without due process of law, nor deny to any person within its jurisdiction the equal protection of the laws.

The only question left to be settled, now, is: Are women persons? And I hardly believe any of our opponents will have the hardihood to say they are not. Being persons, then, women are citizens, and no state has a right to make any new law, or to enforce any old law, that shall abridge their privileges or immunities. Hence, every discrimination against women in the constitutions and laws of the several states is today null and void, precisely as is every one against negroes.

On Getting Out of Bed

by Marcus Aurelius

Marcus Aurelius (121–180 CE) was Emperor of Rome from 161 to 180. This text comes from a translation of Book 5 of Meditations, *a collection of writings in the form of a personal notebook. It is not likely that Aurelius intended these meditations to be published but rather that he used them as a source for personal guidance and self-improvement. One recurring theme in the book concerns the ideas of Stoic philosopher Epictetus. Stoics believed that destructive emotions were caused by errors in judgment. In order to achieve a well-balanced life, individuals must work to improve their morals and ethics.*

In the morning, when you rise unwillingly, let this thought be present — I am rising to do the work of a human being. Why then am I dissatisfied if I am going to do the things for which I exist and for which I was brought into the world? Or have I been made for this, to lie in bed and keep myself warm?

"But this is so pleasant!"

Do you exist then to take your pleasure, and not at all for action or hard work? Do you not see how all other things in the world are — all trees and plants, sparrows and ants, spiders and bees? They are all working together to put in order their various parts of the universe. And are you unwilling to do the work of a human being? Do you hold back from doing the work appropriate for your nature?

"But one must rest, too!"

Rest is necessary, but nature has set boundaries for this, too. 5
She has set boundaries both for eating and drinking, yet you go beyond those boundaries, beyond what is sufficient. However, in your actions, this is not so. You stop short of what you can

do. Thus you do not love yourself, for if you did, you would love your human nature and its will.

Others — as many as take pleasure in their trade and profession — will exhaust themselves for that work. But you value your own nature less than the carpenter values his craft, less than the dancer values his dancing, less than the greedy man values his money, less than the vain man values his applause. These people, when they have a strong attraction to a thing, choose to go without food or sleep for the sake of the things they care about. Do actions taken for the common good of human society appear more vile to you or less worthy of your respect and labor?

The Bill of Rights

On June 8, 1789, James Madison proposed a bill to the United States House of Representatives consisting of nine articles and a series of proposed amendments to the Constitution. Some of this bill was later submitted to the first U.S. Congress and, on December 15, 1791, Articles 3 through 12 were ratified by a required number of states and became the first ten amendments to the Constitution. These ten amendments are collectively known as the Bill of Rights. They express freedoms not directly stated in the main body of the Constitution.

The Preamble to The Bill of Rights

Congress of the United States begun and held at the City of New-York, on Wednesday the fourth of March, one thousand seven hundred and eighty nine.

THE Conventions of a number of the States, having at the time of their adopting the Constitution, expressed a desire, in order to prevent misconstruction or abuse of its powers, that further declaratory and restrictive clauses should be added: And as extending the ground of public confidence in the Government, will best ensure the beneficent ends of its institution.

RESOLVED by the Senate and House of Representatives of the United States of America, in Congress assembled, two thirds of both Houses concurring, that the following Articles be proposed to the Legislatures of the several States, as amendments to the Constitution of the United States, all, or any of which Articles, when ratified by three fourths of the said Legislatures, to be valid to all intents and purposes, as part of the said Constitution; viz.

ARTICLES in addition to, and Amendment of the Constitution of the United States of America, proposed by Congress, and ratified by the Legislatures of the several States, pursuant to the fifth Article of the original Constitution.

Amendment I

Congress shall make no law respecting an establishment of religion, or prohibiting the free exercise thereof; or abridging the freedom of speech, or of the press; or the right of the people peaceably to assemble, and to petition the Government for a redress of grievances.

Amendment II

A well regulated Militia, being necessary to the security of a free State, the right of the people to keep and bear Arms, shall not be infringed.

Amendment III

No Soldier shall, in time of peace be quartered in any house, without the consent of the Owner, nor in time of war, but in a manner to be prescribed by law.

Amendment IV

The right of the people to be secure in their persons, houses, papers, and effects, against unreasonable searches and seizures, shall not be violated, and no Warrants shall issue, but upon probable cause, supported by Oath or affirmation, and particularly describing the place to be searched, and the persons or things to be seized.

Amendment V

No person shall be held to answer for a capital, or otherwise infamous crime, unless on a presentment or indictment of a Grand Jury, except in cases arising in the land or naval forces, or in the Militia, when in actual service in time of War or public danger; nor shall any person be subject for the same offence to be twice put in jeopardy of life or limb; nor shall be compelled in any criminal case to be a witness against himself, nor be deprived of life, liberty, or property, without due process of law; nor shall private property be taken for public use, without just compensation.

Amendment VI

In all criminal prosecutions, the accused shall enjoy the right to a speedy and public trial, by an impartial jury of the State and district wherein the crime shall have been committed, which district shall have been previously ascertained by law, and to be informed of the nature and cause of the accusation; to be confronted with the witnesses against him; to have compulsory process for obtaining witnesses in his favor, and to have the Assistance of Counsel for his defence.

Amendment VII

In Suits at common law, where the value in controversy shall exceed twenty dollars, the right of trial by jury shall be preserved, and no fact tried by a jury, shall be otherwise re-examined in any Court of the United States, than according to the rules of the common law.

Amendment VIII

Excessive bail shall not be required, nor excessive fines imposed, nor cruel and unusual punishments inflicted.

Amendment IX

The enumeration in the Constitution, of certain rights, shall not be construed to deny or disparage others retained by the people.

Amendment X

The powers not delegated to the United States by the Constitution, nor prohibited by it to the States, are reserved to the States respectively, or to the people.

Crime and Criminals: An Address to the Prisoners in the Chicago County Jail

by Clarence Darrow

Clarence Seward Darrow (1857–1938) was an American lawyer and civil libertarian. Darrow is known for defending such notable cases as teenage "thrill killers" Leopold and Loeb, and John T. Scopes, a substitute high-school teacher who was famously charged and fined for teaching human evolution in a public school in what became known as the Scopes Monkey Trial.

Preface

This address is a stenographic report of a talk made to the prisoners in the Chicago jail. Some of my good friends have insisted that while my theories are true, I should not have given them to the inmates of a jail.

Realizing the force of the suggestion that the truth should not be spoken to all people, I have caused these remarks to be printed on rather good paper and in a somewhat expensive form. In this way the truth does not become cheap and vulgar, and is only placed before those whose intelligence and affluence will prevent their being influenced by it.

Crime and Criminals

If I looked at jails and crimes and prisoners in the way the ordinary person does, I should not speak on this subject to you. The reason I talk to you on the question of crime, its cause and cure, is because I really do not in the least believe in crime. There is no such thing as a crime as the word is generally understood. I do not believe there is any sort of distinction between the real moral condition of the people in and out of jail. One is just as good as the other. The people here can no more help being here than the people outside can avoid being outside. I do not believe that people are in jail because they deserve to be. They are in jail simply because they cannot avoid it on account of circumstances which are entirely beyond their control and for which they are in no way responsible. I suppose a great many people on the outside would say I was doing you harm if they should hear what I say to you this afternoon, but you cannot be hurt a great deal anyway, so it will not matter. Good people outside would say that I was really teaching you things that were calculated to injure society, but it's worth while now and then to hear something different from what you ordinarily get from preachers and the like. These will tell you that you should be good and then you will get rich and be happy. Of course we know that people do not get rich by being good, and that is the reason why so many of you people try to get rich some other way, only you do not understand how to do it quite as well as the fellow outside.

There are people who think that everything in this world is an accident. But really there is no such thing as an accident. A great many folks admit that many of the people in jail ought not to be there, and many who are outside ought to be in. I think none of them ought to be here. There ought to be no jails, and if it were not for the fact that the people on the outside are so grasping and heartless in their dealings with the people on the inside, there would be no such institution as jails.

I do not want you to believe that I think all you people here 5
are angels. I do not think that. You are people of all kinds, all of you doing the best you can, and that is evidently not very

well — you are people of all kinds and conditions and under all circumstances. In one sense everybody is equally good and equally bad. We all do the best we can under the circumstances. But as to the exact things for which you are sent here, some of you are guilty and did the particular act because you needed the money. Some of you did it because you are in the habit of doing it, and some of you because you are born to it, and it comes to be as natural as it does, for instance, for me to be good.

Most of you probably have nothing against me, and most of you would treat me the same as any other person would; probably better than some of the people on the outside would treat me, because you think I believe in you and they know I do not believe in them. While you would not have the least thing against me in the world you might pick my pockets. I do not think all of you would, but I think some of you would. You would not have anything against me, but that's your profession, a few of you. Some of the rest of you, if my doors were unlocked, might come in if you saw anything you wanted — not out of malice to me, but because that is your trade. There is no doubt there are quite a number of people in this jail who would pick my pockets. And still I know this, that when I get outside pretty nearly everybody picks my pocket. There may be some of you who would hold up a man on the street, if you did not happen to have something else to do, and needed the money; but when I want to light my house or my office the gas company holds me up. They charge me one dollar for something that is worth twenty-five cents, and still all these people are good people; they are pillars of society and support the churches, and they are respectable.

When I ride on the street cars, I am held up — I pay five cents for a ride that is worth two and a half cents, simply because a body of men have bribed the city council and the legislature, so that all the rest of us have to pay tribute to them.

If I do not wish to fall into the clutches of the gas trust and choose to burn oil instead of gas, then good Mr. Rockefeller holds me up, and he uses a certain portion of his money to build universities and support churches which are engaged in telling us how to be good.

Some of you are here for obtaining property under false pretenses — yet I pick up a great Sunday paper and read the advertisements of a merchant prince — "Shirt waists for 39 cents, marked down from $3.00."

When I read the advertisements in the paper I see they are all lies. When I want to get out and find a place to stand anywhere on the face of the earth, I find that it has all been taken up long ago before I came here, and before you came here, and somebody says, "Get off, swim into the lake, fly into the air; go anywhere, but get off." That is because these people have the police and they have the jails and judges and the lawyers and the soldiers and all the rest of them to take care of the earth and drive everybody off that comes in their way.

A great many people will tell you that all this is true, but that it does not excuse you. These facts do not excuse some fellow who reaches into my pocket and takes out a five dollar bill; the fact that the gas company bribes the members of the legislature from year to year, and fixes the law, so that all you people are compelled to be "fleeced" whenever you deal with them; the fact that the street car companies and the gas companies have control of the streets and the fact that the landlords own all the earth, they say, has nothing to do with you.

Let us see whether there is any connection between the crimes of the respectable classes and your presence in the jail. Many of you people are in jail because you have really committed burglary. Many of you, because you have stolen something; in the meaning of the law, you have taken some other person's property. Some of you have entered a store and carried off a pair of shoes because you did not have the price. Possibly some of you have committed murder. I cannot tell what all of you did. There are a great many people here who have done some of these things who really do not know themselves why they did them. I think I know why you did them — every one of you; you did these things because you were bound to do them. It looked to you at the time as if you had a chance to do them or not, as you saw fit, but still after all you had no choice. There may be people here who had some money in their pockets and who still went out and got some more money in a way society forbids. Now you may not yourselves see exactly why it was you did this thing, but if you look at the question deeply enough and carefully enough you would see that there were circumstances that drove you to do exactly the thing which you did. You could not help it any more than we outside can help taking the positions that we take. The reformers who tell you to be good and you will be happy, and the people on the outside who have property to protect — they think that the only way to do it is by building jails and locking you up in cells on week days and praying for you Sundays.

I think that all of this has nothing whatever to do with right conduct. I think it is very easily seen what has to do with right conduct. Some so-called criminals — and I will use this word because it is handy, it means nothing to me — I speak of the criminals who get caught as distinguished from the criminals who catch them — some of these so-called criminals are in jail for the first offenses, but nine-tenths of you are in jail because you did not have a good lawyer and of course you did not have a good lawyer because you did not have enough money to pay a good lawyer. There is no very great danger of a rich man going to jail.

Some of you may be here for the first time. If we would open the doors and let you out, and leave the laws as they are today, some of you would be back tomorrow. This is about as good a place as you can get anyway. There are many people here who are so in the habit of coming that they would not know where else to go. There are people who are born with the tendency to break into jail every chance they get, and they cannot avoid it. You cannot figure out your life and see why it was, but still there is a reason for it, and if we were all wise and knew all the facts we could figure it out.

In the first place, there are a good many more people who 15
go to jail in the winter time than in summer. Why is this? Is it because people are more wicked in winter? No, it is because the coal trust begins to get in its grip in the winter. A few gentlemen take possession of the coal, and unless the people will pay \$7 or \$8 a ton for something that is worth \$3, they will have to freeze. Then there is nothing to do but break into jail, and so there are many more in jail in the winter than in summer. It costs more for gas in the winter because the nights are longer, and people go to jail to save gas bills. The jails are electric lighted. You may not know it, but these economic laws are working all the time, whether we know it or do not know it.

There are more people go to jail in hard times than in good times — few people comparatively go to jail except when they are hard up. They go to jail because they have no other place to go. They may not know why, but it is true all the same. People are not more wicked in hard times. That is not the reason. The fact is true all over the world that in hard times more people go to jail than in good times, and in winter more people go to jail than in summer. Of course it is pretty hard times for people who go to jail at any time. The people who go to jail are almost always poor people — people who have no other place to live first and last. When times are hard then you find large numbers of people who go to jail who would not otherwise be in jail.

Long ago Mr. Buckle, who was a great philosopher and historian, collected facts and he showed that the number of people who are arrested increased just as the price of food increased.

When they put up the price of gas ten cents a thousand I do not know who will go to jail, but I do know that a certain number of people will go. When the meat combine raises the price of beef I do not know who is going to jail, but I know that a large number of people are bound to go. Whenever the Standard Oil Company raises the price of oil, I know that a certain number of girls who are seamstresses, and who work after night long hours for somebody else, will be compelled to go out on the streets and ply another trade, and I know that Mr. Rockefeller and his associates are responsible and not the poor girls in the jails.

First and last, people are sent to jail because they are poor. Sometimes, as I say, you may not need money at the particular time, but you wish to have thrifty forehanded habits, and do not always wait until you are in absolute want. Some of you people are perhaps plying the trade, the profession, which is called burglary. No man in his right senses will go into a strange house in the dead of night and prowl around with a dark lantern through unfamiliar rooms and take chances of his life if he has plenty of the good things of the world in his own home. You would not take any such chances as that. If a man had clothes in his clothes-press and beefsteak in his pantry, and money in the bank, he would not navigate around nights in houses where he knows nothing about the premises whatever. It always requires experience and education for this profession, and people who fit themselves for it are no more to blame than I am for being a lawyer. A man would not hold up another man on the street if he had plenty of money in his own pocket. He might do it if he had one dollar or two dollars, but he wouldn't if he had as much money as Mr. Rockefeller has. Mr. Rockefeller has a great deal better hold-up game than that.

The more that is taken from the poor by the rich, who have the chance to take it, the more poor people there are who are compelled to resort to these means for a livelihood. They may not understand it, they may not think so at once, but after all they are driven into that line of employment.

There is a bill before the legislature of this State to punish 20
kidnapping of children with death. We have wise members of the legislature. They know the gas trust when they see it and they always see it — they can furnish light enough to be seen, and this legislature thinks it is going to stop kidnapping of children by making a law punishing kidnappers of children with death. I don't believe in kidnapping children, but the legislature is all wrong. Kidnapping children is not a crime, it is a profession. It has been developed with the times. It has been developed with our modern industrial conditions. There are many ways of making money — many new ways that our ancestors knew nothing about. Our ancestors knew nothing about a billion dollar trust; and here comes some poor fellow who has no other trade and he discovers the profession of kidnapping children.

This crime is born, not because people are bad; people don't kidnap other people's children because they want the children or because they are devilish, but because they see a chance to get some money out of it. You cannot cure this crime by passing a law punishing by death kidnappers of children. There is one way to cure it. There is one way to cure all these offenses, and that is to give the people a chance to live. There is no other way, and there never was any other way since the world began, and the world is so blind and stupid that it will not see. If every man and woman and child in the world had a chance to make a decent, fair, honest living, there would be no jails, and no lawyers and no courts. There might be some persons here or there with some peculiar formation of their brain, like Rockefeller, who would do these things simply to be doing them; but they would be very, very few, and those should be sent to a hospital and treated, and not sent to jail, and they would entirely disappear in the second generation, or at least in the third generation. I am not talking pure theory. I will just give you two or three illustrations.

The English people once punished criminals by sending them away. They would load them on a ship and export them to Australia. England was owned by lords and nobles and rich people. They owned the whole earth over there, and the other people had to stay in the streets. They could not get a decent living. They used to take their criminals and send them to Australia — I mean the class of criminals who got caught. When these criminals got over there, and nobody else had come, they had the whole continent to run over, and so they could raise sheep and furnish their own meat, which is easier than stealing it; these criminals then became decent, respectable people because they had a chance to live. They did not commit any crimes. They were just like the English people who sent them there, only better. And in the second generation the descendants of those criminals were as good and respectable a class of people as there were on the face of the earth, and then they began building churches and jails themselves.

A portion of this country was settled in the same way, landing prisoners down on the southern coast; but when they got here and had a whole continent to run over and plenty of chances to make a living, they became respectable citizens, making their own living just like any other citizen in the world; but finally these descendants of the English aristocracy, who sent the people over to Australia, found out they were getting rich, and so they went over to get possession of the earth as they always do, and they organized land syndicates and got control of the land and ores, and then they had just as many criminals in Australia as they did in England. It was not because the world had grown bad; it was because the earth had been taken away from the people.

Some of you people have lived in the country. It's prettier than it is here. And if you have ever lived on a farm you understand that if you put a lot of cattle in a field, when the pasture is short they will jump over the fence; but put them in a good field where there is plenty of pasture, and they will be law-abiding cattle to the end of time. The human animal is just like the rest of the animals, only a little more so. The same thing that governs in the one governs in the other. 25

Everybody makes his living along the lines of least resistance. A wise man who comes into a country early sees a great undeveloped land. For instance, our rich men twenty-five years ago saw that Chicago was small and knew a lot of people would come here and settle, and they readily saw that if they had all the land around here it would be worth a good deal, so they grabbed the land. You cannot be a landlord because somebody has got it all. You must find some other calling. In England and Ireland and Scotland less than five percent own all the land there is, and the people are bound to stay there on any kind of terms the landlords give. They must live the best they can, so they develop all these various professions — burglary, picking pockets and the like.

Again, people find all sorts of ways of getting rich. These are diseases like everything else. You look at people getting rich, organizing trusts, and making a million dollars, and somebody gets the disease and he starts out. He catches it just as a man catches the mumps or the measles; he is not to blame, it is in the air. You will find men speculating beyond their means, because the mania of money-getting is taking possession of them. It is simply a disease; nothing more, nothing less. You cannot avoid catching it; but the fellows who have control of the earth have the advantage of you. See what the law is; when these men get control of things, they make the laws. They do not make the laws to protect anybody; courts are not instruments of justice; when your case gets into court it will make little difference whether you are guilty or innocent; but it's better if you have a smart lawyer. And you cannot have a smart lawyer unless you have money. First and last it's a question of money. Those men who own the earth make the laws to protect what they have. They fix up a sort of fence or pen around what they have, and they fix the law so the fellow on the outside cannot get in. The laws are really organized for the protection of the men who rule the world. They were never organized or enforced to do justice. We have no system for doing justice, not the slightest in the world.

Let me illustrate: Take the poorest person in this room. If the community had provided a system of doing justice the poorest person in this room would have as good a lawyer as the richest, would he not? When you went into court you would have just as long a trial, and just as fair a trial as the richest person in Chicago. Your case would not be tried in fifteen or twenty minutes, whereas it would take fifteen days to get through with a rich man's case.

Then if you were rich and were beaten your case would be taken to the Appellate Court. A poor man cannot take his case to the Appellate Court; he has not the price; and then to the Supreme Court, and if he were beaten there he might perhaps go to the United States Supreme Court. And he might die of old age before he got into jail. If you are poor, it's a quick job. You are almost known to be guilty, else you would not be there. Why should anyone be in the criminal court if he were not guilty? He would not be there if he could be anywhere else. The officials have no time to look after these cases. The people who are on the outside, who are running banks and building churches and making jails, they have no time to examine 600 or 700 prisoners each year to see whether they are guilty or innocent. If the courts were organized to promote justice the people would elect somebody to defend all these criminals, somebody as smart as the prosecutor — and give him as many detectives and as many assistants to help, and pay as much money to defend you as to prosecute you. We have a very able man for State's Attorney, and he has many assistants, detectives and policemen without end, and judges to hear the cases — everything handy.

Most of our criminal code consists in offenses against property. People are sent to jail because they have committed a crime against property. It is of very little consequence whether one hundred people more or less go to jail who ought not to go — you must protect property, because in this world property is of more importance than anything else.

How is it done? These people who have property fix it so they can protect what they have. When somebody commits a crime it does not follow that he has done something that is morally wrong. The man on the outside who has committed no crime may have done something. For instance: to take all the coal in the United States and raise the price two dollars or three dollars when there is no need of it, and thus kills thousands of babies and send thousands of people to the poorhouse and tens of thousands to jail, as is done every year in the United States — this is a greater crime than all the people in our jails ever committed, but the law does not punish it. Why? Because the fellows who control the earth make the laws. If you and I had the making of the laws, the first thing we would do would be to punish the fellow who gets control of the earth. Nature put this coal in the ground for me as well as for them and nature made the prairies up here to raise wheat for me as well as for them, and then the great railroad companies came along and fenced it up.

Most all of the crimes for which we are punished are property crimes. There are a few personal crimes, like murder — but they are very few. The crimes committed are mostly against property. If this punishment is right the criminals must have a lot of property. How much money is there in this crowd? And yet you are all here for crimes against property. The people up and down the Lake Shore have not committed crime, still they have so much property they don't know what to do with it. It is perfectly plain why these people have not committed crimes against property; they make the laws and therefore do not need to break them. And in order for you to get some property you are obliged to break the rules of the game. I don't know but what some of you may have had a very nice chance to get rich by carrying the hod for one dollar a day, twelve hours. Instead of taking that nice, easy profession, you are a burglar. If you had been given a chance to be a banker you would rather follow that. Some of you may have had a chance to work as a switchman on a railroad where you know, according to statistics, that you cannot live and keep all your limbs more than seven years, and you get fifty dollars a month for taking your lives in your hands, and instead of taking that lucrative position you choose to be a sneak thief, or something like that. Some of you made that sort of choice. I don't know which I would take if I was reduced to this choice. I have an easier choice.

I will guarantee to take from this jail, or any jail in the world, five hundred men who have been the worst criminals and law breakers who ever got into jail, and I will go down to our lowest streets and take five hundred of the most hardened prostitutes, and go out somewhere where there is plenty of land, and will give them a chance to make a living, and they will be as good people as the average in the community.

There is a remedy for the sort of condition we see here. The world never finds it out, or when it does find it out it does not enforce it. You may pass a law punishing every person with death for burglary, and it will make no difference. Men will commit it just the same. In England there was a time when one hundred different offenses were punishable with death, and it made no difference. The English people strangely found out that so fast as they repealed the severe penalties and so fast as they did away with punishing men by death, crime decreased instead of increased; that the smaller the penalty the fewer the crimes.

Hanging men in our county jails does not prevent murder. It makes murderers. 35

And this has been the history of the world. It's easy to see how to do away with what we call crime. It is not so easy to do it. I will tell you how to do it. It can be done by giving the people a chance to live — by destroying special privileges. So long as big criminals can get the coal fields, so long as the big criminals have control of the city council and get the public streets for street cars and gas rights, this is bound to send thousands of poor people to jail. So long as men are allowed to monopolize all the earth, and compel others to live on such terms as these men see fit to make, then you are bound to get into jail.

The only way in the world to abolish crime and criminals is to abolish the big ones and the little ones together. Make fair conditions of life. Give men a chance to live. Abolish the right of private ownership of land, abolish monopoly, make the world partners in production, partners in the good things of life. Nobody would steal if he could get something of his own some easier way. Nobody will commit burglary when he has a house full. No girl will go out on the streets when she has a comfortable place at home. The man who owns a sweatshop or a department store may not be to blame himself for the condition of his girls, but when he pays them five dollars, three dollars, and two dollars a week, I wonder where he thinks they will get the rest of their money to live. The only way to cure these conditions is by equality. There should be no jails. They do not accomplish what they pretend to accomplish. If you would wipe them out, there would be no more criminals than now. They terrorize nobody. They are a blot upon civilization, and a jail is an evidence of the lack of charity of the people on the outside who make the jails and fill them with the victims of their greed.

Learning to Read and Write

by Frederick Douglass

Frederick Augustus Washington Bailey (1818–1895) was born into slavery in Maryland around 1818. In 1838, he escaped and later took the last name of Douglass to protect his identity. Douglass became a leading figure in the abolitionist movement, a celebrated orator, and a bestselling author. His 1845 autobiography, Narrative of the Life of Frederick Douglass, an American Slave, *describes his experiences in slavery. "Learning to Read and Write" is excerpted from this work.*

I lived in Master Hugh's family about seven years. During this time, I succeeded in learning to read and write. In accomplishing this, I was compelled to resort to various stratagems. I had no regular teacher. My mistress, who had kindly commenced to instruct me, had, in compliance with the advice and direction of her husband, not only ceased to instruct, but had set her face against my being instructed by anyone else. It is due, however, to my mistress to say of her, that she did not adopt this course of treatment immediately. She at first lacked the depravity indispensable to shutting me up in mental darkness. It was at least necessary for her to have some training in the exercise of irresponsible power, to make her equal to the task of treating me as though I were a brute.

My mistress was, as I have said, a kind and tender hearted woman; and in the simplicity of her soul she commenced, when I first went to live with her, to treat me as she supposed one human being ought to treat another. In entering upon the duties of a slaveholder, she did not seem to perceive that

I sustained to her the relation of a mere chattel, and that for her to treat me as a human being was not only wrong, but dangerously so. Slavery proved as injurious to her as it did to me. When I went there, she was a pious, warm, and tender hearted woman. There was no sorrow or suffering for which she had not a tear. She had bread for the hungry, clothes for the naked, and comfort for every mourner that came within her reach. Slavery soon proved its ability to divest her of these heavenly qualities. Under its influence, the tender heart became stone, and the lamb like disposition gave way to one of tiger like fierceness. The first step in her downward course was in her ceasing to instruct me. She now commenced to practice her husband's precepts. She finally became even more violent in her opposition than her husband himself. She was not satisfied with simply doing as well as he had commanded; she seemed anxious to do better. Nothing seemed to make her more angry than to see me with a newspaper. She seemed to think that here lay the danger. I have had her rush at me with a face made all up of fury, and snatch from me a newspaper, in a manner that fully revealed her apprehension. She was an apt woman; and a little experience soon demonstrated, to her satisfaction, that education and slavery were incompatible with each other.

From this time I was most narrowly watched. If I was in a separate room any considerable length of time, I was sure to be suspected of having a book, and was at once called to give an account of myself. All this, however, was too late. The first step had been taken. Mistress, in teaching me the alphabet, had given me the inch, and no precaution could prevent me from taking the ell.

The plan which I adopted, and the one by which I was most successful, was that of making friends of all the little white boys whom I met in the street. As many of these as I could, I converted into teachers. With their kindly aid, obtained at different times and in different places, I finally succeeded in learning to read. When I was sent to errands, I always took my book with me, and by doing one part of my errand quickly, I found time to get a lesson before my return. I used also to carry bread with me, enough of which was always in the house, and to which I was always welcome; for I was much better off in this regard than many of the poor white children in our neighborhood. This bread I used to bestow upon the hungry little urchins, who, in return, would give me that more valuable bread of knowledge. I am strongly tempted to give the names of two or three of those little boys, as a testimonial of the gratitude and affection I bear them; but prudence forbids not that it would injure me, — but it might embarrass them; for it is almost an unpardonable offense to teach slaves to read in this Christian country. It is enough to say of the dear little fellows, that they lived on Philpot Street, very near Durgin and Bailey's shipyard. I used to talk this matter of slavery over with them. I would sometimes say to them, I wished I could be as free as they would be when they got to be men. "You will be free as soon as you are twenty one, but I am a slave for life! Have not I as good a right to be free as you have. "These words used to trouble them; they would express for me the liveliest sympathy, and console me with the hope that something would occur by which I might be free.

5 I was now about twelve years old, and the thought of being a slave for life began to bear heavily upon my heart. Just about this time, I got hold of a book entitled "The Columbian Orator." Every opportunity I got, I used to read this book. Among much of other interesting matter, I found in it a dialogue between a master and his slave. The slave was represented as having run away from his master three times. The dialogue represented the conversation which took place between them, when the slave was retaken the third time. In this dialogue, the whole argument

in behalf of slavery was brought forward by the master, all of which was disposed of by the slave. The slave was made to say some very smart as, well as impressive things in reply to his master things which had the de sired though unexpected effect; for the conversation resulted in the voluntary emancipation of the slave on the part of the master.

In the same book, I met with one of Sheridan's mighty speeches on and in behalf of Catholic emancipation. These were choice documents to me. I read them over and over again with unabated interest. They gave tongue to interesting thoughts of my own soul, which had frequently flashed through my mind, and died away for want of utterance. The moral which I gained from the dialogue was the power of truth over the conscience of even a slaveholder. What I got from Sheridan was a bold denunciation of slavery, and a powerful vindication of human rights. The reading of these documents enabled me to utter my thoughts, and to meet the arguments brought forward to sustain slavery; but while they relieved me of one difficulty, they brought on another even more painful than the one of which I was relieved. The more I read, the more I was led to abhor and detest my enslavers. I could regard them in no other light than a band of successful robbers, who had left their homes, and gone to Africa, and stolen us from our homes, and in a strange land reduced us to slavery. I loathed them as being the meanest as well as the most wicked of men. As I read and contemplated the subject, behold that very discontentment which Master Hugh had predicted would follow my learning to read had already come, to torment and sting my soul to unutterable anguish. As I writhed under it, I would at times feel that learning to read had been a curse rather than a blessing. It had given me a view of my wretched condition, without the remedy. It opened my eyes to the horrible pit, but to no ladder upon which to get out. In moments of agony, I envied my fellow slaves for their stupidity.

I have often wished myself a beast. I preferred the condition of the meanest reptile to my own. Anything, no matter what, to get rid of thinking! It was this everlasting thinking of my condition that tormented me. There was no getting rid of it. It was pressed upon me by every object within sight or hearing, animate or inanimate. The silver trump of freedom had roused my soul to eternal wakefulness. Freedom now appeared, to disappear no more forever. It was heard in every sound, and seen in every thing. It was ever present to torment me with a sense of my wretched condition. I saw nothing without seeing it, I heard nothing without hearing it, and felt nothing without feeling it. It looked from every star, it smiled in every calm, breathed in every wind, and moved in every storm.

I often found myself regretting my own existence, and wishing myself dead; and but for the hope of being free, I have no doubt but that I should have killed myself, or done something for which I should have been killed. While in this state of mind, I was eager to hear anyone speak of slavery. I was a ready listener. Every little while, I could hear something about the abolitionists. It was some time before I found what the word meant. It was always used in such connections as to make it an interesting word to me. If a slave ran away and succeeded in getting clear, or if a slave killed his master, set fire to a barn, or did anything very wrong in the mind of a slaveholder, it was spoken of as the fruit of abolition. Hearing the word in this connection very often, I set about learning what it meant. The dictionary afforded me little or no help. I found it was "the act of abolishing"; but then I did not know what was to be abolished. Here I was perplexed. I did not dare to ask anyone about its meaning, for I was satisfied that it was something they wanted me to know very little about. After a patient waiting, I got one of our city papers, containing an account of the number of petitions from the North, praying for the abolition of slavery in the District of Columbia, and of the slave trade between the States. From this time I understood the words abolition and abolitionist, and always drew near when that word was spoken, expecting to hear something of importance to myself and fellow-slaves. The light broke in upon me by degrees. I went one day down on the wharf of Mr. Waters; and seeing two Irishmen unloading a scow of stone, I went, unasked, and helped them. When we had finished, one of them came to me and asked me if I were a slave. I told him I was. He asked, "Are ye a slave for life?" I told him that I was. The good Irishman seemed to be deeply affected by the statement. He said to the other that it was a pity so fine a little fellow as myself should be a slave for life. He said it was a shame to hold me. They both advised me to run away to the North; that I should find friends there, and that I should be free. I pretended not to be interested in what they said, and treated them as if I did not understand them; for I feared they might be treacherous. White men have been known to encourage slaves to escape, and then, to get the reward, catch them and return them to their masters. I was afraid that these seemingly good men might use me so; but I nevertheless remembered their advice, and from that time I resolved to run away. I looked forward to a time at which it would be safe for me to escape. I was too young to think of doing so immediately; besides, I wished to learn how to write, as I might have occasion to write my own pass. I consoled myself with the hope that I should one day find a good chance. Meanwhile, I would learn to write.

The idea as to how I might learn to write was suggested to me by being in Durgin and Bailey's ship yard, and frequently seeing the ship carpenters, after hewing, and getting a piece of timber ready for use, write on the timber the name of that part of the ship for which it was intended. When a piece of timber was intended for the larboard side, it would be marked thus "L." When apiece was for the starboard side, it would be marked thus

S. F." A piece for the larboard side forward, would be marked thus "L. F." When apiece was for starboard side forward, it would be marked thus "S. F." For larboard aft, it would be marked thus "L. A." For starboard aft, it would be marked thus "S. A." I soon learned the names of these letters, and for what they were intended when placed upon a piece of timber in the shipyard. I immediately commenced copying them, and in a short time was able to make the four letters named. After that, when I met with any boy who I knew could write, I would tell him I could write as well as he. The next word would be, "1 don't believe you. Let me see you try it." I would then make the letters which I had been so fortunate as to learn, and ask him to beat that. In this way I got a good many lessons in writing, which it is quite possible I should never have gotten in any other way. During this time, my copybook was the board fence, brick wall, and pavement; my pen and ink was a lump of chalk. With these, I learned mainly how to write. I then commenced and continued copying the Italics in Webster's Spelling Book, until I could make them all without looking in the book. By this time, my little Master Thomas had gone to school, and learned how to write, and had written over a number of copybooks. These had been brought home, and shown to some of our near neighbors, and then laid aside. My mistress used to go to class meeting at the Wilk Street meeting house every Monday afternoon, and leave me to take care of the house. When left thus, I used to spend the time in writing in the spaces left in master Thomas's copybook, copying what he had written. I continued to do this until I could write a hand very similar to that of Master Thomas. Thus, after a long, tedious effort for years, I finally succeeded in learning how to write.

What to the Slave Is the Fourth of July?

by Frederick Douglass

Frederick Augustus Washington Bailey (1818–1895) was born into slavery in Maryland around 1818. In 1838, he escaped and later took the last name of Douglass to protect his identity. Douglass became a leading figure in the abolitionist movement, a celebrated orator, and a bestselling author. "What to the Slave is the Fourth of July?" is a speech Douglass delivered to a crowd of 500–600 people in Rochester, New York, on July 5, 1852. It was immediately reprinted in local newspapers and later published as a 45-page pamphlet.

Fellow-Citizens — Pardon me, and allow me to ask, why am I called upon to speak here today? What have I, or those I represent, to do with your national independence? Are the great principles of political freedom and of natural justice, embodied in that Declaration of Independence, extended to us? and am I, therefore, called upon to bring our humble offering to the national altar, and to confess the benefits, and express devout gratitude for the blessings, resulting from your independence to us?

Would to God, both for your sakes and ours, that an affirmative answer could be truthfully returned to these questions! Then would my task be light, and my burden easy and delightful. For who is there so cold that a nation's sympathy could not warm him? Who so obdurate and dead to the claims of gratitude, that would not thankfully acknowledge such priceless benefits? Who so stolid and selfish, that would not give his voice to swell the hallelujahs of a nation's jubilee, when the chains of servitude had been torn from his limbs? I am not that man. In a case like that, the dumb might eloquently speak, and the "lame man leap as an hart."

But, such is not the state of the case. I say it with a sad sense of the disparity between us. I am not included within the pale of this glorious anniversary! Your high independence only reveals the immeasurable distance between us. The blessings in which you this day rejoice, are not enjoyed in common. The rich inheritance of justice, liberty, prosperity, and independence, bequeathed by your fathers, is shared by you, not by me. The sunlight that brought life and healing to you, has brought stripes and death to me. This Fourth of July is *yours*, not mine. You may rejoice, I must mourn. To drag a man in fetters into the grand illuminated temple of liberty, and call upon him to join you in joyous anthems, were inhuman mockery and sacrilegious irony. Do you mean, citizens, to mock me, by asking me to speak today? If so, there is a parallel to your conduct. And let me warn you that it is dangerous to copy the example of a nation whose crimes, towering up to heaven, were thrown down by the breath of the Almighty, burying that nation in irrecoverable ruin! I can today take up the plaintive lament of a peeled and woe-smitten people.

"By the rivers of Babylon, there we sat down. Yea! we wept when we remembered Zion. We hanged our harps upon the willows in the midst thereof. For there, they that carried us away captive, required of us a song; and they who wasted us required of us mirth, saying, Sing us one of the songs of Zion. How can we sing the Lord's song in a strange land? If I forget thee, O Jerusalem, let my right hand forget her cunning. If I do not remember thee, let my tongue cleave to the roof of my mouth."

5 Fellow-citizens, above your national, tumultuous joy, I hear the mournful wail of millions, whose chains, heavy and grievous yesterday, are today rendered more intolerable by the jubilant shouts that reach them. If I do forget, if I do not faithfully remember those bleeding children of sorrow this day, "may my right hand forget her cunning, and may my

tongue cleave to the roof of my mouth!" To forget them, to pass lightly over their wrongs, and to chime in with the popular theme, would be treason most scandalous and shocking, and would make me a reproach before God and the world. My subject, then, fellow-citizens, is *American Slavery.* I shall see this day and its popular characteristics from the slave's point of view. Standing there, identified with the American bondman, making his wrongs mine, I do not hesitate to declare, with all my soul, that the character and conduct of this nation never looked blacker to me than on this Fourth of July. Whether we turn to the declarations of the past, or to the professions of the present, the conduct of the nation seems equally hideous and revolting. America is false to the past, false to the present, and solemnly binds herself to be false to the future. Standing with God and the crushed and bleeding slave on this occasion, I will, in the name of humanity which is outraged, in the name of liberty which is fettered, in the name of the constitution and the bible, which are disregarded and trampled upon, dare to call in question and to denounce, with all the emphasis I can command, everything that serves to perpetuate slavery — the great sin and shame of America! "I will not equivocate; I will not excuse;" I will use the severest language I can command; and yet not one word shall escape me that any man, whose judgment is not blinded by prejudice, or who is not at heart a slaveholder, shall not confess to be right and just.

But I fancy I hear some one of my audience say, it is just in this circumstance that you and your brother abolitionists fail to make a favorable impression on the public mind. Would you argue more, and denounce less, would you persuade more and rebuke less, your cause would be much more likely to succeed. But, I submit, where all is plain there is nothing to be argued. What point in the anti-slavery creed would you have me argue? On what branch of the subject do the people of this country need light? Must I undertake to prove that the slave is a man? That point is conceded already. Nobody doubts it. The slaveholders themselves acknowledge it in the enactment of laws for their government. They acknowledge it when they punish disobedience on the part of the slave. There are seventy-two crimes in the state of Virginia, which, if committed by a black man (no matter how ignorant he be), subject him to the punishment of death; while only two of these same crimes will subject a white man to the like punishment. What is this but the acknowledgement that the slave is a moral, intellectual, and responsible being. The manhood of the slave is conceded. It is admitted in the fact that southern statute books are covered with enactments forbidding, under severe fines and penalties, the teaching of the slave to read or write. When you can point to any such laws, in reference to the beasts of the field, then I may consent to argue the manhood of the slave. When the dogs in your streets, when the fowls of the air, when the cattle on your hills, when the fish of the sea, and the reptiles that crawl, shall be unable to distinguish the slave from a brute, then will I argue with you that the slave is a man!

For the present, it is enough to affirm the equal manhood of the Negro race. Is it not astonishing that, while we are plowing, planting, and reaping, using all kinds of mechanical tools, erecting houses, constructing bridges, building ships, working in metals of brass, iron, copper, silver, and gold; that, while we are reading, writing, and cyphering, acting as clerks, merchants, and secretaries, having among us lawyers, doctors, ministers, poets, authors, editors, orators, and teachers; that, while we are engaged in all manner of enterprises common to other men — digging gold in California, capturing the whale in the Pacific, feeding sheep and cattle on the hillside, living, moving, acting, thinking, planning, living in families as husbands, wives, and children, and, above all, confessing and worshiping the Christian's God, and looking hopefully for life and immortality beyond the grave — we are called upon to prove that we are men!

Would you have me argue that man is entitled to liberty? that he is the rightful owner of his own body? You have already declared it. Must I argue the wrongfulness of slavery? Is that a question for republicans? Is it to be settled by the rules of logic and argumentation, as a matter beset with great difficulty, involving a doubtful application of the principle of justice, hard to be understood? How should I look today in the presence of Americans, dividing and subdividing a discourse, to show that men have a natural right to freedom, speaking of it relatively and positively, negatively and affirmatively? To do so, would be to make myself ridiculous, and to offer an insult to your understanding. There is not a man beneath the canopy of heaven that does not know that slavery is wrong for *him*.

What! am I to argue that it is wrong to make men brutes, to rob them of their liberty, to work them without wages, to keep them ignorant of their relations to their fellow-men, to beat them with sticks, to flay their flesh with the lash, to load their limbs with irons, to hunt them with dogs, to sell them at auction, to sunder their families, to knock out their teeth, to burn their flesh, to starve them into obedience and submission to their masters? Must I argue that a system, thus marked with blood and stained with pollution, is wrong? No; I will not. I have better employment for my time and strength than such arguments would imply.

What, then, remains to be argued? Is it that slavery is not 10
divine; that God did not establish it; that our doctors of divinity are mistaken? There is blasphemy in the thought. That which is inhuman cannot be divine. Who can reason on such a proposition! They that can, may! I cannot. The time for such argument is past.

At a time like this, scorching irony, not convincing argument, is needed. Oh! had I the ability, and could I reach the nation's ear, I would today pour out a fiery stream of biting ridicule, blasting reproach, withering sarcasm, and stern rebuke.

For it is not light that is needed, but fire; it is not the gentle shower, but thunder. We need the storm, the whirlwind, and the earthquake. The feeling of the nation must be quickened; the conscience of the nation must be roused; the propriety of the nation must be startled; the hypocrisy of the nation must be exposed; and its crimes against God and man must be proclaimed and denounced.

What to the American slave is your Fourth of July? I answer, a day that reveals to him, more than all other days in the year, the gross injustice and cruelty to which he is the constant victim. To him, your celebration is a sham; your boasted liberty, an unholy license; your national greatness, swelling vanity; your sounds of rejoicing are empty and heartless; your denunciations of tyrants, brass-fronted impudence; your shouts of liberty and equality, hollow mockery; your prayers and hymns, your sermons and thanksgivings, with all your religious parade and solemnity, are to him mere bombast, fraud, deception, impiety, and hypocrisy — a thin veil to cover up crimes which would disgrace a nation of savages. There is not a nation on the earth guilty of practices more shocking and bloody, than are the people of these United States, at this very hour.

Go where you may, search where you will, roam through all the monarchies and despotisms of the old world, travel through South America, search out every abuse, and when you have found the last, lay your facts by the side of the every-day practices of this nation, and you will say with me, that, for revolting barbarity and shameless hypocrisy, America reigns without a rival.

Of Our Spiritual Strivings

by W. E. B. DuBois

William Edward Burghardt DuBois (1868–1963) was an American sociologist, historian, author, and civil rights activist. He was the first African American to earn a doctorate from Harvard College, and after his education, he became professor of history, sociology, and economics at Atlanta University. His writing and activism primarily addressed discrimination and racism in the U.S. and the independence of people of color globally. "Of Our Spiritual Strivings" is the first chapter of his book, The Souls of Black Folk.

O water, voice of my heart, crying in the sand,
All night long crying with a mournful cry,
As I lie and listen, and cannot understand
The voice of my heart in my side or the voice of the sea,
O water, crying for rest, is it I, is it I?
All night long the water is crying to me.

Unresting water, there shall never be rest
Till the last moon droop and the last tide fail,
And the fire of the end begin to burn in the west;
And the heart shall be weary and wonder and cry like
the sea,
All life long crying without avail,
As the water all night long is crying to me.

— Arthur Symons

Between me and the other world there is ever an unasked question: unasked by some through feelings of delicacy; by others through the difficulty of rightly framing it. All, nevertheless, flutter round it. They approach me in a half-hesitant sort of way, eye me curiously or compassionately, and then, instead of saying directly, How does it feel to be a problem? they say, I know an excellent colored man in my town; or, I fought at Mechanicsville; or, Do not these Southern outrages make your blood boil? At these I smile, or am interested, or reduce the boiling to a simmer, as the occasion may require. To the real question, How does it feel to be a problem? I answer seldom a word.

And yet, being a problem is a strange experience, — peculiar even for one who has never been anything else, save perhaps in babyhood and in Europe. It is in the early days of rollicking boyhood that the revelation first bursts upon one, all in a day, as it were. I remember well when the shadow swept across me. I was a little thing, away up in the hills of New England, where the dark Housatonic winds between Hoosac and Taghkanic to the sea. In a wee wooden schoolhouse, something put it into the boys' and girls' heads to buy gorgeous visiting-cards — ten cents a package — and exchange. The exchange was merry, till one girl, a tall newcomer, refused my card, — refused it peremptorily, with a glance. Then it dawned upon me with a certain suddenness that I was different from the others; or like, mayhap, in heart and life and longing, but shut out from their world by a vast veil. I had thereafter no desire to tear down that veil, to creep through; I held all beyond it in common contempt, and lived above it in a region of blue sky and great wandering shadows. That sky was bluest when I could beat my mates at examination-time, or beat them at a foot-race, or even beat their stringy heads. Alas, with the years all this fine contempt began to fade; for the words I longed for, and all their dazzling opportunities, were theirs, not mine. But they should not keep these prizes, I said; some, all, I would wrest from them. Just how I would do it I could never decide: by reading law, by healing the sick, by telling the wonderful tales that swam in my head, — some way. With other black boys the strife was not so fiercely sunny: their youth shrunk into tasteless sycophancy, or into silent hatred of the pale world about them and mocking distrust of everything white; or wasted itself in a bitter cry, Why did God make me an outcast and a stranger in mine own house? The shades of the prison-house closed round about us all: walls strait and stubborn to the whitest, but relentlessly narrow, tall, and unscalable to sons of night who must plod darkly on in resignation, or beat unavailing palms against the stone, or steadily, half hopelessly, watch the streak of blue above.

After the Egyptian and Indian, the Greek and Roman, the Teuton and Mongolian, the Negro is a sort of seventh son, born with a veil, and gifted with second-sight in this American world, — a world which yields him no true self-consciousness, but only lets him see himself through the revelation of the other world. It is a peculiar sensation, this double-consciousness, this sense of always looking at one's self through the eyes of others, of measuring one's soul by the tape of a world that looks on in amused contempt and pity. One ever feels his twoness, — an American, a Negro; two souls, two thoughts, two unreconciled strivings; two warring ideals in one dark body, whose dogged strength alone keeps it from being torn asunder.

The history of the American Negro is the history of this strife, — this longing to attain self-conscious manhood, to merge his double self into a better and truer self. In this merging he wishes neither of the older selves to be lost. He would not Africanize America, for America has too much to teach the world and Africa. He would not bleach his Negro soul in a flood of white Americanism, for he knows that Negro blood has a message for the world. He simply wishes to make it possible for a man to be both a Negro and an American, without being cursed and spit upon by his fellows, without having the doors of Opportunity closed roughly in his face.

This, then, is the end of his striving: to be a co-worker in the kingdom of culture, to escape both death and isolation, to husband and use his best powers and his latent genius. These powers of body and mind have in the past been strangely wasted, dispersed, or forgotten. The shadow of a mighty Negro past flits through the tale of Ethiopia the Shadowy and of Egypt the Sphinx. Through history, the powers of single black men flash here and there like falling stars, and die sometimes before the world has rightly gauged their brightness. Here in America, in the few days since Emancipation, the black man's turning hither and thither in hesitant and doubtful striving has often made his very strength to lose effectiveness, to seem like absence of power, like weakness. And yet it is not weakness, — it is the contradiction of double aims. The double-aimed struggle of the black artisan — on the one hand to escape white contempt for a nation of mere hewers of wood and drawers of water, and on the other hand to plough and nail and dig for a poverty-stricken horde — could only result in making him a poor craftsman, for he had but half a heart in either cause. By the poverty and ignorance of his people, the Negro minister or doctor was tempted toward quackery and demagogy; and by the criticism of the other world, toward ideals that made him ashamed of his lowly tasks. The would-be black savant was confronted by the paradox that the knowledge his people needed was a twice-told tale to his white neighbors, while the knowledge which would teach the white world was Greek to his own flesh and blood. The innate love of harmony and beauty that set the ruder souls of his people a-dancing and a-singing raised but confusion and doubt in the soul of the black artist; for the beauty revealed to him was the soul-beauty of a race which his larger audience despised, and he could not articulate the message of another people. This waste of double aims, this seeking to satisfy two unreconciled ideals, has wrought sad havoc with the courage and faith and deeds of ten thousand thousand people, — has sent them often wooing false gods and invoking false means of salvation, and at times has even seemed about to make them ashamed of themselves.

Away back in the days of bondage they thought to see in one divine event the end of all doubt and disappointment; few men ever worshipped Freedom with half such unquestioning faith as did the American Negro for two centuries. To him, so far as he thought and dreamed, slavery was indeed the sum of all villainies, the cause of all sorrow, the root of all prejudice; Emancipation was the key to a promised land of sweeter beauty than ever stretched before the eyes of wearied Israelites. In song and exhortation swelled one refrain — Liberty; in his tears and curses the God he implored had Freedom in his right hand. At last it came, — suddenly, fearfully, like a dream. With one wild carnival of blood and passion came the message in his own plaintive cadences: —

> "Shout, O children!
> Shout, you're free!
> For God has bought your liberty!"

Years have passed away since then, — ten, twenty, forty; forty years of national life, forty years of renewal and development, and yet the swarthy specter sits in its accustomed seat at the Nation's feast. In vain do we cry to this our vastest social problem: —

> "Take any shape but that, and my firm nerves
> Shall never tremble!"

The Nation has not yet found peace from its sins; the freedman has not yet found in freedom his promised land. Whatever of good may have come in these years of change, the shadow of a deep disappointment rests upon the Negro people, — a disappointment all the more bitter because the unattained ideal was unbounded save by the simple ignorance of a lowly people.

The first decade was merely a prolongation of the vain search for freedom, the boon that seemed ever barely to elude their grasp, — like a tantalizing will-o'-the-wisp, maddening and misleading the headless host. The holocaust of war, the terrors of the Ku-Klux Klan, the lies of carpet-baggers, the disorganization of industry, and the contradictory advice of friends and foes, left the bewildered serf with no new watchword beyond the old cry for freedom. As the time flew, however, he began to grasp a new idea. The ideal of liberty demanded for its attainment powerful means, and these the Fifteenth Amendment gave him. The ballot, which before he had looked upon as a visible sign of freedom, he now regarded as the chief means of gaining and perfecting the liberty with which war had partially endowed him. And why not? Had not votes made war and emancipated millions? Had not votes enfranchised the freedmen? Was anything impossible to a power that had done all this? A million black men started with renewed zeal to vote themselves into the kingdom. So the decade flew away, the revolution of 1876 came, and left the half-free serf weary, wondering, but still inspired. Slowly but steadily, in the following years, a new vision began gradually to replace the dream of political power, — a powerful movement, the rise of another ideal to guide the unguided, another pillar of fire by night after a clouded day. It was the ideal of "book-learning"; the curiosity, born of compulsory ignorance, to know and test the power of the cabalistic letters of the white man, the longing to know. Here at last seemed to have been discovered the mountain path to Canaan; longer than the highway of Emancipation and law, steep and rugged, but straight, leading to heights high enough to overlook life.

Up the new path the advance guard toiled, slowly, heavily, doggedly; only those who have watched and guided the faltering feet, the misty minds, the dull understandings, of the dark pupils of these schools know how faithfully, how piteously, this people strove to learn. It was weary work. The cold statistician wrote down the inches of progress here and there, noted also where here and there a foot had slipped or some one had fallen. To the tired climbers, the horizon was ever dark, the mists were often cold, the Canaan was always dim and far away. If, however, the vistas disclosed as yet no goal, no resting-place, little but flattery and criticism, the journey at least gave leisure for reflection and self-examination; it changed the child of Emancipation to the youth with dawning self-consciousness, self-realization, self-respect. In those sombre forests of his striving his own soul rose before him, and he saw himself, — darkly as through a veil; and yet he saw in himself some faint revelation of his power, of his mission. He began to have a dim feeling that, to attain his place in the world, he must be himself, and not another. For the first time he sought to analyze the burden he bore upon his back, that dead-weight of social degradation partially masked behind a half-named Negro problem. He felt his poverty; without a cent, without a home, without land, tools, or savings, he had entered into competition with rich, landed, skilled neighbors. To be a poor man is hard, but to be a poor race in a land of dollars is the very bottom of hardships. He felt the weight of his ignorance, — not simply of letters, but of life, of business, of the humanities; the accumulated sloth and shirking and awkwardness of decades and centuries shackled his hands and feet. Nor was his burden all poverty and ignorance. The red stain of bastardy, which two centuries of systematic legal defilement of Negro women had stamped upon his race, meant not only the loss of ancient African chastity, but also the hereditary weight of a mass of corruption from white adulterers, threatening almost the obliteration of the Negro home.

A people thus handicapped ought not to be asked to race with the world, but rather allowed to give all its time and thought to its own social problems. But alas! while sociologists gleefully count his bastards and his prostitutes, the very soul of the toiling, sweating black man is darkened by the shadow of a vast despair. Men call the shadow prejudice, and learnedly explain it as the natural defense of culture against barbarism, learning against ignorance, purity against crime, the "higher" against the "lower" races. To which the Negro cries Amen! and swears that to so much of this strange prejudice as is founded on just homage to civilization, culture, righteousness, and progress, he humbly bows and meekly does obeisance. But before that nameless prejudice that leaps beyond all this he stands helpless, dismayed, and well-nigh speechless; before that personal disrespect and mockery, the ridicule and systematic humiliation, the distortion of fact and wanton license of fancy, the cynical ignoring of the better and the boisterous welcoming of the worse, the all-pervading desire to inculcate disdain for everything black, from Toussaint to the devil, — before this there rises a sickening despair that would disarm and discourage any nation save that black host to whom "discouragement" is an unwritten word.

But the facing of so vast a prejudice could not but bring the inevitable self-questioning, self-disparagement, and lowering of ideals which ever accompany repression and breed in an atmosphere of contempt and hate. Whisperings and portents came home upon the four winds: Lo! we are diseased and dying, cried the dark hosts; we cannot write, our voting is vain; what need of education, since we must always cook and serve? And the Nation echoed and enforced this self-criticism, saying: Be content to be servants, and nothing more; what need of higher culture for half-men? Away with the black man's ballot, by force or fraud, — and behold the suicide of a race! Nevertheless, out of the evil came something of good, — the more careful adjustment of education to real life, the clearer perception of the Negroes' social responsibilities, and the sobering realization of the meaning of progress.

So dawned the time of *Sturm und Drang*: storm and stress today rocks our little boat on the mad waters of the world-sea; there is within and without the sound of conflict, the burning of body and rending of soul; inspiration strives with doubt, and faith with vain questionings. The bright ideals of the past, — physical freedom, political power, the training of brains and the training of hands, — all these in turn have waxed and waned, until even the last grows dim and overcast. Are they all wrong, — all false? No, not that, but each alone was over-simple and incomplete, — the dreams of a credulous race-childhood, or the fond imaginings of the other world which does not know and does not want to know our power. To be really true, all these ideals must be melted and welded into one. The training of the schools we need today more than ever, — the training of deft hands, quick eyes and ears, and above all the broader, deeper, higher culture of gifted minds and pure hearts. The power of the ballot we need in sheer self-defense, — else what shall save us from a second slavery? Freedom, too, the long-sought, we still seek, — the freedom of life and limb, the freedom to work and think, the freedom to love and aspire. Work, culture, liberty, — all these we need, not singly but together, not successively but together, each growing and aiding each, and all striving toward that vaster ideal that swims before the Negro people, the ideal of human brotherhood, gained through the unifying ideal of Race; the ideal of fostering and developing the traits and talents of the Negro, not in opposition to or contempt for other races, but rather in large conformity to the greater ideals of the American Republic, in order that some day on American soil two world-races may give each to each those characteristics both so sadly lack. We the darker ones come even now not altogether empty-handed: there are today no truer exponents of the pure human spirit of the Declaration of Independence than the American Negroes; there is no true American music but the wild sweet melodies of the Negro slave; the American fairy tales and folklore are Indian and African; and, all in all, we black men seem the sole oasis of simple faith and reverence in a dusty desert of dollars and smartness. Will America be poorer if she replaces her brutal dyspeptic blundering with light-hearted but determined Negro humility? or her coarse and cruel wit with loving jovial good-humor? or her vulgar music with the soul of the Sorrow Songs?

Merely a concrete test of the underlying principles of the great republic is the Negro Problem, and the spiritual striving of the freedmen's sons is the travail of souls whose burden is almost beyond the measure of their strength, but who bear it in the name of an historic race, in the name of this the land of their fathers' fathers, and in the name of human opportunity.

15 And now what I have briefly sketched in large outline let me on coming pages tell again in many ways, with loving emphasis and deeper detail, that men may listen to the striving in the souls of black folk.

Farewell Address

by Dwight D. Eisenhower

Dwight David Eisenhower (1890–1969) was the thirty-fourth President of the United States, serving from 1953 until 1961. Prior to his presidency he was a five-star general in the U.S. Army and Supreme Commander of the Allied troops in Europe during World War II. This farewell address was delivered on January 7, 1961.

My fellow Americans:

Three days from now, after half a century in the service of our country, I shall lay down the responsibilities of office as, in traditional and solemn ceremony, the authority of the Presidency is vested in my successor.

This evening I come to you with a message of leave-taking and farewell, and to share a few final thoughts with you, my countrymen.

Like every other citizen, I wish the new President, and all who will labor with him, Godspeed. I pray that the coming years will be blessed with peace and prosperity for all.

Our people expect their President and the Congress to 5
find essential agreement on issues of great moment, the wise resolution of which will better shape the future of the Nation.

My own relations with the Congress, which began on a remote and tenuous basis when, long ago, a member of the Senate appointed me to West Point, have since ranged to the intimate during the war and immediate post-war period, and, finally, to the mutually interdependent during these past eight years.

In this final relationship, the Congress and the Administration have, on most vital issues, cooperated well, to serve the national good rather than mere partisanship, and so have assured that the business of the Nation should go forward. So, my official relationship with the Congress ends in a feeling, on my part, of gratitude that we have been able to do so much together.

II.

We now stand ten years past the midpoint of a century that has witnessed four major wars among great nations. Three of these involved our own country. Despite these holocausts America is today the strongest, the most influential and most productive nation in the world. Understandably proud of this pre-eminence, we yet realize that America's leadership and prestige depend, not merely upon our unmatched material progress, riches and military strength, but on how we use our power in the interests of world peace and human betterment.

III.

Throughout America's adventure in free government, our basic purposes have been to keep the peace, to foster progress in human achievement, and to enhance liberty, dignity and integrity among people and among nations. To strive for less would be unworthy of a free and religious people. Any failure traceable to arrogance, or our lack of comprehension or readiness to sacrifice would inflict upon us grievous hurt both at home and abroad.

10 Progress toward these noble goals is persistently threatened by the conflict now engulfing the world. It commands our whole attention, absorbs our very beings. We face a hostile ideology — global in scope, atheistic in character, ruthless in purpose, and insidious in method. Unhappily the danger it poses promises to be of indefinite duration. To meet it successfully, there is called for, not so much the emotional and transitory sacrifices of crisis, but rather those which enable us to carry forward steadily, surely, and without complaint the burdens of a prolonged and

complex struggle — with liberty the stake. Only thus shall we remain, despite every provocation, on our charted course toward permanent peace and human betterment.

Crises there will continue to be. In meeting them, whether foreign or domestic, great or small, there is a recurring temptation to feel that some spectacular and costly action could become the miraculous solution to all current difficulties. A huge increase in newer elements of our defense; development of unrealistic programs to cure every ill in agriculture; a dramatic expansion in basic and applied research — these and many other possibilities, each possibly promising in itself, may be suggested as the only way to the road we wish to travel.

But each proposal must be weighed in the light of a broader consideration: the need to maintain balance in and among national programs — balance between the private and the public economy, balance between cost and hoped for advantage — balance between the clearly necessary and the comfortably desirable; balance between our essential requirements as a nation and the duties imposed by the nation upon the individual; balance between actions of the moment and the national welfare of the future. Good judgment seeks balance and progress; lack of it eventually finds imbalance and frustration.

The record of many decades stands as proof that our people and their government have, in the main, understood these truths and have responded to them well, in the face of stress and threat. But threats, new in kind or degree, constantly arise. I mention two only.

IV.

A vital element in keeping the peace is our military establishment. Our arms must be mighty, ready for instant action, so that no potential aggressor may be tempted to risk his own destruction.

15 Our military organization today bears little relation to that known by any of my predecessors in peacetime, or indeed by the fighting men of World War II or Korea.

Until the latest of our world conflicts, the United States had no armaments industry. American makers of plowshares could, with time and as required, make swords as well. But now we can no longer risk emergency improvisation of national defense; we have been compelled to create a permanent armaments industry of vast proportions. Added to this, three and a half million men and women are directly engaged in the defense establishment. We annually spend on military security more than the net income of all United States corporations.

This conjunction of an immense military establishment and a large arms industry is new in the American experience. The total influence — economic, political, even spiritual — is felt in every city, every State house, every office of the Federal government. We recognize the imperative need for this development. Yet we must not fail to comprehend its grave implications. Our toil, resources and livelihood are all involved; so is the very structure of our society.

In the councils of government, we must guard against the acquisition of unwarranted influence, whether sought or unsought, by the military/industrial complex. The potential for the disastrous rise of misplaced power exists and will persist.

We must never let the weight of this combination endanger our liberties or democratic processes. We should take nothing for granted. Only an alert and knowledgeable citizenry can compel the proper meshing of the huge industrial and military machinery of defense with our peaceful methods and goals, so that security and liberty may prosper together.

20 Akin to, and largely responsible for the sweeping changes in our industrial-military posture, has been the technological revolution during recent decades.

In this revolution, research has become central; it also becomes more formalized, complex, and costly. A steadily increasing share is conducted for, by, or at the direction of, the Federal government.

Today, the solitary inventor, tinkering in his shop, has been overshadowed by task forces of scientists in laboratories and testing fields. In the same fashion, the free university, historically the fountainhead of free ideas and scientific discovery, has experienced a revolution in the conduct of research. Partly because of the huge costs involved, a government contract becomes virtually a substitute for intellectual curiosity. For every old blackboard there are now hundreds of new electronic computers.

The prospect of domination of the nation's scholars by Federal employment, project allocations, and the power of money is ever present and is gravely to be regarded. Yet, in holding scientific research and discovery in respect, as we should, we must also be alert to the equal and opposite danger that public policy could itself become the captive of a scientific/technological elite.

It is the task of statesmanship to mold, to balance, and to integrate these and other forces, new and old, within the principles of our democratic system — ever aiming toward the supreme goals of our free society.

V.

Another factor in maintaining balance involves the element of 25
time. As we peer into society's future, we — you and I, and our government — must avoid the impulse to live only for today, plundering, for our own ease and convenience, the precious resources of tomorrow. We cannot mortgage the material assets of our grandchildren without risking the loss also of their political and spiritual heritage. We want democracy to survive for all generations to come, not to become the insolvent phantom of tomorrow.

VI.

Down the long lane of the history yet to be written America knows that this world of ours, ever growing smaller, must avoid becoming a community of dreadful fear and hate, and be instead, a proud confederation of mutual trust and respect.

Such a confederation must be one of equals. The weakest must come to the conference table with the same confidence as do we, protected as we are by our moral, economic, and military strength. That table, though scarred by many past frustrations, cannot be abandoned for the certain agony of the battlefield.

Disarmament, with mutual honor and confidence, is a continuing imperative. Together we must learn how to compose differences, not with arms, but with intellect and decent purpose. Because this need is so sharp and apparent I confess that I lay down my official responsibilities in this field with a definite sense of disappointment. As one who has witnessed the horror and the lingering sadness of war — as one who knows that another war could utterly destroy this civilization which has been so slowly and painfully built over thousands of years — I wish I could say tonight that a lasting peace is in sight.

Happily, I can say that war has been avoided. Steady progress toward our ultimate goal has been made. But, so much remains to be done. As a private citizen, I shall never cease to do what little I can to help the world advance along that road.

VII.

30 So — in this my last good night to you as your President — I thank you for the many opportunities you have given me for public service in war and peace. I trust that in that service you find some things worthy; as for the rest of it, I know you will find ways to improve performance in the future.

You and I — my fellow citizens — need to be strong in our faith that all nations, under God, will reach the goal of peace with justice. May we be ever unswerving in devotion to principle, confident but humble with power, diligent in pursuit of the Nation's great goals.

To all the peoples of the world, I once more give expression to America's prayerful and continuing aspiration:

We pray that peoples of all faiths, all races, all nations, may have their great human needs satisfied; that those now denied opportunity shall come to enjoy it to the full; that all who yearn for freedom may experience its spiritual blessings; that those who have freedom will understand, also, its heavy responsibilities; that all who are insensitive to the needs of others will learn charity; that the scourges of poverty, disease and ignorance will be made to disappear from the earth, and that, in the goodness of time, all peoples will come to live together in a peace guaranteed by the binding force of mutual respect and love.

Self-Reliance

by Ralph Waldo Emerson

Ralph Waldo Emerson (1803–1882) was an American essayist, philosopher, and poet known for his central role in developing transcendentalism, a religious and philosophical movement popular in the 1820s and '30s. In this essay, Emerson articulates the transcendentalist philosophies about individualism and nonconformity.

"Ne te quaesiveris extra."

"Man is his own star; and the soul that can
Render an honest and a perfect man,
Commands all light, all influence, all fate;
Nothing to him falls early or too late.
Our acts our angels are, or good or ill,
Our fatal shadows that walk by us still."

— Epilogue to Beaumont and Fletcher's
Honest Man's Fortune

Cast the bantling on the rocks,
Suckle him with the she-wolf's teat,
Wintered with the hawk and fox.
Power and speed be hands and feet.

I read the other day some verses written by an eminent painter which were original and not conventional. The soul always hears an admonition in such lines, let the subject be what it may. The sentiment they instill is of more value than any thought they may contain. To believe your own thought, to believe that what is true for you in your private heart is true for all men, — that is genius. Speak your latent conviction, and it shall be the universal sense; for the inmost in due time becomes the outmost, and our first thought is rendered back to us by the trumpets of the Last Judgment. Familiar as the voice of the mind is to each, the highest merit we ascribe to Moses, Plato and Milton is that they set at naught books and traditions, and spoke not what men, but what they thought. A man should learn to detect and watch that gleam of light which flashes across his mind from within, more than the luster of the firmament of bards and sages. Yet he dismisses without notice his thought, because it is his. In every work of genius we recognize our own rejected thoughts; they come back to us with a certain alienated majesty. Great works of art have no more affecting lesson for us than this. They teach us to abide by our spontaneous impression with good-humored inflexibility then most when the whole cry of voices is on the other side. Else tomorrow a stranger will say with masterly good sense precisely what we have thought and felt all the time, and we shall be forced to take with shame our own opinion from another.

There is a time in every man's education when he arrives at the conviction that envy is ignorance; that imitation is suicide; that he must take himself for better for worse as his portion; that though the wide universe is full of good, no kernel of nourishing corn can come to him but through his toil bestowed on that plot of ground which is given to him to till. The power which resides in him is new in nature, and none but he knows what that is which he can do, nor does he know until he has tried.

Not for nothing one face, one character, one fact, makes much impression on him, and another none. This sculpture in the memory is not without pre-established harmony. The eye was placed where one ray should fall, that it might testify of that particular ray. We but half express ourselves, and are ashamed of that divine idea which each of us represents. It may be safely trusted as proportionate and of good issues, so it be faithfully imparted, but God will not have his work made manifest by cowards. A man is relieved and gay when he has put his heart into his work and done his best; but what he has said or done otherwise shall give him no peace. It is a deliverance which does not deliver. In the attempt his genius deserts him; no muse befriends; no invention, no hope.

Trust thyself: every heart vibrates to that iron string. Accept the place the divine providence has found for you, the society of your contemporaries, the connection of events. Great men have always done so, and confided themselves childlike to the genius of their age, betraying their perception that the absolutely trustworthy was seated at their heart, working through their hands, predominating in all their being. And we are now men, and must accept in the highest mind the same transcendent destiny; and not minors and invalids in a protected corner, not cowards fleeing before a revolution, but guides, redeemers and benefactors, obeying the Almighty effort and advancing on Chaos and the Dark.

What pretty oracles nature yields us on this text in the face and behavior of children, babes, and even brutes! That divided and rebel mind, that distrust of a sentiment because our arithmetic has computed the strength and means opposed to our purpose, these have not. Their mind being whole, their eye is as yet unconquered, and when we look in their faces we are disconcerted. Infancy conforms to nobody; all conform to it; so that one babe commonly makes four or five out of the adults who prattle and play to it. So God has armed youth and puberty and manhood no less with its own piquancy and charm, and made it enviable and gracious and its claims not to be put by, if it will stand by itself. Do not think the youth has no force, because he cannot speak to you and me. Hark! in the next room his voice is sufficiently clear and emphatic. It seems he knows how to speak to his contemporaries. Bashful or bold then, he will know how to make us seniors very unnecessary.

The nonchalance of boys who are sure of a dinner, and would 5
disdain as much as a lord to do or say aught to conciliate one, is the healthy attitude of human nature. A boy is in the parlor what the pit is in the playhouse; independent, irresponsible, looking out from his corner on such people and facts as pass by, he tries and sentences them on their merits, in the swift, summary way of boys, as good, bad, interesting, silly, eloquent, troublesome. He cumbers himself never about consequences, about interests; he gives an independent, genuine verdict. You must court him; he does not court you. But the man is as it were clapped into jail by his consciousness. As soon as he has once acted or spoken with eclat he is a committed person, watched by the sympathy or the hatred of hundreds, whose affections must now enter into his account. There is no Lethe for this. Ah, that he could pass again into his neutrality! Who can thus avoid all pledges and, having observed, observe again from the same unaffected, unbiased, unbribable, unaffrighted innocence, — must always be formidable. He would utter opinions on all passing affairs, which being seen to be not private but necessary, would sink like darts into the ear of men and put them in fear.

These are the voices which we hear in solitude, but they grow faint and inaudible as we enter into the world. Society everywhere is in conspiracy against the manhood of every one of its members. Society is a joint-stock company, in which the members agree, for the better securing of his bread to each shareholder, to surrender the liberty and culture of the eater. The virtue in most request is conformity. Self-reliance is its aversion. It loves not realities and creators, but names and customs.

Whoso would be a man, must be a nonconformist. He who would gather immortal palms must not be hindered by the name of goodness, but must explore if it be goodness. Nothing is at last sacred but the integrity of your own mind. Absolve you to yourself, and you shall have the suffrage of the world. I remember an answer which when quite young I was prompted to make to a valued adviser who was wont to importune me with the dear old doctrines of the church. On my saying, "What have I to do with the sacredness of traditions, if I live wholly from within?" my friend suggested, — "But these impulses may be from below, not from above." I replied, "They do not seem to me to be such; but if I am the Devil's child, I will live then from the Devil." No law can be sacred to me but that of my nature. Good and bad are but names very readily transferable to that or this; the only right is what is after my constitution; the only wrong what is against it. A man is to carry himself in the presence of all opposition as if every thing were titular and ephemeral but he. I am ashamed to think how easily we capitulate to badges and names, to large societies and dead institutions. Every decent and well-spoken individual affects and sways me more than is right. I ought to go upright and vital, and speak the rude truth in all ways. If malice and vanity wear the coat of philanthropy, shall that pass? If an angry bigot assumes this bountiful cause of Abolition, and comes to me with his last news from Barbadoes, why should I not say to him, 'Go love thy infant; love thy wood-chopper; be good-natured and modest; have that grace; and never varnish your hard, uncharitable ambition with this incredible tenderness for black folk a thousand miles off. Thy love afar is spite at home.' Rough and graceless would be such greeting, but truth is handsomer than the affectation of love. Your goodness must have some edge to it, — else it is none. The doctrine of hatred must be preached, as the counteraction of the doctrine of love, when that pules and whines. I shun father and mother and wife and brother when my genius calls me. I would write on the lintels of the door-post, *Whim*. I hope it is somewhat better than whim at last, but we cannot spend the day in explanation. Expect me not to show cause why I seek or why I exclude company. Then again, do not tell me, as a good man did today, of my obligation to put all poor men in good situations. Are they my poor? I tell thee thou foolish philanthropist that I grudge the dollar, the dime, the cent, I give to such men as do not belong to me and to whom I do not belong. There is a class of persons to whom by all spiritual affinity I am bought and sold; for them I will go to prison if need be; but your miscellaneous popular charities; the education at college of fools; the building of meeting-houses to the vain end to which many now stand; alms to sots, and the thousand-fold Relief Societies; — though I confess with shame I sometimes succumb and give the dollar, it is a wicked dollar which by and by I shall have the manhood to withhold.

Virtues are, in the popular estimate, rather the exception than the rule. There is the man and his virtues. Men do what is called a good action, as some piece of courage or charity, much as they would pay a fine in expiation of daily non-appearance on parade. Their works are done as an apology or extenuation of their living in the world, — as invalids and the insane pay a high board. Their virtues are penances. I do not wish to expiate, but to live. My life is for itself and not for a spectacle. I much prefer that it should be of a lower strain, so it be genuine and equal, than that it should be glittering and unsteady. I wish it to be sound and sweet, and not to need diet and bleeding. I ask primary evidence that you are a man, and refuse this appeal from the man to his actions. I know that for myself it makes no difference whether I do or forbear those actions which are reckoned excellent. I cannot consent to pay for a privilege where

I have intrinsic right. Few and mean as my gifts may be, I actually am, and do not need for my own assurance or the assurance of my fellows any secondary testimony.

What I must do is all that concerns me, not what the people think. This rule, equally arduous in actual and in intellectual life, may serve for the whole distinction between greatness and meanness. It is the harder because you will always find those who think they know what is your duty better than you know it. It is easy in the world to live after the world's opinion; it is easy in solitude to live after our own; but the great man is he who in the midst of the crowd keeps with perfect sweetness the independence of solitude.

10 The objection to conforming to usages that have become dead to you is that it scatters your force. It loses your time and blurs the impression of your character. If you maintain a dead church, contribute to a dead Bible-society, vote with a great party either for the government or against it, spread your table like base housekeepers, — under all these screens I have difficulty to detect the precise man you are: and of course so much force is withdrawn from your proper life. But do your work, and I shall know you. Do your work, and you shall reinforce yourself. A man must consider what a blindman's-buff is this game of conformity. If I know your sect, I anticipate your argument. I hear a preacher announce for his text and topic the expediency of one of the institutions of his church. Do I not know beforehand that not possibly can he say a new and spontaneous word? Do I not know that with all this ostentation of examining the grounds of the institution he will do no such thing? Do I not know that he is pledged to himself not to look but at one side, the permitted side, not as a man, but as a parish minister? He is a retained attorney, and these airs of the bench are the emptiest affectation. Well, most men have bound their eyes with one or another handkerchief, and attached themselves to some one of these communities of opinion. This

conformity makes them not false in a few particulars, authors of a few lies, but false in all particulars. Their every truth is not quite true. Their two is not the real two, their four not the real four; so that every word they say chagrins us and we know not where to begin to set them right. Meantime nature is not slow to equip us in the prison-uniform of the party to which we adhere. We come to wear one cut of face and figure, and acquire by degrees the gentlest asinine expression. There is a mortifying experience in particular, which does not fail to wreak itself also in the general history; I mean "the foolish face of praise," the forced smile which we put on in company where we do not feel at ease in answer to conversation which does not interest us. The muscles, not spontaneously moved but moved by a low usurping wilfulness, grow tight about the outline of the face with the most disagreeable sensation.

For nonconformity the world whips you with its displeasure. And therefore a man must know how to estimate a sour face. The by-standers look askance on him in the public street or in the friend's parlor. If this aversation had its origin in contempt and resistance like his own he might well go home with a sad countenance; but the sour faces of the multitude, like their sweet faces, have no deep cause, but are put on and off as the wind blows and a newspaper directs. Yet is the discontent of the multitude more formidable than that of the senate and the college. It is easy enough for a firm man who knows the world to brook the rage of the cultivated classes. Their rage is decorous and prudent, for they are timid, as being very vulnerable themselves. But when to their feminine rage the indignation of the people is added, when the ignorant and the poor are aroused, when the unintelligent brute force that lies at the bottom of society is made to growl and mow, it needs the habit of magnanimity and religion to treat it godlike as a trifle of no concernment.

The other terror that scares us from self-trust is our consistency; a reverence for our past act or word because the eyes of others have no other data for computing our orbit than our past acts, and we are loath to disappoint them.

But why should you keep your head over your shoulder? Why drag about this corpse of your memory, lest you contradict somewhat you have stated in this or that public place? Suppose you should contradict yourself; what then? It seems to be a rule of wisdom never to rely on your memory alone, scarcely even in acts of pure memory, but to bring the past for judgment into the thousand-eyed present, and live ever in a new day. In your metaphysics you have denied personality to the Deity, yet when the devout motions of the soul come, yield to them heart and life, though they should clothe God with shape and color. Leave your theory, as Joseph his coat in the hand of the harlot, and flee.

A foolish consistency is the hobgoblin of little minds, adored by little statesmen and philosophers and divines. With consistency a great soul has simply nothing to do. He may as well concern himself with his shadow on the wall. Speak what you think now in hard words and tomorrow speak what tomorrow thinks in hard words again, though it contradict every thing you said today. — 'Ah, so you shall be sure to be misunderstood.' — Is it so bad then to be misunderstood? Pythagoras was misunderstood, and Socrates, and Jesus, and Luther, and Copernicus, and Galileo, and Newton, and every pure and wise spirit that ever took flesh. To be great is to be misunderstood.

15 I suppose no man can violate his nature. All the sallies of his will are rounded in by the law of his being, as the inequalities of Andes and Himmaleh are insignificant in the curve of the sphere. Nor does it matter how you gauge and try him. A character is like an acrostic or Alexandrian stanza; — read it forward, backward, or across, it still spells the same thing. In this pleasing contrite wood-life which God allows me, let me record day by day my honest thought without prospect or

retrospect, and, I cannot doubt, it will be found symmetrical, though I mean it not and see it not. My book should smell of pines and resound with the hum of insects. The swallow over my window should interweave that thread or straw he carries in his bill into my web also. We pass for what we are. Character teaches above our wills. Men imagine that they communicate their virtue or vice only by overt actions, and do not see that virtue or vice emit a breath every moment.

There will be an agreement in whatever variety of actions, so they be each honest and natural in their hour. For of one will, the actions will be harmonious, however unlike they seem. These varieties are lost sight of at a little distance, at a little height of thought. One tendency unites them all. The voyage of the best ship is a zigzag line of a hundred tacks. See the line from a sufficient distance, and it straightens itself to the average tendency. Your genuine action will explain itself and will explain your other genuine actions. Your conformity explains nothing. Act singly, and what you have already done singly will justify you now. Greatness appeals to the future. If I can be firm enough today to do right and scorn eyes, I must have done so much right before as to defend me now. Be it how it will, do right now. Always scorn appearances and you always may. The force of character is cumulative. All the foregone days of virtue work their health into this. What makes the majesty of the heroes of the senate and the field, which so fills the imagination? The consciousness of a train of great days and victories behind. They shed an united light on the advancing actor. He is attended as by a visible escort of angels. That is it which throws thunder into Chatham's voice, and dignity into Washington's port, and America into Adams's eye. Honor is venerable to us because it is no ephemera. It is always ancient virtue. We worship it today because it is not of today. We love it and pay it homage because it is not a trap for our love and homage, but is self-dependent, self-derived, and therefore of an old immaculate pedigree, even if shown in a young person.

I hope in these days we have heard the last of conformity and consistency. Let the words be gazetted and ridiculous henceforward. Instead of the gong for dinner, let us hear a whistle from the Spartan fife. Let us never bow and apologize more. A great man is coming to eat at my house. I do not wish to please him; I wish that he should wish to please me. I will stand here for humanity, and though I would make it kind, I would make it true. Let us affront and reprimand the smooth mediocrity and squalid contentment of the times, and hurl in the face of custom and trade and office, the fact which is the upshot of all history, that there is a great responsible Thinker and Actor working wherever a man works; that a true man belongs to no other time or place, but is the center of things. Where he is, there is nature. He measures you and all men and all events. Ordinarily, every body in society reminds us of somewhat else, or of some other person. Character, reality, reminds you of nothing else; it takes place of the whole creation. The man must be so much that he must make all circumstances indifferent. Every true man is a cause, a country, and an age; requires infinite spaces and numbers and time fully to accomplish his design; — and posterity seem to follow his steps as a train of clients. A man Caesar is born, and for ages after we have a Roman Empire. Christ is born, and millions of minds so grow and cleave to his genius that he is confounded with virtue and the possible of man. An institution is the lengthened shadow of one man; as, Monachism, of the Hermit Antony; the Reformation, of Luther; Quakerism, of Fox; Methodism, of Wesley; Abolition, of Clarkson. Scipio, Milton called "the height of Rome"; and all history Resolves itself very easily into the biography of a few stout and earnest persons.

Let a man then know his worth, and keep things under his feet. Let him not peep or steal, or skulk up and down with the air of a charity-boy, a bastard, or an interloper in the world which exists for him. But the man in the street, finding no worth in himself which corresponds to the force which built a tower or sculptured a marble god, feels poor when he looks on these. To him a palace, a statue, or a costly book have an alien and forbidding air, much like a gay equipage, and seem to say like that, 'Who are you, Sir?' Yet they all are his, suitors for his notice, petitioners to his faculties that they will come out and take possession. The picture waits for my verdict; it is not to command me, but I am to settle its claims to praise. That popular fable of the sot who was picked up dead drunk in the street, carried to the duke's house, washed and dressed and laid in the duke's bed, and, on his waking, treated with all obsequious ceremony like the duke, and assured that he had been insane, owes its popularity to the fact that it symbolizes so well the state of man, who is in the world a sort of sot, but now and then wakes up, exercises his reason and finds himself a true prince.

Our reading is mendicant and sycophantic. In history our imagination plays us false. Kingdom and lordship, power and estate, are a gaudier vocabulary than private John and Edward in a small house and common day's work; but the things of life are the same to both; the sum total of both is the same. Why all this deference to Alfred and Scanderbeg and Gustavus? Suppose they were virtuous; did they wear out virtue? As great a stake depends on your private act today, as followed their public and renowned steps. When private men shall act with original views, the luster will be transferred from the actions of kings to those of gentlemen.

The world has been instructed by its kings, who have so 20
magnetized the eyes of nations. It has been taught by this colossal symbol the mutual reverence that is due from man to man. The joyful loyalty with which men have everywhere suffered the king, the noble, or the great proprietor to walk among them by a law

of his own, make his own scale of men and things and reverse theirs, pay for benefits not with money but with honor, and represent the law in his person, was the hieroglyphic by which they obscurely signified their consciousness of their own right and comeliness, the right of every man.

The magnetism which all original action exerts is explained when we inquire the reason of self-trust. Who is the Trustee? What is the aboriginal Self, on which a universal reliance may be grounded? What is the nature and power of that science-baffling star, without parallax, without calculable elements, which shoots a ray of beauty even into trivial and impure actions, if the least mark of independence appear? The inquiry leads us to that source, at once the essence of genius, of virtue, and of life, which we call Spontaneity or Instinct. We denote this primary wisdom as Intuition, whilst all later teachings are tuitions. In that deep force, the last fact behind which analysis cannot go, all things find their common origin. For the sense of being which in calm hours rises, we know not how, in the soul, is not diverse from things, from space, from light, from time, from man, but one with them and proceeds obviously from the same source whence their life and being also proceed. We first share the life by which things exist and afterwards see them as appearances in nature and forget that we have shared their cause. Here is the fountain of action and of thought. Here are the lungs of that inspiration which giveth man wisdom and which cannot be denied without impiety and atheism. We lie in the lap of immense intelligence, which makes us receivers of its truth and organs of its activity. When we discern justice, when we discern truth, we do nothing of ourselves, but allow a passage to its beams. If we ask whence this comes, if we seek to pry into the soul that causes, all philosophy is at fault. Its presence or its absence is all we can affirm. Every man discriminates between the voluntary acts of his mind and his involuntary perceptions, and knows that to his involuntary perceptions a perfect faith is due. He may err in the expression of them, but he knows that these things are so, like day and night, not to be disputed. My willful actions and acquisitions are but roving; — the idlest reverie, the faintest native emotion, command my curiosity and respect. Thoughtless people contradict as readily the statement of perceptions as of opinions, or rather much more readily; for they do not distinguish between perception and notion. They fancy that I choose to see this or that thing. But perception is not whimsical, but fatal. If I see a trait, my children will see it after me, and in course of time all mankind, — although it may chance that no one has seen it before me. For my perception of it is as much a fact as the sun.

The relations of the soul to the divine spirit are so pure that it is profane to seek to interpose helps. It must be that when God speaketh he should communicate, not one thing, but all things; should fill the world with his voice; should scatter forth light, nature, time, souls, from the center of the present thought; and new date and new create the whole. Whenever a mind is simple and receives a divine wisdom, old things pass away, — means, teachers, texts, temples fall; it lives now, and absorbs past and future into the present hour. All things are made sacred by relation to it, — one as much as another. All things are dissolved to their center by their cause, and in the universal miracle petty and particular miracles disappear. If therefore a man claims to know and speak of God and carries you backward to the phraseology of some old moldered nation in another country, in another world, believe him not. Is the acorn better than the oak which is its fullness and completion? Is the parent better than the child into whom he has cast his ripened being? Whence then this worship of the past? The centuries are conspirators against the sanity and authority of the soul. Time and space are but physiological colors which the eye makes, but the soul is light: where it is, is day; where it was, is night; and history is an impertinence and an injury if it be any thing more than a cheerful apologue or parable of my being and becoming.

Man is timid and apologetic; he is no longer upright; he dares not say 'I think,' 'I am,' but quotes some saint or sage. He is ashamed before the blade of grass or the blowing rose. These roses under my window make no reference to former roses or to better ones; they are for what they are; they exist with God today. There is no time to them. There is simply the rose; it is perfect in every moment of its existence. Before a leaf-bud has burst, its whole life acts; in the full-blown flower there is no more; in the leafless root there is no less. Its nature is satisfied and it satisfies nature in all moments alike. But man postpones or remembers; he does not live in the present, but with reverted eye laments the past, or, heedless of the riches that surround him, stands on tiptoe to foresee the future. He cannot be happy and strong until he too lives with nature in the present, above time.

This should be plain enough. Yet see what strong intellects dare not yet hear God himself unless he speak the phraseology of I know not what David, or Jeremiah, or Paul. We shall not always set so great a price on a few texts, on a few lives. We are like children who repeat by rote the sentences of grandames and tutors, and, as they grow older, of the men of talents and character they chance to see, — painfully recollecting the exact words they spoke; afterwards, when they come into the point of view which those had who uttered these sayings, they understand them and are willing to let the words go; for at any time they can use words as good when occasion comes. If we live truly, we shall see truly. It is as easy for the strong man to be strong, as it is for the weak to be weak. When we have new perception, we shall gladly disburden the memory of its hoarded treasures as old rubbish. When a man lives with God, his voice shall be as sweet as the murmur of the brook and the rustle of the corn.

And now at last the highest truth on this subject remains 25
unsaid; probably cannot be said; for all that we say is the far-off remembering of the intuition. That thought by what I can now nearest approach to say it, is this. When good is near you, when you have life in yourself, it is not by any known or accustomed way; you shall not discern the footprints of any other; you shall not see the face of man; you shall not hear any name; — the way, the thought, the good shall be wholly strange and new. It shall exclude example and experience. You take the way from man, not to man. All persons that ever existed are its forgotten ministers. Fear and hope are alike beneath it. There is somewhat low even in hope. In the hour of vision there is nothing that can be called gratitude, nor properly joy. The soul raised over passion beholds identity and eternal causation, perceives the self-existence of Truth and Right, and calms itself with knowing that all things go well. Vast spaces of nature, the Atlantic Ocean, the South Sea; long intervals of time, years, centuries, are of no account. This which I think and feel underlay every former state of life and circumstances, as it does underlie my present, and what is called life, and what is called death.

Life only avails, not the having lived. Power ceases in the instant of repose; it resides in the moment of transition from a past to a new state, in the shooting of the gulf, in the darting to an aim. This one fact the world hates; that the soul *becomes*; for that for ever degrades the past, turns all riches to poverty, all reputation to a shame, confounds the saint with the rogue, shoves Jesus and Judas equally aside. Why then do we prate of self-reliance? Inasmuch as the soul is present there will be power not confident but agent. To talk of reliance is a poor external way of speaking. Speak rather of that which relies because it works and is. Who has more obedience than I masters me, though he should not raise his finger. Round him I must revolve by the gravitation of spirits. We fancy it rhetoric when we speak of eminent virtue. We do not yet see that virtue is Height, and that a man or a company of men, plastic and permeable to principles, by the law of nature must overpower and ride all cities, nations, kings, rich men, poets, who are not.

This is the ultimate fact which we so quickly reach on this, as on every topic, the resolution of all into the ever-blessed ONE. Self-existence is the attribute of the Supreme Cause, and it constitutes the measure of good by the degree in which it enters into all lower forms. All things real are so by so much virtue as they contain. Commerce, husbandry, hunting, whaling, war, eloquence, personal weight, are somewhat, and engage my respect as examples of its presence and impure action. I see the same law working in nature for conservation and growth. Power is, in nature, the essential measure of right. Nature suffers nothing to remain in her kingdoms which cannot help itself. The genesis and maturation of a planet, its poise and orbit, the bended tree recovering itself from the strong wind, the vital resources of every animal and vegetable, are demonstrations of the self-sufficing and therefore self-relying soul.

Thus all concentrates: let us not rove; let us sit at home with the cause. Let us stun and astonish the intruding rabble of men and books and institutions, by a simple declaration of the divine fact. Bid the invaders take the shoes from off their feet, for God is here within. Let our simplicity judge them, and our docility to our own law demonstrate the poverty of nature and fortune beside our native riches.

But now we are a mob. Man does not stand in awe of man, nor is his genius admonished to stay at home, to put itself in communication with the internal ocean, but it goes abroad to beg a cup of water of the urns of other men. We must go alone. I like the silent church before the service begins, better than any preaching. How far off, how cool, how chaste the persons look, begirt each one with a precinct or sanctuary! So let us always sit. Why should we assume the faults of our friend, or wife, or father, or child, because they sit around our hearth, or are said to have the same blood? All men have my blood and I have all men's. Not for that will I adopt their petulance or folly, even to the extent of being ashamed of it. But your isolation must not be mechanical, but spiritual, that is, must be elevation. At times the whole world seems to be in conspiracy to importune you with emphatic trifles. Friend, client, child, sickness, fear, want, charity, all knock at once at thy closet door and say, — 'Come out unto us.' But keep thy state; come not into their confusion. The power men possess to annoy me I give them by a weak curiosity. No man can come near me but through my act. "What we love that we have, but by desire we bereave ourselves of the love."

30 If we cannot at once rise to the sanctities of obedience and faith, let us at least resist our temptations; let us enter into the state of war and wake Thor and Woden, courage and constancy, in our Saxon breasts. This is to be done in our smooth times by speaking the truth. Check this lying hospitality and lying affection. Live no longer to the expectation of these deceived and deceiving people with whom we converse. Say to them, 'O father, O mother, O wife, O brother, O friend, I have lived with you after appearances hitherto. Henceforward I am the truth's. Be it known unto you that henceforward I obey no law less than the eternal law. I will have no covenants but proximities. I shall endeavor to nourish my parents, to support my family, to be the chaste husband of one wife, — but these relations I must fill after a new and unprecedented way. I appeal from your customs. I must be myself. I cannot break myself any longer for you, or you. If you can love me for what I am, we shall be the happier. If you cannot, I will still seek to deserve that you should. I will not hide my tastes or aversions. I will so trust that what is deep is holy, that I will do strongly before the sun and moon whatever inly rejoices me and the heart appoints. If

you are noble, I will love you: if you are not, I will not hurt you and myself by hypocritical attentions. If you are true, but not in the same truth with me, cleave to your companions; I will seek my own. I do this not selfishly but humbly and truly. It is alike your interest, and mine, and all men's, however long we have dwelt in lies, to live in truth. Does this sound harsh today? You will soon love what is dictated by your nature as well as mine, and if we follow the truth it will bring us out safe at last.' — But so may you give these friends pain. Yes, but I cannot sell my liberty and my power, to save their sensibility. Besides, all persons have their moments of reason, when they look out into the region of absolute truth; then will they justify me and do the same thing.

The populace think that your rejection of popular standards is a rejection of all standard, and mere antinomianism; and the bold sensualist will use the name of philosophy to gild his crimes. But the law of consciousness abides. There are two confessionals, in one or the other of which we must be shriven. You may fulfill your round of duties by clearing yourself in the *direct*, or in the *reflex* way. Consider whether you have satisfied your relations to father, mother, cousin, neighbor, town, cat, and dog; whether any of these can upbraid you. But I may also neglect this reflex standard and absolve me to myself. I have my own stern claims and perfect circle. It denies the name of duty to many offices that are called duties. But if I can discharge its debts it enables me to dispense with the popular code. If any one imagines that this law is lax, let him keep its commandment one day.

And truly it demands something godlike in him who has cast off the common motives of humanity and has ventured to trust himself for a taskmaster. High be his heart, faithful his will, clear his sight, that he may in good earnest be doctrine, society, law, to himself, that a simple purpose may be to him as strong as iron necessity is to others!

If any man consider the present aspects of what is called by distinction *society*, he will see the need of these ethics. The sinew and heart of man seem to be drawn out, and we are become timorous, desponding whimperers. We are afraid of truth, afraid of fortune, afraid of death and afraid of each other. Our age yields no great and perfect persons. We want men and women who shall renovate life and our social state, but we see that most natures are insolvent, cannot satisfy their own wants, have an ambition out of all proportion to their practical force and do lean and beg day and night continually. Our housekeeping is mendicant, our arts, our occupations, our marriages, our religion we have not chosen, but society has chosen for us. We are parlor soldiers. We shun the rugged battle of fate, where strength is born.

If our young men miscarry in their first enterprises they lose all heart. If the young merchant fails, men say he is *ruined.* If the finest genius studies at one of our colleges and is not installed in an office within one year afterwards in the cities or suburbs of Boston or New York, it seems to his friends and to himself that he is right in being disheartened and in complaining the rest of his life. A sturdy lad from New Hampshire or Vermont, who in turn tries all the professions, who *teams it, farms it, peddles*, keeps a school, preaches, edits a newspaper, goes to Congress, buys a township, and so forth, in successive years, and always like a cat falls on his feet, is worth a hundred of these city dolls. He walks abreast with his days and feels no shame in not 'studying a profession,' for he does not postpone his life, but lives already. He has not one chance, but a hundred chances. Let a Stoic open the resources of man and tell men they are not leaning willows, but can and must detach themselves; that with the exercise of self-trust, new powers shall appear; that a man is the word made flesh, born to shed healing to the nations; that he should be ashamed of our compassion, and that the moment he acts from himself, tossing the laws, the books, idolatries and customs out of the window, we pity him no more but thank and revere him; — and that teacher shall restore the life of man to splendor and make his name dear to all history.

35 It is easy to see that a greater self-reliance must work a revolution in all the offices and relations of men; in their religion; in their education; in their pursuits; their modes of living; their association; in their property; in their speculative views.

1. In what prayers do men allow themselves! That which they call a holy office is not so much as brave and manly. Prayer looks abroad and asks for some foreign addition to come through some foreign virtue, and loses itself in endless mazes of natural and supernatural, and mediatorial and miraculous. Prayer that craves a particular commodity, any thing less than all good, is vicious. Prayer is the contemplation of the facts of life from the highest point of view. It is the soliloquy of a beholding and jubilant soul. It is the spirit of God pronouncing his works good. But prayer as a means to effect a private end is meanness and theft. It supposes dualism and not unity in nature and consciousness. As soon as the man is at one with God, he will not beg. He will then see prayer in all action. The prayer of the farmer kneeling in his field to weed it, the prayer of the rower kneeling with the stroke of his oar, are true prayers heard throughout nature, though for cheap ends. Caratach, in Fletcher's Bonduca, when admonished to inquire the mind of the god Audate, replies, —

> "His hidden meaning lies in our endeavors; Our valors are our best gods."

Another sort of false prayers are our regrets. Discontent is the want of self-reliance: it is infirmity of will. Regret calamities if you can thereby help the sufferer; if not, attend your own work and already the evil begins to be repaired. Our sympathy is just as base. We come to them who weep foolishly and sit down and cry for company, instead of imparting to them truth and health in rough electric shocks, putting them once more in communication with their own reason. The secret of fortune is joy in our hands. Welcome evermore to gods and men is the self-helping man. For him all doors are flung wide; him all tongues greet, all honors crown, all eyes follow with desire. Our love goes out to him and embraces him because he did not need it. We solicitously and apologetically caress and celebrate him because he held on his way and scorned our disapprobation. The gods love him because men hated him. "To the persevering mortal," said Zoroaster, "the blessed Immortals are swift."

As men's prayers are a disease of the will, so are their creeds a disease of the intellect. They say with those foolish Israelites, 'Let not God speak to us, lest we die. Speak thou, speak any man with us, and we will obey.' Everywhere I am hindered of meeting God in my brother, because he has shut his own temple doors and recites fables merely of his brother's, or his brother's brother's God. Every new mind is a new classification. If it prove a mind of uncommon activity and power, a Locke, a Lavoisier, a Hutton, a Bentham, a Fourier, it imposes its classification on other men, and lo! a new system. In proportion to the depth of the thought, and so to the number of the objects it touches and brings within reach of the pupil, is his complacency. But chiefly is this apparent in creeds and churches, which are also classifications of some powerful mind acting on the elemental thought of duty, and man's relation to the Highest. Such is Calvinism, Quakerism, Swedenborgism. The pupil takes the same delight in subordinating every thing to the new terminology as a girl who has just learned botany in seeing a new earth and new seasons thereby. It will happen for a time that the pupil will find his intellectual power has grown by the study of his master's mind. But in all unbalanced minds the classification is idolized, passes for the end and not for a speedily exhaustible means, so that the walls of the system blend to their eye in the remote horizon with the walls of the universe; the luminaries of heaven seem to them hung on the arch their master built. They cannot imagine how you aliens have any right to see, — how you can see; 'It must be somehow that you stole the light from us.' They do not yet perceive that light, unsystematic, indomitable, will break into any cabin, even into theirs. Let them chirp awhile and call it their own. If they are honest and do well, presently their neat new pinfold will be too strait and low, will crack, will lean, will rot and vanish, and the immortal light, all young and joyful, million-orbed, million-colored, will beam over the universe as on the first morning.

2. It is for want of self-culture that the superstition of Travelling, whose idols are Italy, England, Egypt, retains its fascination for all educated Americans. They who made England, Italy, or Greece venerable in the imagination did so by sticking fast where they were, like an axis of the earth. In manly hours we feel that duty is our place. The soul is no traveller; the wise man stays at home, and when his necessities, his duties, on any occasion call him from his house, or into foreign lands, he is at home still and shall make men sensible by the expression of his countenance that he goes, the missionary of wisdom and virtue, and visits cities and men like a sovereign and not like an interloper or a valet.

40 I have no churlish objection to the circumnavigation of the globe for the purposes of art, of study, and benevolence, so that the man is first domesticated, or does not go abroad with the hope of finding somewhat greater than he knows. He who travels to be amused, or to get somewhat which he does not carry, travels away from himself, and grows old even in youth among old things. In Thebes, in Palmyra, his will and mind have become old and dilapidated as they. He carries ruins to ruins.

Travelling is a fool's paradise. Our first journeys discover to us the indifference of places. At home I dream that at Naples, at Rome, I can be intoxicated with beauty and lose my sadness. I pack my trunk, embrace my friends, embark on the sea and at last wake up in Naples, and there beside me is the stern fact, the sad self, unrelenting, identical, that I fled from. I seek the Vatican and the palaces. I affect to be intoxicated with sights and suggestions, but I am not intoxicated. My giant goes with me wherever I go.

3. But the rage of travelling is a symptom of a deeper unsoundness affecting the whole intellectual action. The intellect is vagabond, and our system of education fosters restlessness. Our minds travel when our bodies are forced to stay at home. We imitate; and what is imitation but the travelling of the mind? Our houses are built with foreign taste; our shelves are garnished with foreign ornaments; our opinions, our tastes, our faculties, lean, and follow the Past and the Distant. The soul created the arts wherever they have flourished. It was in his own mind that the artist sought his model. It was an application of his own thought to the thing to be done and the conditions to be observed. And why need we copy the Doric or the Gothic model? Beauty, convenience, grandeur of thought and quaint expression are as near to us as to any, and if the American artist will study with hope and love the precise thing to be done by him, considering the climate, the soil, the length of the day, the wants of the people, the habit and form of the government, he will create a house in which all these will find themselves fitted, and taste and sentiment will be satisfied also.

Insist on yourself; never imitate. Your own gift you can present every moment with the cumulative force of a whole life's cultivation; but of the adopted talent of another you have only an extemporaneous half possession. That which each can do best, none but his Maker can teach him. No man yet knows what it is, nor can, till that person has exhibited it. Where is the master who could have taught Shakespeare? Where is the master who could have instructed Franklin, or Washington, or Bacon, or Newton? Every great man is a unique. The Scipionism of Scipio is precisely that part he could not borrow. Shakespeare will never be made by the study of Shakespeare. Do that which is assigned you, and you cannot hope too much or dare too much. There is at this moment for you an utterance brave and grand as that of the colossal chisel of Phidias, or trowel of the Egyptians, or the pen of Moses or Dante, but different from all these. Not possibly will the soul, all rich, all eloquent, with thousand-cloven tongue, deign to repeat itself; but if you can hear what these patriarchs say, surely you can reply to them in the same pitch of voice; for the ear and the tongue are two organs of one nature. Abide in the simple and noble regions of thy life, obey thy heart and thou shalt reproduce the Foreworld again.

4. As our Religion, our Education, our Art look abroad, so does our spirit of society. All men plume themselves on the improvement of society, and no man improves.

45 Society never advances. It recedes as fast on one side as it gains on the other. It undergoes continual changes; it is barbarous, it is civilized, it is christianized, it is rich, it is scientific; but this change is not amelioration. For every thing that is given something is taken. Society acquires new arts and loses old instincts. What a contrast between the well-clad, reading, writing, thinking American, with a watch, a pencil and a bill of exchange in his pocket, and the naked New Zealander, whose property is a club, a spear, a mat and an undivided twentieth of a shed to sleep under! But compare the health of the two men and you shall see that the white man has lost his aboriginal strength. If the traveller tell us truly, strike the savage with a broad axe and in a day or two the flesh shall unite and heal as if you struck the blow into soft pitch, and the same blow shall send the white to his grave.

The civilized man has built a coach, but has lost the use of his feet. He is supported on crutches, but lacks so much support of muscle. He has a fine Geneva watch, but he fails of the skill to tell the hour by the sun. A Greenwich nautical almanac he has, and so being sure of the information when he wants it, the man in the street does not know a star in the sky. The solstice he does not observe; the equinox he knows as little; and the whole bright calendar of the year is without a dial in his mind. His note-books impair his memory; his libraries overload his wit; the insurance-office increases the number of accidents; and it may be a question whether machinery does not encumber; whether we have not lost by refinement some energy, by a Christianity entrenched in establishments and forms some vigor of wild virtue. For every Stoic was a Stoic; but in Christendom where is the Christian?

There is no more deviation in the moral standard than in the standard of height or bulk. No greater men are now than ever were. A singular equality may be observed between the great men of the first and of the last ages; nor can all the science, art, religion, and philosophy of the nineteenth century avail to educate greater men than Plutarch's heroes, three or four and twenty centuries ago. Not in time is the race progressive. Phocion, Socrates, Anaxagoras, Diogenes, are great men, but they leave no class. He who is really of their class will not be called by their name, but will be his own man, and in his turn the founder of a sect. The arts and inventions of each period are only its costume and do not invigorate men. The harm of the improved machinery may compensate its good. Hudson and Behring accomplished so much in their fishing-boats as to astonish Parry and Franklin, whose equipment exhausted the resources of science and art. Galileo, with an opera-glass, discovered a more splendid series of celestial phenomena than any one since. Columbus found the New World in an undecked boat. It is curious to see the periodical disuse and perishing of means and machinery which were introduced with loud laudation a few years or centuries before. The great genius returns to essential man. We reckoned the improvements of the art of war among the triumphs of science, and yet Napoleon conquered Europe by the bivouac, which consisted of falling back on naked valor and disencumbering it of all aids. The Emperor held it impossible to make a perfect army, says Las Cases, "without abolishing our arms, magazines, commissaries and carriages, until, in imitation of the Roman custom, the soldier should receive his supply of corn, grind it in his hand-mill, and bake his bread himself."

Society is a wave. The wave moves onward, but the water of which it is composed does not. The same particle does not rise from the valley to the ridge. Its unity is only phenomenal. The persons who make up a nation today, next year die, and their experience with them.

And so the reliance on Property, including the reliance on governments which protect it, is the want of self-reliance. Men have looked away from themselves and at things so long that they have come to esteem the religious, learned and civil institutions as guards of property, and they deprecate assaults on these, because they feel them to be assaults on property. They measure their esteem of each other by what each has, and not by what each is. But a cultivated man becomes ashamed of his property, out of new respect for his nature. Especially he hates what he has if he see that it is accidental, — came to him by inheritance, or gift, or crime; then he feels that it is not having; it does not belong to him, has no root in him and merely lies there because no revolution or no robber takes it away. But that which a man is, does always by necessity acquire, and what the man acquires is living property, which does not wait the beck of rulers, or mobs, or revolutions, or fire, or storm, or bankruptcies, but perpetually renews itself wherever the man breathes. "Thy lot or portion of life," said the Caliph Ali, "is seeking after thee;

therefore be at rest from seeking after it." Our dependence on these foreign goods leads us to our slavish respect for numbers. The political parties meet in numerous conventions; the greater the concourse and with each new uproar of announcement, The delegation from Essex! The Democrats from New Hampshire! The Whigs of Maine! the young patriot feels himself stronger than before by a new thousand of eyes and arms. In like manner the reformers summon conventions and vote and resolve in multitude. Not so, O friends! will the God deign to enter and inhabit you, but by a method precisely the reverse. It is only as a man puts off all foreign support and stands alone that I see him to be strong and to prevail. He is weaker by every recruit to his banner. Is not a man better than a town? Ask nothing of men, and, in the endless mutation, thou only firm column must presently appear the upholder of all that surrounds thee. He who knows that power is inborn, that he is weak because he has looked for good out of him and elsewhere, and so perceiving, throws himself unhesitatingly on his thought, instantly rights himself, stands in the erect position, commands his limbs, works miracles; just as a man who stands on his feet is stronger than a man who stands on his head.

So use all that is called Fortune. Most men gamble with her, 50
and gain all, and lose all, as her wheel rolls. But do thou leave as unlawful these winnings, and deal with Cause and Effect, the chancellors of God. In the Will work and acquire, and thou hast chained the wheel of Chance, and shalt sit hereafter out of fear from her rotations. A political victory, a rise of rents, the recovery of your sick or the return of your absent friend, or some other favorable event raises your spirits, and you think good days are preparing for you. Do not believe it. Nothing can bring you peace but yourself. Nothing can bring you peace but the triumph of principles.

On the Slave-Trade

by Benjamin Franklin

Benjamin Franklin (1706–1790) was one of the Founding Fathers of the United States. Throughout his adult life, he was an author, printer, scientist, inventor, statesman, and diplomat. He often wrote anonymously or under a false name in order to attack those with whom he disagreed, as he did in this satirical piece that was written three weeks prior to his death.

To the Editor of the *Federal Gazette*
March 23d, 1790.

Sir: Reading last night in your excellent paper the speech of Mr. Jackson in Congress against their meddling with the affair of slavery, or attempting to mend the condition of the slaves, it put me in mind of a similar one made about 100 years since by Sidi Mehemet Ibrahim, a member of the Divan of Algiers, which may be seen in Martin's account of his consulship, anno 1687. It was against granting the petition of the sect called *Erika*, or purists who prayed for the abolition of piracy and slavery as being unjust. Mr. Jackson does not quote it; perhaps he has not seen it. If, therefore, some of its reasonings are to be found in his eloquent speech, it may only show that men's interests and intellects operate and are operated on with surprising similarity in all countries and climates, when under similar circumstances. The African's speech, as translated, is as follows:

Allah Bismillah, etc. God is great, and Mahomet is his prophet.

Have these *Erika* considered the consequences of granting their petition? If we cease our cruises against the Christians, how shall we be furnished with the commodities their countries produce, and which are so necessary for us? If we forbear to make slaves of their people, who in this hot climate are to cultivate our lands? Who are to perform the common labors of our city, and in our families? Must we not then be our own slaves? And is there not more compassion and more favor due to us as Mussulmen than to these Christian dogs? We have now about 50,000 Slaves in and near Algiers. This number, if not kept up by fresh supplies, will soon diminish, and be gradually annihilated.

If we then cease taking and plundering the infidel ships, and making slaves of the seamen and passengers, our lands will become of no value for want of cultivation; the rents of houses in the city will sink one half; and the revenues of government arising from its share of prizes be totally destroyed! And for what? To gratify the whims of a whimsical sect, who would have us, not only forbear making more slaves, but even to manumit those we have.

But who is to indemnify their masters for the loss? Will the state do it? Is our treasury sufficient? Will the *Erika* do it? Can they do it? Or would they, to do what they think justice to the slaves, do a greater injustice to the owners? And it we set our slaves free, what is to be done with them? Few of them will return to their countries; they know too well the great hardships they must there be subject to; they will not embrace our holy religion; they will not adopt our manners; our people will not pollute themselves by intermarrying with them. Must we maintain them as beggars in our streets, or suffer our properties to be the prey of their pillage? For men long accustomed to slavery will not work for a livelihood when not compelled. And what is there so pitiable in their present condition? Were they not slaves in their own countries?

Are not Spain, Portugal, France, and the Italian states governed by despots, who hold all their subjects in slavery, without exception? Even England treats its sailors as slaves; for they are, whenever the government pleases, seized, and confined in ships of war, condemned not only to work, but to fight, for small wages, or a mere subsistence, not better than our slaves are allowed by us. Is their condition then made worse by their falling into our hands? No; they have only exchanged on slavery for another, and I may say a better; for here they are brought into a land where the sun of Islamism gives forth its light, and shines in full splendor, and they have an opportunity of making themselves acquainted with the true doctrine, and thereby saving their immortal souls. Those who remain at home have not that happiness. Sending the slaves home then would be sending them out of light into darkness.

I repeat the question, what is to be done with them? I have heard it suggested, that they may be planted in the wilderness, where there is plenty of land for them to subsist on, and where they may flourish as a free state; but they are, I doubt, to little disposed to labor without compulsion, as well as too ignorant to establish a good government, and the wild Arabs would soon molest and destroy or again enslave them. While serving us, we take care to provide them with every thing, and they are treated with humanity. The laborers in their own country are, as I am well informed, worse fed, lodged, and clothed. The condition of most of them is therefore already mended, and requires no further improvement. Here their lives are in safety. They are not liable to be impressed for soldiers, and forced to cut one another's Christian throats, as in the wars of their own countries. If some of the religious mad bigots, who now tease us with their silly petitions, have in a fit of blind zeal freed their slaves, it was not generosity, it was not humanity, that moved them to the action; it was from the conscious burden of a load of sins, and hope, from the supposed merits of so good a work, to be excused damnation.

How grossly are they mistaken in imagining slavery to be 10
disallowed by the Alcoran? Are not the two precepts, to quote no more, "Masters, treat your slaves with kindness; slaves, serve your masters with cheerfulness and fidelity," clear proofs to the contrary? Nor can the plundering of infidels be in that sacred book forbidden, since it is well known from it, that God has given the world, and all that it contains, to his faithful Mussulmen, who are to enjoy it of right as fast as they conquer it. Let us then hear no more of this detestable proposition, the manumission of Christian slaves, the adoption of which would, by depreciating our lands and houses, and thereby depriving so many good citizens of their properties, create universal discontent, and provoke insurrections, to the endangering of government and producing general confusion. I have therefore no doubt, but this wise council will prefer the comfort and happiness of a whole nation of true believers to the whim of a few *Erika*, and dismiss their petition.

The result was, as Martin tells us, that the Divan came to this resolution: "The doctrine, that plundering and enslaving the Christians is unjust, is at best *problematical*; but that it is the interest of this state to continue the practice, is clear; therefore let the petition be rejected."

And it was rejected accordingly.

And since like motives are apt to produce in the minds of men like opinions and resolutions, may we not, Mr. Brown, venture to predict, from this account, that the petitions to the parliament of England for abolishing the slave-trade, to say nothing of other legislatures, and the debates upon them, will have a similar conclusion? I am, sir, your constant reader and humble servant,

— Historicus

Anarchism: What It Really Stands For

by Emma Goldman

Emma Goldman (1869–1940) was a writer and orator known for drawing out crowds that numbered in the thousands. She was a pivotal figure in the development of anarchist political thought in the United States. The following essay comes from the 1917 edition of Anarchism and Other Essays.

Anarchy

Ever reviled, accursed, ne'er understood,
Thou art the grisly terror of our age.
"Wreck of all order," cry the multitude,
"Art thou, and war and murder's endless rage."
O, let them cry. To them that ne'er have striven
The truth that lies behind a word to find,
To them the word's right meaning was not given.
They shall continue blind among the blind.
But thou, O word, so clear, so strong, so pure,
Thou sayest all which I for goal have taken.
I give thee to the future! Thine secure
When each at least unto himself shall waken.
Comes it in sunshine? In the tempest's thrill?
I cannot tell — but it the earth shall see!
I am an Anarchist! Wherefore I will
Not rule, and also ruled I will not be!

— John Henry Mackay

The history of human growth and development is at the same time the history of the terrible struggle of every new idea heralding the approach of a brighter dawn. In its tenacious hold on tradition, the Old has never hesitated to make use of the foulest and cruelest means to stay the advent of the New, in whatever form or period the latter may have asserted itself. Nor need we retrace our steps into the distant past to realize the enormity of opposition, difficulties, and hardships placed in the path of every progressive idea. The rack, the thumbscrew, and the knout are still with us; so are the convict's garb and the social wrath, all conspiring against the spirit that is serenely marching on.

Anarchism could not hope to escape the fate of all other ideas of innovation. Indeed, as the most revolutionary and uncompromising innovator, Anarchism must needs meet with the combined ignorance and venom of the world it aims to reconstruct.

To deal even remotely with all that is being said and done against Anarchism would necessitate the writing of a whole volume. I shall therefore meet only two of the principal objections. In so doing, I shall attempt to elucidate what Anarchism really stands for.

The strange phenomenon of the opposition to Anarchism is that it brings to light the relation between so-called intelligence and ignorance. And yet this is not so very strange when we consider the relativity of all things. The ignorant mass has in its favor that it makes no pretense of knowledge or tolerance. Acting, as it always does, by mere impulse, its reasons are like those of a child. "Why?" "Because." Yet the opposition of the uneducated to Anarchism deserves the same consideration as that of the intelligent man.

What, then, are the objections? First, Anarchism is im- 5
practical, though a beautiful ideal. Second, Anarchism stands for violence and destruction, hence it must be repudiated as

vile and dangerous. Both the intelligent man and the ignorant mass judge not from a thorough knowledge of the subject, but either from hearsay or false interpretation.

A practical scheme, says Oscar Wilde, is either one already in existence, or a scheme that could be carried out under the existing conditions; but it is exactly the existing conditions that one objects to, and any scheme that could accept these conditions is wrong and foolish. The true criterion of the practical, therefore, is not whether the latter can keep intact the wrong or foolish; rather is it whether the scheme has vitality enough to leave the stagnant waters of the old, and build, as well as sustain, new life. In the light of this conception, Anarchism is indeed practical. More than any other idea, it is helping to do away with the wrong and foolish; more than any other idea, it is building and sustaining new life.

The emotions of the ignorant man are continuously kept at a pitch by the most blood-curdling stories about Anarchism. Not a thing too outrageous to be employed against this philosophy and its exponents. Therefore Anarchism represents to the unthinking what the proverbial bad man does to the child, — a black monster bent on swallowing everything; in short, destruction and violence.

Destruction and violence! How is the ordinary man to know that the most violent element in society is ignorance; that its power of destruction is the very thing Anarchism is combating? Nor is he aware that Anarchism, whose roots, as it were, are part of nature's forces, destroys, not healthful tissue, but parasitic growths that feed on the life's essence of society. It is merely clearing the soil from weeds and sagebrush, that it may eventually bear healthy fruit.

Someone has said that it requires less mental effort to condemn than to think. The widespread mental indolence, so prevalent in society, proves this to be only too true. Rather than to go to the bottom of any given idea, to examine into its origin and meaning, most people will either condemn it altogether, or rely on some superficial or prejudicial definition of non-essentials.

Anarchism urges man to think, to investigate, to analyze every proposition; but that the brain capacity of the average reader be not taxed too much, I also shall begin with a definition, and then elaborate on the latter.

> ANARCHISM: — The philosophy of a new social order based on liberty unrestricted by man-made law; the theory that all forms of government rest on violence, and are therefore wrong and harmful, as well as unnecessary.

The new social order rests, of course, on the materialistic basis of life; but while all Anarchists agree that the main evil today is an economic one, they maintain that the solution of that evil can be brought about only through the consideration of *every phase* of life, — individual, as well as the collective; the internal, as well as the external phases.

A thorough perusal of the history of human development will disclose two elements in bitter conflict with each other; elements that are only now beginning to be understood, not as foreign to each other, but as closely related and truly harmonious, if only placed in proper environment: the individual and social instincts. The individual and society have waged a relentless and bloody battle for ages, each striving for supremacy, because each was blind to the value and importance of the other. The individual and social instincts, — the one a most potent factor for individual endeavor, for growth, aspiration, self-realization; the other an equally potent factor for mutual helpfulness and social well-being.

The explanation of the storm raging within the individual, and between him and his surroundings, is not far to seek. The primitive man, unable to understand his being, much less the unity of all life, felt himself absolutely dependent on blind, hidden forces ever ready to mock and taunt him. Out of that attitude grew the religious concepts of man as a mere speck of dust dependent on superior powers on high, who can only be appeased by complete surrender. All the early sagas rest on that idea, which continues to be the *Leitmotiv* of the biblical tales dealing with the relation of man to God, to the State, to society. Again and again the same motif, *man is nothing, the powers are everything*. Thus Jehovah would only endure man on condition of complete surrender. Man can have all the glories of the earth, but he must not become conscious of himself. The State, society, and moral laws all sing the same refrain: Man can have all the glories of the earth, but he must not become conscious of himself.

Anarchism is the only philosophy which brings to man the consciousness of himself; which maintains that God, the State, and society are non-existent, that their promises are null and void, since they can be fulfilled only through man's subordination. Anarchism is therefore the teacher of the unity of life; not merely in nature, but in man. There is no conflict between the individual and the social instincts, any more than there is between the heart and the lungs: the one the receptacle of a precious life essence, the other the repository of the element that keeps the essence pure and strong. The individual is the heart of society, conserving the essence of social life; society is the lungs which are distributing the element to keep the life essence — that is, the individual — pure and strong.

15 "The one thing of value in the world," says Emerson, "is the active soul; this every man contains within him. The soul active sees absolute truth and utters truth and creates." In other words, the individual instinct is the thing of value in the world. It is the true soul that sees and creates the truth alive, out of which is to come a still greater truth, the re-born social soul.

Anarchism is the great liberator of man from the phantoms that have held him captive; it is the arbiter and pacifier of the two forces for individual and social harmony. To accomplish that unity, Anarchism has declared war on the pernicious influences which have so far prevented the harmonious blending of individual and social instincts, the individual and society.

Religion, the dominion of the human mind; Property, the dominion of human needs; and Government, the dominion of human conduct, represent the stronghold of man's enslavement and all the horrors it entails. Religion! How it dominates man's mind, how it humiliates and degrades his soul. God is everything, man is nothing, says religion. But out of that nothing God has created a kingdom so despotic, so tyrannical, so cruel, so terribly exacting that naught but gloom and tears and blood have ruled the world since gods began. Anarchism rouses man to rebellion against this black monster. Break your mental fetters, says Anarchism to man, for not until you think and judge for yourself will you get rid of the dominion of darkness, the greatest obstacle to all progress.

Property, the dominion of man's needs, the denial of the right to satisfy his needs. Time was when property claimed a divine right, when it came to man with the same refrain, even as religion, "Sacrifice! Abnegate! Submit!" The spirit of Anarchism has lifted man from his prostrate position. He now stands erect, with his face toward the light. He has learned to see the insatiable, devouring, devastating nature of property, and he is preparing to strike the monster dead.

"Property is robbery," said the great French Anarchist, Proudhon. Yes, but without risk and danger to the robber. Monopolizing the accumulated efforts of man, property has robbed him of his birthright, and has turned him loose a pauper and an outcast. Property has not even the time-worn excuse that man does not create enough to satisfy all needs. The A B C student of economics knows that the productivity of labor within the last few decades far exceeds normal demand a hundredfold. But what are normal demands to an abnormal institution? The only demand that property recognizes is its own gluttonous appetite for greater wealth, because wealth means power; the power to subdue, to crush, to exploit, the power to enslave, to outrage, to degrade. America is particularly boastful of her great power, her enormous national wealth. Poor America, of what avail is all her wealth, if the individuals comprising the nation are wretchedly poor? If they live in squalor, in filth, in crime, with hope and joy gone, a homeless, soilless army of human prey.

It is generally conceded that unless the returns of any business venture exceed the cost, bankruptcy is inevitable. But those engaged in the business of producing wealth have not yet learned even this simple lesson. Every year the cost of production in human life is growing larger (50,000 killed, 100,000 wounded in America last year); the returns to the masses, who help to create wealth, are ever getting smaller. Yet America continues to be blind to the inevitable bankruptcy of our business of production. Nor is this the only crime of the latter. Still more fatal is the crime of turning the producer into a mere particle of a machine, with less will and decision than his master of steel and iron. Man is being robbed not merely of the products of his labor, but of the power of free initiative, of originality, and the interest in, or desire for, the things he is making.

Real wealth consists in things of utility and beauty, in things that help to create strong, beautiful bodies and surroundings inspiring to live in. But if man is doomed to wind cotton around a spool, or dig coal, or build roads for thirty years of his life, there can be no talk of wealth. What he gives to the world is only gray and hideous things, reflecting a dull and hideous existence, — too weak to live, too cowardly to die. Strange to say, there are people who extol this deadening method of centralized production as the proudest achievement of our age. They fail utterly to realize that if we are to continue in machine subserviency, our slavery is more complete than was our bondage to the King. They do not want to know that centralization is not only the death-knell of liberty, but also of health and beauty, of art and science, all these being impossible in a clock-like, mechanical atmosphere.

Anarchism cannot but repudiate such a method of production: its goal is the freest possible expression of all the latent powers of the individual. Oscar Wilde defines a perfect personality as "one who develops under perfect conditions, who is not wounded, maimed, or in danger." A perfect personality, then, is only possible in a state of society where man is free to choose the mode of work, the conditions of work, and the freedom to work. One to whom the making of a table, the building of a house, or the tilling of the soil, is what the painting is to the artist and the discovery to the scientist, — the result of inspiration, of intense longing, and deep interest in work as a creative force. That being the ideal of Anarchism, its economic arrangements must consist of voluntary productive and distributive associations, gradually developing into free communism, as the best means of producing with the least waste of human energy. Anarchism, however, also recognizes the right of the individual, or numbers of individuals, to arrange at all times for other forms of work, in harmony with their tastes and desires.

Such free display of human energy being possible only under complete individual and social freedom, Anarchism directs its forces against the third and greatest foe of all social equality; namely, the State, organized authority, or statutory law, — the dominion of human conduct.

Just as religion has fettered the human mind, and as property, or the monopoly of things, has subdued and stifled man's needs, so has the State enslaved his spirit, dictating every phase of conduct. "All government in essence," says Emerson, "is tyranny." It matters not whether it is government by divine right or majority rule. In every instance its aim is the absolute subordination of the individual.

25 Referring to the American government, the greatest American Anarchist, David Thoreau, said: "Government, what is it but a tradition, though a recent one, endeavoring to transmit itself unimpaired to posterity, but each instance losing its integrity; it has not the vitality and force of a single living man. Law never made man a whit more just; and by means of their respect for it, even the well disposed are daily made agents of injustice."

Indeed, the keynote of government is injustice. With the arrogance and self-sufficiency of the King who could do no wrong, governments ordain, judge, condemn, and punish the most insignificant offenses, while maintaining themselves by the greatest of all offenses, the annihilation of individual liberty. Thus Ouida is right when she maintains that "the State only aims at instilling those qualities in its public by which its demands are obeyed, and its exchequer is filled. Its highest attainment is the reduction of mankind to clockwork. In its atmosphere all those finer and more delicate liberties, which require treatment and spacious expansion, inevitably dry up and perish. The State requires a taxpaying machine in which there is no hitch, an exchequer in which there is never a deficit, and a public, monotonous, obedient, colorless, spiritless, moving humbly like a flock of sheep along a straight high road between two walls."

Yet even a flock of sheep would resist the chicanery of the State, if it were not for the corruptive, tyrannical, and oppressive methods it employs to serve its purposes. Therefore Bakunin repudiates the State as synonymous with the surrender of the liberty of the individual or small minorities, — the destruction of social relationship, the curtailment, or complete denial even, of life itself, for its own aggrandizement. The State is the altar of political freedom and, like the religious altar, it is maintained for the purpose of human sacrifice.

In fact, there is hardly a modern thinker who does not agree that government, organized authority, or the State, is necessary ONLY to maintain or protect property and monopoly. It has proven efficient in that function only.

Even George Bernard Shaw, who hopes for the miraculous from the State under Fabianism, nevertheless admits that "it is at present a huge machine for robbing and slave-driving of the poor by brute force." This being the case, it is hard to see why the clever prefacer wishes to uphold the State after poverty shall have ceased to exist.

Unfortunately there are still a number of people who con- 30
tinue in the fatal belief that government rests on natural laws, that it maintains social order and harmony, that it diminishes crime, and that it prevents the lazy man from fleecing his fellows. I shall therefore examine these contentions.

A natural law is that factor in man which asserts itself freely and spontaneously without any external force, in harmony with the requirements of nature. For instance, the demand for nutrition, for sex gratification, for light, air, and exercise, is a natural law. But its expression needs not the machinery of government, needs not the club, the gun, the handcuff, or the prison. To obey such laws, if we may call it obedience, requires only spontaneity and free opportunity. That governments do not maintain themselves through such harmonious factors is proven by the terrible array of violence, force, and coercion all governments use in order to live. Thus Blackstone is right when he says, "Human laws are invalid, because they are contrary to the laws of nature."

Unless it be the order of Warsaw after the slaughter of thousands of people, it is difficult to ascribe to governments any capacity for order or social harmony. Order derived through submission and maintained by terror is not much of a safe guaranty; yet that is the only "order" that governments have ever maintained. True social harmony grows naturally out of solidarity of interests. In a society where those who always work never have anything, while those who never work enjoy everything, solidarity of interests is non-existent; hence social harmony is but a myth. The only way organized authority meets this grave situation is by extending still greater privileges to those who have already monopolized the earth, and by still further enslaving the disinherited masses. Thus the entire arsenal of government — laws, police, soldiers, the courts, legislatures, prisons, — is strenuously engaged in "harmonizing" the most antagonistic elements in society.

The most absurd apology for authority and law is that they serve to diminish crime. Aside from the fact that the State is itself the greatest criminal, breaking every written and natural law, stealing in the form of taxes, killing in the form of war and capital punishment, it has come to an absolute standstill in coping with crime. It has failed utterly to destroy or even minimize the horrible scourge of its own creation.

Crime is naught but misdirected energy. So long as every institution of today, economic, political, social, and moral, conspires to misdirect human energy into wrong channels; so long as most people are out of place doing the things they hate to do, living a life they loathe to live, crime will be inevitable, and all the laws on the statutes can only increase, but never do away with, crime. What does society, as it exists today, know of the process of despair, the poverty, the horrors, the fearful struggle the human soul must pass on its way to crime and degradation. Who that knows this terrible process can fail to see the truth in these words of Peter Kropotkin:

35 "Those who will hold the balance between the benefits thus attributed to law and punishment and the degrading effect of

the latter on humanity; those who will estimate the torrent of depravity poured abroad in human society by the informer, favored by the Judge even, and paid for in clinking cash by governments, under the pretext of aiding to unmask crime; those who will go within prison walls and there see what human beings become when deprived of liberty, when subjected to the care of brutal keepers, to coarse, cruel words, to a thousand stinging, piercing humiliations, will agree with us that the entire apparatus of prison and punishment is an abomination which ought to be brought to an end."

The deterrent influence of law on the lazy man is too absurd to merit consideration. If society were only relieved of the waste and expense of keeping a lazy class, and the equally great expense of the paraphernalia of protection this lazy class requires, the social tables would contain an abundance for all, including even the occasional lazy individual. Besides, it is well to consider that laziness results either from special privileges, or physical and mental abnormalities. Our present insane system of production fosters both, and the most astounding phenomenon is that people should want to work at all now. Anarchism aims to strip labor of its deadening, dulling aspect, of its gloom and compulsion. It aims to make work an instrument of joy, of strength, of color, of real harmony, so that the poorest sort of a man should find in work both recreation and hope.

To achieve such an arrangement of life, government, with its unjust, arbitrary, repressive measures, must be done away with. At best it has but imposed one single mode of life upon all, without regard to individual and social variations and needs. In destroying government and statutory laws, Anarchism proposes to rescue the self-respect and independence of the individual from all restraint and invasion by authority. Only in freedom can man grow to his full stature. Only in freedom will he learn to think and move, and give the very best in him. Only in freedom will he realize the true force of the social bonds which knit men together, and which are the true foundation of a normal social life.

But what about human nature? Can it be changed? And if not, will it endure under Anarchism?

Poor human nature, what horrible crimes have been committed in thy name! Every fool, from king to policeman, from the flatheaded parson to the visionless dabbler in science, presumes to speak authoritatively of human nature. The greater the mental charlatan, the more definite his insistence on the wickedness and weaknesses of human nature. Yet, how can any one speak of it today, with every soul in a prison, with every heart fettered, wounded, and maimed?

40 John Burroughs has stated that experimental study of animals in captivity is absolutely useless. Their character, their habits, their appetites undergo a complete transformation when torn from their soil in field and forest. With human nature caged in a narrow space, whipped daily into submission, how can we speak of its potentialities?

Freedom, expansion, opportunity, and, above all, peace and repose, alone can teach us the real dominant factors of human nature and all its wonderful possibilities.

Anarchism, then, really stands for the liberation of the human mind from the dominion of religion; the liberation of the human body from the dominion of property; liberation from the shackles and restraint of government. Anarchism stands for a social order based on the free grouping of individuals for the purpose of producing real social wealth; an order that will guarantee to every human being free access to the earth and full enjoyment of the necessities of life, according to individual desires, tastes, and inclinations.

This is not a wild fancy or an aberration of the mind. It is the conclusion arrived at by hosts of intellectual men and women the world over; a conclusion resulting from the close and studious observation of the tendencies of modern society: individual liberty and economic equality, the twin forces for the birth of what is fine and true in man.

As to methods. Anarchism is not, as some may suppose, a theory of the future to be realized through divine inspiration. It is a living force in the affairs of our life, constantly creating new conditions. The methods of Anarchism therefore do not comprise an iron-clad program to be carried out under all circumstances. Methods must grow out of the economic needs of each place and clime, and of the intellectual and temperamental requirements of the individual. The serene, calm character of a Tolstoy will wish different methods for social reconstruction than the intense, overflowing personality of a Michael Bakunin or a Peter Kropotkin. Equally so it must be apparent that the economic and political needs of Russia will dictate more drastic measures than would England or America. Anarchism does not stand for military drill and uniformity; it does, however, stand for the spirit of revolt, in whatever form, against everything that hinders human growth. All Anarchists agree in that, as they also agree in their opposition to the political machinery as a means of bringing about the great social change.

"All voting," says Thoreau, "is a sort of gaming, like checkers, or backgammon, a playing with right and wrong; its obligation never exceeds that of expediency. Even voting for the right thing is doing nothing for it. A wise man will not leave the right to the mercy of chance, nor wish it to prevail through the power of the majority." A close examination of the machinery of politics and its achievements will bear out the logic of Thoreau.

What does the history of parliamentarism show? Nothing but failure and defeat, not even a single reform to ameliorate the economic and social stress of the people. Laws have been passed and enactments made for the improvement and protection of labor. Thus it was proven only last year that Illinois, with the most rigid laws for mine protection, had the greatest mine disasters. In States where child labor laws prevail, child exploitation is at its highest, and though with us the workers enjoy full political opportunities, capitalism has reached the most brazen zenith.

Even were the workers able to have their own representatives, for which our good Socialist politicians are clamoring, what chances are there for their honesty and good faith? One has but to bear in mind the process of politics to realize that its path of good intentions is full of pitfalls: wire-pulling, intriguing, flattering, lying, cheating; in fact, chicanery of every description, whereby the political aspirant can achieve success. Added to that is a complete demoralization of character and conviction, until nothing is left that would make one hope for anything from such a human derelict. Time and time again the people were foolish enough to trust, believe, and support with their last farthing aspiring politicians, only to find themselves betrayed and cheated.

It may be claimed that men of integrity would not become corrupt in the political grinding mill. Perhaps not; but such men would be absolutely helpless to exert the slightest influence in behalf of labor, as indeed has been shown in numerous instances. The State is the economic master of its servants. Good men, if such there be, would either remain true to their political faith and lose their economic support, or they would cling to their economic master and be utterly unable to do the slightest good. The political arena leaves one no alternative, one must either be a dunce or a rogue.

The political superstition is still holding sway over the hearts and minds of the masses, but the true lovers of liberty will have no more to do with it. Instead, they believe with Stirner that man has as much liberty as he is willing to take. Anarchism therefore stands for direct action, the open defiance of, and resistance to, all laws and restrictions, economic, social, and moral. But defiance and resistance are illegal. Therein lies the salvation of man. Everything illegal necessitates integrity, self-reliance, and courage. In short, it calls for free, independent spirits, for "men who are men, and who have a bone in their backs which you cannot pass your hand through."

Universal suffrage itself owes its existence to direct action. If 50
not for the spirit of rebellion, of the defiance on the part of the American revolutionary fathers, their posterity would still wear the King's coat. If not for the direct action of a John Brown and his comrades, America would still trade in the flesh of the black man. True, the trade in white flesh is still going on; but that, too, will have to be abolished by direct action. Trade-unionism, the economic arena of the modern gladiator, owes its existence to direct action. It is but recently that law and government have attempted to crush the trade-union movement, and condemned the exponents of man's right to organize to prison as conspirators. Had they sought to assert their cause through begging, pleading, and compromise, trade-unionism would today be a negligible quantity. In France, in Spain, in Italy, in Russia, nay even in England (witness the growing rebellion of English labor unions) direct, revolutionary, economic action has become so strong a force in the battle for industrial liberty as to make the world realize the tremendous importance of labor's power. The General Strike, the supreme expression of the economic consciousness of the workers, was ridiculed in America but a short time ago. Today every great strike, in order to win, must realize the importance of the solidaric general protest.

Direct action, having proven effective along economic lines, is equally potent in the environment of the individual. There a hundred forces encroach upon his being, and only persistent resistance to them will finally set him free. Direct action against the authority in the shop, direct action against the authority of the law, direct action against the invasive, meddlesome authority of our moral code, is the logical, consistent method of Anarchism.

Will it not lead to a revolution? Indeed, it will. No real social change has ever come about without a revolution. People are either not familiar with their history, or they have not yet learned that revolution is but thought carried into action.

Anarchism, the great leaven of thought, is today permeating every phase of human endeavor. Science, art, literature, the drama, the effort for economic betterment, in fact every individual and social opposition to the existing disorder of things, is illumined by the spiritual light of Anarchism. It is the philosophy of the sovereignty of the individual. It is the theory of social harmony. It is the great, surging, living truth that is reconstructing the world, and that will usher in the Dawn.

Politeness
by Florence Hartley

There is little information available about Florence Hartley. Her book The Ladies' Book of Etiquette, and Manual of Politeness *was published in 1860. This text is the introduction to that book.*

In preparing a book of etiquette for ladies, I would lay down as the first rule, "Do unto others as you would others should do to you." You can never be rude if you bear the rule always in mind, for what lady likes to be treated rudely? True Christian politeness will always be the result of an unselfish regard for the feelings of others, and though you may err in the ceremonious points of etiquette, you will never be impolite.

Politeness, founded upon such a rule, becomes the expression, in graceful manner, of social virtues. The spirit of politeness consists in a certain attention to forms and ceremonies, which are meant both to please others and ourselves, and to make others pleased with us; a still clearer definition may be given by saying that politeness is goodness of heart put into daily practice; there can be no *true* politeness without kindness, purity, singleness of heart, and sensibility.

Many believe that politeness is but a mask worn in the world to conceal bad passions and impulses, and to make a show of possessing virtues not really existing in the heart; thus, that politeness is merely hypocrisy and dissimulation. Do not believe this; be certain that those who profess such a doctrine are practicing themselves the deceit they condemn so much. Such people scout politeness, because, to be truly a lady, one must carry the principles into every circumstance of life, into the family circle, the most intimate friendship, and never forget to extend the gentle courtesies of life to every one. This they find too much trouble, and so deride the idea of being polite and call it deceitfulness.

True politeness is the language of a good heart, and those possessing that heart will never, under any circumstances, be rude. They may not enter a crowded saloon gracefully; they may be entirely ignorant of the *forms* of good society; they may be awkward at table, ungrammatical in speech; but they will never be heard speaking so as to wound the feelings of another; they will never be seen making others uncomfortable by seeking solely for their own *personal* convenience; they will always endeavor to set every one around them at ease; they will be self-sacrificing, friendly, unselfish; truly in word and deed, *polite*. Give to such a woman the knowledge of the forms and customs of society, teach her how best to show the gentle courtesies of life, and you have a *lady*, created by God, only indebted for the *outward* polish to the world.

5 It is true that society demands this same unselfishness and courtesy, but when there is no heart in the work, the time is frittered away on the mere ceremonies, forms of etiquette, and customs of society, and this politeness seeks only its own ends; to be known as courteous, spoken of as lady-like, and not beloved as unselfish and womanly.

Etiquette exists in some form in all countries, has existed and will exist in all ages. From the rudest savage who dares not approach his ignorant, barbarous ruler without certain forms and ceremonies, to the most polished courts in Europe, or the home circles of America, etiquette reigns.

True politeness will be found, its basis in the human heart, the same in all these varied scenes and situations, but the outward forms of etiquette will vary everywhere. Even in the same scene, time will alter every form, and render the exquisite polish of last year, obsolete rudeness next year.

Politeness, being based upon real kindness of heart, cannot exist where there is selfishness or brutality to warp its growth. It is founded upon love of the neighbor, and a desire to be beloved, and to show love. Thus, where such pure, noble feelings do not exist, the mere forms of politeness become hypocrisy and deceit.

Rudeness will repel, where courtesy would attract friends.

Never by word or action notice the defects of another; be 10
charitable, for all need charity. Remember who said, "Let him that is without fault cast the first stone." Remember that the laws of politeness require the consideration of the feelings of others; the endeavor to make every one feel at ease; and frank courtesy towards all. Never meet rudeness in others with rudeness upon your own part; even the most brutal and impolite will be more shamed by being met with courtesy and kindness, than by any attempt to annoy them by insolence on your part.

Politeness forbids any display of resentment. The polished surface throws back the arrow.

Remember that a favor becomes doubly valuable if granted with courtesy, and that the pain of a refusal may be softened if the manner expresses polite regret.

Kindness, even to the most humble, will never lose anything by being offered in a gentle, courteous manner, and the most commonplace action will admit of grace and ease in its execution.

Let every action, while it is finished in strict accordance with etiquette, be, at the same time, easy, as if dictated solely by the heart.

To be truly polite, remember you must be polite at *all* times, 15
and under *all* circumstances.

Give Me Liberty, or Give Me Death

by Patrick Henry

A Founding Father of the United States, Patrick Henry (1736–1799) delivered this speech at the second Virginia Convention in March 1775. The text of this speech was first written out and published by William Wirt, Henry's grandson and biographer, many years after Henry's death.

Mr. President: No man thinks more highly than I do of the patriotism, as well as abilities, of the very worthy gentlemen who have just addressed the house. But different men often see the same subject in different lights; and, therefore, I hope it will not be thought disrespectful to those gentlemen if, entertaining as I do opinions of a character very opposite to theirs, I shall speak forth my sentiments freely and without reserve. This is no time for ceremony. The question before the House is one of awful moment to this country. For my own part, I consider it as nothing less than a question of freedom or slavery; and in proportion to the magnitude of the subject ought to be the freedom of the debate. It is only in this way that we can hope to arrive at truth, and fulfill the great responsibility which we hold to God and our country. Should I keep back my opinions at such a time, through fear of giving offense, I should consider myself as guilty of treason towards my country, and of an act of disloyalty toward the Majesty of Heaven, which I revere above all earthly kings.

Mr. President, it is natural to man to indulge in the illusions of hope. We are apt to shut our eyes against a painful truth, and listen to the song of that siren till she transforms us into beasts. Is this the part of wise men, engaged in a great and arduous struggle for liberty? Are we disposed to be of the number of those who, having eyes, see not, and, having ears, hear not, the things which so nearly concern their temporal salvation? For my part, whatever anguish of spirit it may cost, I am willing to know the whole truth; to know the worst, and to provide for it.

I have but one lamp by which my feet are guided, and that is the lamp of experience. I know of no way of judging of the future but by the past. And judging by the past, I wish to know what there has been in the conduct of the British ministry for the last ten years to justify those hopes with which gentlemen have been pleased to solace themselves and the House. Is it that insidious smile with which our petition has been lately received? Trust it not, sir; it will prove a snare to your feet. Suffer not yourselves to be betrayed with a kiss. Ask yourselves how this gracious reception of our petition comports with those warlike preparations which cover our waters and darken our land. Are fleets and armies necessary to a work of love and reconciliation? Have we shown ourselves so unwilling to be reconciled that force must be called in to win back our love? Let us not deceive ourselves, sir. These are the implements of war and subjugation; the last arguments to which kings resort. I ask gentlemen, sir, what means this martial array, if its purpose be not to force us to submission? Can gentlemen assign any other possible motive for it? Has Great Britain any enemy, in this quarter of the world, to call for all this accumulation of navies and armies? No, sir, she has none. They are meant for us: they can be meant for no other. They are sent over to bind and rivet upon us those chains which the British ministry have been so long forging. And what have we to oppose to them? Shall we try argument? Sir, we have been trying that for the last ten years. Have we anything new to offer upon the subject? Nothing. We have held the subject up in every light of which it is capable; but it has been all in vain. Shall we resort to entreaty and humble supplication? What terms shall we find which have not been already exhausted? Let us not, I beseech you, sir, deceive ourselves. Sir, we have done everything that could be done to avert the storm which is now coming on. We have petitioned; we have remonstrated; we have supplicated; we have prostrated ourselves before the throne, and have implored its interposition to arrest the tyrannical hands of the ministry and parliament. Our petitions have been slighted; our remonstrances have produced additional violence and insult; our supplications have been disregarded; and we have been spurned, with contempt, from the foot of the throne! In vain, after these things, may we indulge the fond hope of peace and reconciliation. There is no longer any room for hope. If we wish to be free — if we mean to preserve inviolate those inestimable privileges for which we have been so long contending — if we mean not basely to abandon the noble struggle in which we have been so long engaged, and which we have pledged ourselves never to abandon until the glorious object of our contest shall be obtained — we must fight! I repeat it, sir, we must fight! An appeal to arms and to the God of hosts is all that is left us!

They tell us, sir, that we are weak; unable to cope with so formidable an adversary. But when shall we be stronger? Will it be the next week, or the next year? Will it be when we are totally disarmed, and when a British guard shall be stationed in every house? Shall we gather strength by irresolution and inaction? Shall we acquire the means of effectual resistance by lying supinely on our backs and hugging the delusive phantom of hope, until our enemies shall have bound us hand and foot? Sir, we are not weak if we make a proper use of those means which the God of nature hath placed in our power. The millions of people, armed in the holy cause of liberty, and in such a country as that which we possess, are invincible by any force which our enemy can send against us. Besides, sir, we shall not fight our battles alone. There is a just God who presides over the destinies of nations, and who will raise up friends to fight our battles for us. The battle, sir, is not to the strong alone; it is to the vigilant, the active, the brave. Besides, sir, we have no election. If we were base enough to desire it, it is now too late to retire from the contest. There is no retreat but in submission and slavery! Our chains are forged! Their clanking may be heard on the plains of Boston! The war is inevitable — and let it come! I repeat it, sir, let it come.

It is in vain, sir, to extenuate the matter. Gentlemen may 5
cry, Peace, peace — but there is no peace. The war is actually begun! The next gale that sweeps from the north will bring to our ears the clash of resounding arms! Our brethren are already in the field! Why stand we here idle? What is it that gentlemen wish? What would they have? Is life so dear, or peace so sweet, as to be purchased at the price of chains and slavery? Forbid it, Almighty God! I know not what course others may take; but as for me, give me liberty, or give me death!

How It Feels to Be Colored Me

by Zora Neale Hurston

Zora Neal Hurston (1891–1960) was an American writer best known for her novel Their Eyes Were Watching God. *She also published several works as an anthropologist. This essay was first published in* The World Tomorrow, *May 1928. The essay was never collected by Hurston or reprinted during her lifetime.*

I am colored but I offer nothing in the way of extenuating circumstances except the fact that I am the only Negro in the United States whose grandfather on the mother's side was *not* an Indian chief.

I remember the very day that I became colored. Up to my thirteenth year I lived in the little Negro town of Eatonville, Florida. It is exclusively a colored town. The only white people I knew passed through the town going to or coming from Orlando. The native whites rode dusty horses, the Northern tourists chugged down the sandy village road in automobiles. The town knew the Southerners and never stopped cane chewing when they passed. But the Northerners were something else again. They were peered at cautiously from behind curtains by the timid. The more venturesome would come out on the porch to watch them go past and got just as much pleasure out of the tourists as the tourists got out of the village.

The front porch might seem a daring place for the rest of the town, but it was a gallery seat to me. My favorite place was atop the gate-post. Proscenium box for a born first-nighter. Not only did I enjoy the show, but I didn't mind the actors knowing that I liked it. I actually spoke to them in passing. I'd wave at them and when they returned my salute, I would say something like this: "Howdy-do-well-I-thank-you-where you-goin'?" Usually automobile or the horse paused at this, and after a queer exchange of compliments, I would probably "go a piece of the way" with them, as we say in farthest Florida. If one of my family happened to come to the front in time to see me, of course negotiations would be rudely broken off. But even so, it is clear that I was the first "welcome-to-our-state" Floridian, and I hope the Miami Chamber of Commerce will please take notice.

During this period, white people differed from colored to me only in that they rode through town and never lived there. They liked to hear me "speak pieces" and sing and wanted to see me dance the parse-me-la, and gave me generously of their small silver for doing these things, which seemed strange to me for I wanted to do them so much that I needed bribing to stop. Only they didn't know it. The colored people gave no dimes. They deplored any joyful tendencies in me, but I was their Zora nevertheless. I belonged to them, to the nearby hotels, to the county — everybody's Zora.

But changes came in the family when I was thirteen, and I 5
was sent to school in Jacksonville. I left Eatonville, the town of the oleanders, as Zora. When I disembarked from the riverboat at Jacksonville, she was no more. It seemed that I had suffered a sea change. I was not Zora of Orange County any more, I was now a little colored girl. I found it out in certain ways. In my heart as well as in the mirror, I became a fast brown — warranted not to rub nor run.

But I am not tragically colored. There is no great sorrow dammed up in my soul, nor lurking behind my eyes. I do not mind at all. I do not belong to the sobbing school of Negrohood who hold that nature somehow has given them a low-down dirty deal and whose feelings are all hurt about it. Even in the helter-skelter skirmish that is my life, I have seen that the world is to the strong regardless of a little pigmentation more or less. No, I do not weep at the world — I am too busy sharpening my oyster knife.

Someone is always at my elbow reminding me that I am the granddaughter of slaves. It fails to register depression with me. Slavery is sixty years in the past. The operation was successful and the patient is doing well, thank you. The terrible struggle that made me an American out of a potential slave said "On the line!" The Reconstruction said "Get set!"; and the generation before said "Go!" I am off to a flying start and I must not halt in the stretch to look behind and weep. Slavery is the price I paid for civilization, and the choice was not with me. It is a bully adventure and worth all that I have paid through my ancestors for it. No one on earth ever had a greater chance for glory. The world to be won and nothing to be lost. It is thrilling to think — to know that for any act of mine, I shall get twice as much praise or twice as much blame. It is quite exciting to hold the center of the national stage, with the spectators not knowing whether to laugh or to weep.

The position of my white neighbor is much more difficult. No brown specter pulls up a chair beside me when I sit down to eat. No dark ghost thrusts its leg against mine in bed. The game of keeping what one has is never so exciting as the game of getting.

I do not always feel colored. Even now I often achieve the unconscious Zora of Eatonville before the Hegira. I feel most colored when I am thrown against a sharp white background.

10 For instance at Barnard. "Beside the waters of the Hudson" I feel my race. Among the thousand white persons, I am a dark rock surged upon, overswept by a creamy sea. I am surged upon and overswept, but through it all, I remain myself. When covered by the waters, I am; and the ebb but reveals me again.

Sometimes it is the other way around. A white person is set down in our midst, but the contrast is just as sharp for me. For instance, when I sit in the drafty basement that is the New World Cabaret with a white person, my color comes. We enter chatting about any little nothing that we have in common and are seated by the jazz waiters. In the abrupt way that jazz orchestras have, this one plunges into a number. It loses no time in circumlocutions, but gets right down to business. It constricts the thorax and splits the heart with its tempo and narcotic harmonies. This orchestra grows rambunctious, rears on its hind legs and attacks the tonal veil with primitive fury, rending it, clawing it until it breaks through to the jungle beyond. I follow those heathen — follow them exultingly. I dance wildly inside myself; I yell within, I whoop; I shake my assegai above my head, I hurl it true to the mark *yeeeeooww*! I am in the jungle and living in the jungle way. My face is painted red and yellow, and my body is painted blue. My pulse is throbbing like a war drum. I want to slaughter something — give pain, give death to what, I do not know. But the piece ends. The men of the orchestra wipe their lips and rest their fingers. I creep back slowly to the veneer we call civilization with the last tone and find the white friend sitting motionless in his seat, smoking calmly.

"Good music they have here," he remarks, drumming the table with his fingertips.

Music! The great blobs of purple and red emotion have not touched him. He has only heard what I felt. He is far away and I see him but dimly across the ocean and the continent that have fallen between us. He is so pale with his whiteness then and I am *so* colored.

At certain times I have no race, I am *me*. When I set my hat at a certain angle and saunter down Seventh Avenue, Harlem City, feeling as snooty as the lions in front of the Forty-Second Street Library, for instance. So far as my feelings are concerned, Peggy Hopkins Joyce on the Boule Mich with her gorgeous raiment, stately carriage, knees knocking together in a most aristocratic manner, has nothing on me. The cosmic Zora emerges. I belong to no race nor time, I am the eternal feminine with its string of beads.

15 I have no separate feeling about being an American citizen and colored. I am merely a fragment of the Great Soul that surges within the boundaries. My country, right or wrong.

Sometimes, I feel discriminated against, but it does not make me angry. It merely astonishes me. How *can* any deny themselves the pleasure of my company! It's beyond me.

But in the main, I feel like a brown bag of miscellany propped against a wall. Against a wall in company with other bags, white, red and yellow. Pour out the contents, and there is discovered a jumble of small things priceless and worthless. A first-water diamond, an empty spool, bits of broken glass, lengths of string, a key to a door long since crumbled away, a rusty knife-blade, old shoes saved for a road that never was and never will be, a nail bent under the weight of things too heavy for any nail, a dried flower or two, still a little fragrant. In your hand is the brown bag. On the ground before you is the jumble it held — so much like the jumble in the bags, could they be emptied, that all might be dumped in a single heap and the bags refilled without altering the content of any greatly. A bit of colored glass more or less would not matter. Perhaps that is how the Great Stuffer of Bags filled them in the first place — who knows?

The Declaration of Independence of the United States of America

by Thomas Jefferson

Thomas Jefferson (1743–1826) was one of the Founding Fathers of the United States. He represented Virginia at the Continental Congress, where he wrote the initial draft of the Declaration of Independence. The Declaration was edited by the Continental Congress and approved on July 4, 1776. It was then published as a printed broadsheet that was widely distributed throughout the American colonies. Jefferson later became the third president of the United States.

The unanimous Declaration of the thirteen united States of America,

When in the Course of human events, it becomes necessary for one people to dissolve the political bands which have connected them with another, and to assume among the powers of the earth, the separate and equal station to which the Laws of Nature and of Nature's God entitle them, a decent respect to the opinions of mankind requires that they should declare the causes which impel them to the separation.

We hold these truths to be self-evident, that all men are created equal, that they are endowed by their Creator with certain unalienable Rights, that among these are Life, Liberty and the pursuit of Happiness. — That to secure these rights, Governments are instituted among Men, deriving their just powers from the consent of the governed, — That whenever any Form of Government becomes destructive of these ends, it is the Right of the People to alter or to abolish it, and to institute new Government, laying its foundation on such principles and organizing its powers in such form, as to them shall seem most likely to effect their Safety and Happiness. Prudence, indeed, will dictate that Governments long established should not be changed for light and transient causes; and accordingly all experience hath shewn, that mankind are more disposed to suffer, while evils are sufferable, than to right themselves by abolishing the forms to which they are accustomed. But when a long train of abuses and usurpations, pursuing invariably the same Object evinces a design to reduce them under absolute Despotism, it is their right, it is their duty, to throw off such Government, and to provide new Guards for their future security. — Such has been the patient sufferance of these Colonies; and such is now the necessity which constrains them to alter their former Systems of Government. The history of the present King of Great Britain is a history of repeated injuries and usurpations, all having in direct object the establishment of an absolute Tyranny over these States. To prove this, let Facts be submitted to a candid world.

He has refused his Assent to Laws, the most wholesome and necessary for the public good.

He has forbidden his Governors to pass Laws of immediate 5
and pressing importance, unless suspended in their operation till his Assent should be obtained; and when so suspended, he has utterly neglected to attend to them.

He has refused to pass other Laws for the accommodation of large districts of people, unless those people would relinquish the right of Representation in the Legislature, a right inestimable to them and formidable to tyrants only.

He has called together legislative bodies at places unusual, uncomfortable, and distant from the depository of their public Records, for the sole purpose of fatiguing them into compliance with his measures.

He has dissolved Representative Houses repeatedly, for opposing with manly firmness his invasions on the rights of the people.

He has refused for a long time, after such dissolutions, to cause others to be elected; whereby the Legislative powers, incapable of Annihilation, have returned to the People at large for their exercise; the State remaining in the mean time exposed to all the dangers of invasion from without, and convulsions within.

He has endeavoured to prevent the population of these States; for that purpose obstructing the Laws for Naturalization of Foreigners; refusing to pass others to encourage their migrations hither, and raising the conditions of new Appropriations of Lands.

He has obstructed the Administration of Justice, by refusing his Assent to Laws for establishing Judiciary powers.

He has made Judges dependent on his Will alone, for the tenure of their offices, and the amount and payment of their salaries.

He has erected a multitude of New Offices, and sent hither swarms of Officers to harrass our people, and eat out their substance.

He has kept among us, in times of peace, Standing Armies without the Consent of our legislatures.

He has affected to render the Military independent of and superior to the Civil power.

He has combined with others to subject us to a jurisdiction foreign to our constitution, and unacknowledged by our laws; giving his Assent to their Acts of pretended Legislation:

For Quartering large bodies of armed troops among us:

For protecting them, by a mock Trial, from punishment for any Murders which they should commit on the Inhabitants of these States:

For cutting off our Trade with all parts of the world:

For imposing Taxes on us without our Consent:

For depriving us in many cases, of the benefits of Trial by Jury:

For transporting us beyond Seas to be tried for pretended offences

For abolishing the free System of English Laws in a neighbouring Province, establishing therein an Arbitrary government, and enlarging its Boundaries so as to render it at once an example and fit instrument for introducing the same absolute rule into these Colonies:

For taking away our Charters, abolishing our most valuable Laws, and altering fundamentally the Forms of our Governments:

25 For suspending our own Legislatures, and declaring themselves invested with power to legislate for us in all cases whatsoever.

He has abdicated Government here, by declaring us out of his Protection and waging War against us.

He has plundered our seas, ravaged our Coasts, burnt our towns, and destroyed the lives of our people.

He is at this time transporting large Armies of foreign Mercenaries to compleat the works of death, desolation and tyranny, already begun with circumstances of Cruelty & perfidy scarcely paralleled in the most barbarous ages, and totally unworthy the Head of a civilized nation.

He has constrained our fellow Citizens taken Captive on the high Seas to bear Arms against their Country, to become the executioners of their friends and Brethren, or to fall themselves by their Hands.

30 He has excited domestic insurrections amongst us, and has endeavoured to bring on the inhabitants of our frontiers, the merciless Indian Savages, whose known rule of warfare, is an undistinguished destruction of all ages, sexes and conditions.

In every stage of these Oppressions We have Petitioned for Redress in the most humble terms: Our repeated Petitions have been answered only by repeated injury. A Prince whose character is thus marked by every act which may define a Tyrant, is unfit to be the ruler of a free people.

Nor have We been wanting in attentions to our Brittish brethren. We have warned them from time to time of attempts by their legislature to extend an unwarrantable jurisdiction over us. We have reminded them of the circumstances of our emigration and settlement here. We have appealed to their native justice and magnanimity, and we have conjured them by the ties of our common kindred to disavow these usurpations, which, would inevitably interrupt our connections and correspondence. They too have been deaf to the voice of justice and of consanguinity. We must, therefore, acquiesce in the necessity, which denounces our Separation, and hold them, as we hold the rest of mankind, Enemies in War, in Peace Friends.

We, therefore, the Representatives of the united States of America, in General Congress, Assembled, appealing to the Supreme Judge of the world for the rectitude of our intentions, do, in the Name, and by Authority of the good People of these Colonies, solemnly publish and declare, That these United Colonies are, and of Right ought to be Free and Independent States; that they are Absolved from all Allegiance to the British Crown, and that all political connection between them and the State of Great Britain, is and ought to be totally dissolved; and that as Free and Independent States, they have full Power to levy War, conclude Peace, contract Alliances, establish Commerce, and to do all other Acts and Things which Independent States may of right do. And for the support of this Declaration, with a firm reliance on the protection of divine Providence, we mutually pledge to each other our Lives, our Fortunes and our sacred Honor.

Strike Against War

by Helen Keller

Helen Adams Keller (1880–1968) is remembered as an advocate for the rights of people with disabilities, but she was also a major figure in many other political movements during her lifetime, notably women's and worker's rights, socialism, and pacifism. She gave this speech in 1916 in Carnegie Hall in New York City.

To begin with, I have a word to say to my good friends, the editors, and others who are moved to pity me. Some people are grieved because they imagine I am in the hands of unscrupulous persons who lead me astray and persuade me to espouse unpopular causes and make me the mouthpiece of their propaganda. Now, let it be understood once and for all that I do not want their pity; I would not change places with one of them. I know what I am talking about. My sources of information are as good and reliable as anybody else's. I have papers and magazines from England, France, Germany and Austria that I can read myself. Not all the editors I have met can do that. Quite a number of them have to take their French and German second hand. No, I will not disparage the editors. They are an overworked, misunderstood class. Let them remember, though, that if I cannot see the fire at the end of their cigarettes, neither can they thread a needle in the dark. All I ask, gentlemen, is a fair field and no favor. I have entered the fight against preparedness and against the economic system under which we live. It is to be a fight to the finish, and I ask no quarter.

The future of the world rests in the hands of America. The future of America rests on the backs of 80,000,000 working men and women and their children. We are facing a grave crisis in our national life. The few who profit from the labor of the masses want to organize the workers into an army which will protect the interests of the capitalists. You are urged to add to the heavy burdens you already bear the burden of a larger army and many additional warships. It is in your power to refuse to carry the artillery and the dreadnoughts and to shake off some of the burdens, too, such as limousines, steam yachts and country estates. You do not need to make a great noise about it. With the silence and dignity of creators you can end wars and the system of selfishness and exploitation that causes wars. All you need to do to bring about this stupendous revolution is to straighten up and fold your arms.

We are not preparing to defend our country. Even if we were as helpless as Congressman Gardner says we are, we have no enemies foolhardy enough to attempt to invade the United States. The talk about attack from Germany and Japan is absurd. Germany has its hands full and will be busy with its own affairs for some generations after the European war is over.

With full control of the Atlantic Ocean and the Mediterranean Sea, the allies failed to land enough men to defeat the Turks at Gallipoli; and then they failed again to land an army at Salonica in time to check the Bulgarian invasion of Serbia. The conquest of America by water is a nightmare confined exclusively to ignorant persons and members of the Navy League.

Yet, everywhere, we hear fear advanced as argument for 5
armament. It reminds me of a fable I read. A certain man found a horseshoe. His neighbor began to weep and wail because, as he justly pointed out, the man who found the horseshoe might someday find a horse. Having found the shoe, he might shoe him. The neighbor's child might some day go so near the horse's hells as to be kicked, and die. Undoubtedly the two families

would quarrel and fight, and several valuable lives would be lost through the finding of the horseshoe. You know the last war we had we quite accidentally picked up some islands in the Pacific Ocean which may some day be the cause of a quarrel between ourselves and Japan. I'd rather drop those islands right now and forget about them than go to war to keep them. Wouldn't you?

Congress is not preparing to defend the people of the United States. It is planning to protect the capital of American speculators and investors in Mexico, South America, China, and the Philippine Islands. Incidentally this preparation will benefit the manufacturers of munitions and war machines.

Until recently there were uses in the United States for the money taken from the workers. But American labor is exploited almost to the limit now, and our national resources have all been appropriated. Still the profits keep piling up new capital. Our flourishing industry in implements of murder is filling the vaults of New York's banks with gold. And a dollar that is not being used to make a slave of some human being is not fulfilling its purpose in the capitalistic scheme. That dollar must be invested in South America, Mexico, China, or the Philippines.

It was no accident that the Navy League came into prominence at the same time that the National City Bank of New York established a branch in Buenos Aires. It is not a mere coincidence that six business associates of J.P. Morgan are officials of defense leagues. And chance did not dictate that Mayor Mitchel could appoint to his Committee of Safety a thousand men that represent a fifth of the wealth of the United States. These men want their foreign investments protected.

Every modern war has had its root in exploitation. The Civil War was fought to decide whether to slaveholders of the South or the capitalists of the North should exploit the West. The Spanish-American War decided that the United States should exploit Cuba and the Philippines. The South African War decided that the British should exploit the diamond mines. The Russo-Japanese War decided that Japan should exploit Korea. The present war is to decide who shall exploit the Balkans, Turkey, Persia, Egypt, India, China, Africa. And we are whetting our sword to scare the victors into sharing the spoils with us. Now, the workers are not interested in the spoils; they will not get any of them anyway.

The preparedness propagandists have still another object, and a very important one. They want to give the people something to think about besides their own unhappy condition. They know the cost of living is high, wages are low, employment is uncertain and will be much more so when the European call for munitions stops. No matter how hard and incessantly the people work, they often cannot afford the comforts of life; many cannot obtain the necessities.

Every few days we are given a new war scare to lend realism to their propaganda. They have had us on the verge of war over the Lusitania, the Gulflight, the Ancona, and now they want the workingmen to become excited over the sinking of the Persia. The workingman has no interest in any of these ships. The Germans might sink every vessel on the Atlantic Ocean and the Mediterranean Sea, and kill Americans with every one — the American workingman would still have no reason to go to war.

All the machinery of the system has been set in motion. Above the complaint and din of the protest from the workers is heard the voice of authority.

"Friends," it says, "fellow workmen, patriots; your country is in danger! There are foes on all sides of us. There is nothing between us and our enemies except the Pacific Ocean and the Atlantic Ocean. Look at what has happened to Belgium. Consider the fate of Serbia. Will you murmur about low wages when your country, your very liberties, are in jeopardy? What are the miseries you endure compared to the humiliation of having a victorious German army sail up the East River? Quit your whining, get busy and prepare to defend your firesides and your flag. Get an army, get a navy; be ready to meet the invaders like the loyal-hearted freemen you are."

Will the workers walk into this trap? Will they be fooled again? I am afraid so. The people have always been amenable to oratory of this sort. The workers know they have no enemies except their masters. They know that their citizenship papers are no warrant for the safety of themselves or their wives and children. They know that honest sweat, persistent toil and years of struggle bring them nothing worth holding on to, worth fighting for. Yet, deep down in their foolish hearts they believe they have a country. Oh blind vanity of slaves!

The clever ones, up in the high places know how childish and silly the workers are. They know that if the government dresses them up in khaki and gives them a rifle and starts them off with a brass band and waving banners, they will go forth to fight valiantly for their own enemies. They are taught that brave men die for their country's honor. What a price to pay for an abstraction — the lives of millions of young men; other millions crippled and blinded for life; existence made hideous for still more millions of human being; the achievement and inheritance of generations swept away in a moment — and nobody better off for all the misery! This terrible sacrifice would be comprehensible if the thing you die for and call country fed, clothed, housed and warmed you, educated and cherished your children. I think the workers are the most unselfish of the children of men; they toil and live and die for other people's country, other people's sentiments, other people's liberties and other people's happiness! The workers have no liberties of their own; they are not free when they are compelled to work twelve or ten or eight hours a day. They are not free when they are ill paid for their exhausting toil. They are not free when their children must labor in mines, mills and factories or starve, and when their women may be driven by poverty to lives of shame. They are not free when they are clubbed and imprisoned because they go on strike for a raise of wages and for the elemental justice that is their right as human beings.

We are not free unless the men who frame and execute the laws represent the interests of the lives of the people and no other interest. The ballot does not make a free man out of a wage slave. There has never existed a truly free and democratic nation in the world. From time immemorial men have followed with blind loyalty the strong men who had the power of money and of armies. Even while battlefields were piled high with their own dead they have tilled the lands of the rulers and have been robbed of the fruits of their labor. They have built palaces and pyramids, temples and cathedrals that held no real shrine of liberty.

As civilization has grown more complex the workers have become more and more enslaved, until today they are little more than parts of the machines they operate. Daily they face the dangers of railroad, bridge, skyscraper, freight train, stokehold, stockyard, lumber raft and mine. Panting and training at the docks, on the railroads and underground and on the seas, they move the traffic and pass from land to land the precious commodities that make it possible for us to live. And what is their reward? A scanty wage, often poverty, rents, taxes, tributes and war indemnities.

The kind of preparedness the workers want is reorganization and reconstruction of their whole life, such as has never been attempted by statesmen or governments. The Germans found out years ago that they could not raise good soldiers in the slums so they abolished the slums. They saw to it that all the people had at least a few of the essentials of civilization — decent lodging, clean streets, wholesome if scanty food, proper medical care and proper safeguards for the workers in their occupations. That is only a small part of what should be done, but what wonders that one step toward the right sort of preparedness has wrought for Germany! For eighteen months it has kept itself free from invasion while carrying on an extended war of conquest, and its armies are still pressing on with unabated vigor. It is your business to force these reforms on the Administration. Let there be no more talk about what a government can or cannot do. All these things have been done by all the belligerent nations in the hurly-burly of war. Every fundamental industry has been managed better by the governments than by private corporations.

It is your duty to insist upon still more radical measure. It is your business to see that no child is employed in an industrial establishment or mine or store, and that no worker is needlessly exposed to accident or disease. It is your business to make them give you clean cities, free from smoke, dirt and congestion. It is your business to make them pay you a living wage. It is your business to see that this kind of preparedness is carried into every department on the nation, until everyone has a chance to be well born, well nourished, rightly educated, intelligent and serviceable to the country at all times.

20 Strike against all ordinances and laws and institutions that continue the slaughter of peace and the butcheries of war. Strike against war, for without you no battles can be fought. Strike against manufacturing shrapnel and gas bombs and all other tools of murder. Strike against preparedness that means death and misery to millions of human beings. Be not dumb, obedient slaves in an army of destruction. Be heroes in an army of construction.

Inaugural Address

by John F. Kennedy

John Fitzgerald Kennedy (1917–1963) was the thirty-fourth President of the United States, serving from 1961 until his assassination in 1963. He delivered this inaugural address on January 20, 1961.

Vice President Johnson, Mr. Speaker, Mr. Chief Justice, President Eisenhower, Vice President Nixon, President Truman, reverend clergy, fellow citizens:

We observe today not a victory of party, but a celebration of freedom — symbolizing an end, as well as a beginning — signifying renewal, as well as change. For I have sworn before you and Almighty God the same solemn oath our forebears prescribed nearly a century and three-quarters ago.

The world is very different now. For man holds in his mortal hands the power to abolish all forms of human poverty and all forms of human life. And yet the same revolutionary beliefs for which our forebears fought are still at issue around the globe — the belief that the rights of man come not from the generosity of the state, but from the hand of God.

We dare not forget today that we are the heirs of that first revolution. Let the word go forth from this time and place, to friend and foe alike, that the torch has been passed to a new generation of Americans — born in this century, tempered by war, disciplined by a hard and bitter peace, proud of our ancient heritage, and unwilling to witness or permit the slow undoing of those human rights to which this nation has always been committed, and to which we are committed today at home and around the world.

5 Let every nation know, whether it wishes us well or ill, that we shall pay any price, bear any burden, meet any hardship, support any friend, oppose any foe, to assure the survival and the success of liberty.

This much we pledge — and more.

To those old allies whose cultural and spiritual origins we share, we pledge the loyalty of faithful friends. United there is little we cannot do in a host of cooperative ventures. Divided there is little we can do — for we dare not meet a powerful challenge at odds and split asunder.

To those new states whom we welcome to the ranks of the free, we pledge our word that one form of colonial control shall not have passed away merely to be replaced by a far more iron tyranny. We shall not always expect to find them supporting our view. But we shall always hope to find them strongly supporting their own freedom — and to remember that, in the past, those who foolishly sought power by riding the back of the tiger ended up inside.

To those people in the huts and villages of half the globe struggling to break the bonds of mass misery, we pledge our best efforts to help them help themselves, for whatever period is required — not because the Communists may be doing it, not because we seek their votes, but because it is right. If a free society cannot help the many who are poor, it cannot save the few who are rich.

10 To our sister republics south of our border, we offer a special pledge: to convert our good words into good deeds, in a new alliance for progress, to assist free men and free governments in casting off the chains of poverty. But this peaceful revolution of hope cannot become the prey of hostile powers. Let all our neighbors know that we shall join with them to oppose aggression or subversion anywhere in the Americas. And let every other power know that this hemisphere intends to remain the master of its own house.

To that world assembly of sovereign states, the United Nations, our last best hope in an age where the instruments of war have far outpaced the instruments of peace, we renew our pledge of support — to prevent it from becoming merely a forum for invective, to strengthen its shield of the new and the weak, and to enlarge the area in which its writ may run.

Finally, to those nations who would make themselves our adversary, we offer not a pledge but a request: that both sides begin anew the quest for peace, before the dark powers of destruction unleashed by science engulf all humanity in planned or accidental self-destruction.

We dare not tempt them with weakness. For only when our arms are sufficient beyond doubt can we be certain beyond doubt that they will never be employed.

But neither can two great and powerful groups of nations take comfort from our present course — both sides overburdened by the cost of modern weapons, both rightly alarmed by the steady spread of the deadly atom, yet both racing to alter that uncertain balance of terror that stays the hand of mankind's final war.

So let us begin anew — remembering on both sides that 15
civility is not a sign of weakness, and sincerity is always subject to proof. Let us never negotiate out of fear, but let us never fear to negotiate.

Let both sides explore what problems unite us instead of belaboring those problems which divide us.

Let both sides, for the first time, formulate serious and precise proposals for the inspection and control of arms, and bring the absolute power to destroy other nations under the absolute control of all nations.

Let both sides seek to invoke the wonders of science instead of its terrors. Together let us explore the stars, conquer the deserts, eradicate disease, tap the ocean depths, and encourage the arts and commerce.

Let both sides unite to heed, in all corners of the earth, the command of Isaiah — to "undo the heavy burdens, and [to] let the oppressed go free."

20 And, if a beachhead of cooperation may push back the jungle of suspicion, let both sides join in creating a new endeavor — not a new balance of power, but a new world of law — where the strong are just, and the weak secure, and the peace preserved.

All this will not be finished in the first one hundred days. Nor will it be finished in the first one thousand days; nor in the life of this Administration; nor even perhaps in our lifetime on this planet. But let us begin.

In your hands, my fellow citizens, more than mine, will rest the final success or failure of our course. Since this country was founded, each generation of Americans has been summoned to give testimony to its national loyalty. The graves of young Americans who answered the call to service surround the globe.

Now the trumpet summons us again — not as a call to bear arms, though arms we need — not as a call to battle, though embattled we are — but a call to bear the burden of a long twilight struggle, year in and year out, "rejoicing in hope; patient in tribulation," a struggle against the common enemies of man: tyranny, poverty, disease, and war itself.

Can we forge against these enemies a grand and global alliance, North and South, East and West, that can assure a more fruitful life for all mankind? Will you join in that historic effort?

25 In the long history of the world, only a few generations have been granted the role of defending freedom in its hour of maximum danger. I do not shrink from this responsibility — I welcome it. I do not believe that any of us would exchange places with any other people or any other generation. The energy, the faith, the devotion which we bring to this endeavor will light our country and all who serve it. And the glow from that fire can truly light the world.

And so, my fellow Americans, ask not what your country can do for you; ask what you can do for your country.

My fellow citizens of the world, ask not what America will do for you, but what together we can do for the freedom of man.

Finally, whether you are citizens of America or citizens of the world, ask of us here the same high standards of strength and sacrifice which we ask of you. With a good conscience our only sure reward, with history the final judge of our deeds, let us go forth to lead the land we love, asking His blessing and His help, but knowing that here on earth God's work must truly be our own.

Our Home on Earth

by Winona LaDuke

Winona LaDuke (b. 1959) is an activist and environmentalist, known for her work on tribal land claims and preservation, as well as sustainable development. A Native American with Ojibwe ancestry, LaDuke was born in Los Angeles and raised in Ashland, Oregon. She now lives on the White Earth Reservation in Minnesota, where she founded the White Earth Land Recovery Project to regain the Anishinaabeg people's original lands. The following piece was posted to Commons Magazine *on May 16, 2012.*

Giiwedinong means "going home" in the Anishinaabeg language — it also means North, which is the place from which we come. This is a key problem that modern industrial society faces today. We cannot restore our relationship with the Earth until we find our place in the world. This is our challenge today: where is home?

I returned to the White Earth Reservation in Minnesota about twenty-five years ago after being raised off-reservation, which is a common circumstance for our people. White Earth is my place in the Universe. It's where the headwaters of the Mississippi and Red Rivers are.

People of the Land Anishinaabeg is our name for ourselves in our own language, it means "people." We are called Ojibwe, referring to "ojibige" (meaning "to write") on our birch bark scrolls. Our aboriginal territory, and where we live today, is in the northern part of five U.S. states and the southern part of four Canadian Provinces. We are people of lakes, rivers, deep woods and lush prairies.

Now, if you look at the United States, about 4 percent of the land is held by Indian people. But if you go to Canada, about 85% of the population north of the fiftieth parallel is native. If you look at the whole of North America, you'll find that the majority of the population is native in about a third of the continent. Within this larger area indigenous people maintain their own ways of living and their cultural practices.

There are a number of countries in the Western Hemisphere 5
in which native peoples are the majority of the population: in Guatemala, Ecuador, Peru, and Bolivia. In some South American countries we control as much as 22 to 40 percent of the land. Overall, the Western Hemisphere is not predominantly white. Indigenous people continue their ways of living based on generations and generations of knowledge and practice on the land. On a worldwide scale there are about five thousand indigenous nations.

Nations are groups of indigenous peoples who share common language, culture, history, territory and government institutions. It is said that there are currently about five hundred million of us in the world today, depending on how you define the term indigenous. I define it as peoples who have continued their way of living for thousands of years. In 2007 the United Nations finally passed the U.N. Declaration of the Rights of Indigenous Peoples, recognizing our unique status in the world. Four countries opposed this: the US, Canada, New Zealand and Australia. However New Zealand recently signed this declaration.

Indigenous peoples believe fundamentally in a state of balance. We believe that all societies and cultural practices must exist in accordance with the laws of nature in order to be sustainable. We also believe that cultural diversity is as essential as biological diversity in maintaining sustainable societies.

Indigenous people have lived on Earth sustainably for thousands of years, and I suggest to you that indigenous ways of living are the only sustainable ways of living. Most indigenous ceremonies, if you look to their essence, are about the restoration of balance — they are a reaffirmation of our relationship to creation. That is our intent: to restore, and then to retain balance and honor our part in creation.

Therefore, when I harvest wild rice on our reservation, I always offer asemaa (tobacco) because when you take something, you must always give thanks to its spirit for giving itself to you. We are very careful when we harvest. Anthropologists call this reciprocity. This means that when you take, you always give. We also say that you must take only what you need and leave the rest. Because if you take more than you need, you have brought about imbalance, you have been selfish. To do this in our community is a very big disgrace. It is a violation of natural law, and it leaves you with no guarantee that you will be able to continue harvesting.

We have a word in our language which describes the prac-
10 tice of living in harmony with natural law: minocimaatisiiwin. This word describes how you behave as an individual in a relationship with other individuals and in relationship with the land and all things. We have tried to retain this way of living and this way of thinking in spite of all that has happened to us over the centuries. I believe we do retain most of these practices in our community, even if they are overshadowed at times by individualism.

The Clash of Indigenous and Industrial Worldviews

I would like to contrast indigenous thinking with what I call "industrial thinking," which is characterized by five key ideas that run counter to what we as native people believe.

1) Instead of believing that natural law is preeminent, industrial society believes that humans are entitled to full dominion over nature. It believes that man — and it is usually man of course — has some God-given right to all that is around him. Industrial society puts its faith in man's laws: that

pollution regulations, allowable catches, etc. are sustainable.

2) In indigenous societies, we notice that much in nature is cyclical: the movement of moons, the tides, the seasons, and our bodies. Time itself is cyclical. Instead of modeling itself on the cyclical structure of nature, industrial society is patterned on linear thinking. Industrial society strives to continually move in one direction defined by things like technology and economic growth.

3) Industrial society holds a different attitude toward what is wild as opposed to what is cultivated or "tame." In our language we have the word indinawayuuganitoog (all our relations). That is what we believe — that our relatives may have wings, fins, roots or hooves. Industrial society believes wilderness must be tamed. This is also the idea behind colonialism: that some people have the right to civilize other people.

4) Industrial society speaks in a language of inanimate nouns. 15
Things of all kinds are not spoken of as being alive and having spirit; they are described as mere objects, commodities. When things are inanimate, "man" can take them, buy and sell them, or destroy them. Some scholars refer to this as the "comodification of the sacred."

5) The last aspect of industrial thinking is the idea of capitalism itself (which is always unpopular to question in America). The capitalist goal is to use the least labor, capital, and resources to make the most profit. The intent of capitalism is accumulation. So the capitalist's method is always to take more than is needed. With accumulation as its core, industrial society practices conspicuous consumption. Indigenous societies, on the other hand, practice what I would call "conspicuous distribution." We focus on the potlatch — the act of giving away. In fact, the more you give away, the greater your honor.

Modern industrial societies must begin to see the interlocking interests between their own ability to survive and the survival of indigenous peoples' culture. Indigenous peoples have lived sustainably on the land for thousands of years. I am absolutely sure that our societies could live without yours, but I'm not so sure that your society can continue to live without ours.

Sustainability in Action

All across the continent there are small groups of native peoples who are trying to regain control of and restore their communities.

I'll use my own people as an example. The White Earth Reservation is thirty-six by thirty-six miles square, which is about 837,000 acres. A treaty reserved it for our people in 1867 in return for relinquishing a much larger area of northern Minnesota. Out of all our territory we chose this land for its richness and diversity. There are forty-seven lakes on the reservation. There's maple sugar, there are hardwoods, and there are all the different medicine plants my people use. We have wild rice, we have deer, we have beaver, we have fish — we have every food we need. On the eastern part of the reservation there are stands of white pine; to the west is prairieland where the buffalo once roamed. Our word for prairie is mashkode (place of burned medicine) referring to native practices of burning as a form of nurturing the soil and plants.

20 Our traditional forms of land use and ownership are similar to those found in community land trusts being established today. The land is owned collectively, and each family has traditional areas where it fishes and hunts. We call our concept of land ownership Anishinaabeg akiing: "the land of the people," which doesn't imply that we own our land, but that we belong on it. Unfortunately, our definition doesn't stand up well in court because this country's legal system upholds the concept of private property.

We have maintained our land by means of careful management. For example, we traditionally have "hunting bosses" and "rice chiefs," who make sure that resources are used sustainably in each region. Hunting bosses oversee rotation of trap lines, a system by which people trap in an area for two years and then move to a different area to let the land rest. Rice chiefs coordinate wild rice harvesting. The rice on each lake has its own unique taste and ripens at its own time. Traditionally, we have a "tallyman," who makes sure there are enough animals for each family in a given area. If a family can't sustain itself, the tallyman moves them to a new place where animals are more plentiful. These practices are essential to sustainability, and to maintaining what some now call the commons.

The Loss of White Earth, and How We Plan to Get It Back

Our reservation was reserved by treaty in 1867. In 1887 the Nelson Act and subsequently the General Allotment Act was passed to teach Indians the concept of private property, but also to facilitate the removal of more land from Indian Nations. The federal government divided our reservation into eighty-acre parcels of land and allotted each parcel to an individual Indian, hoping that this would somehow force us to become farmers and adopt the notion of progress — in short, to be civilized.

The allotment system was alien to our traditional concepts of land. In our society a person harvested rice in one place, trapped in another place, gathered medicines in a third place, and picked berries in a fourth. These locations depended on the ecosystem; they were not necessarily contiguous. But the government said to each Indian, "Here are your eighty acres; this is where you'll live." Then, after each Indian had received an allotment, the rest of the land was declared "surplus" and given to white people to homestead or "develop." What happened to my reservation happened to reservations all across the country.

The state of Minnesota took our pine forests away and sold them to timber companies, and then taxed us for the land that was left. When the Indians couldn't pay the taxes, the state confiscated the land. But how could these people pay taxes? In 1910, they could not even read or write English.

I'll tell you a story about how my great-grandma was cheated by a loan shark. She lived on Many-Point Lake, where she was allotted land. She had run up a bill at the local store because she was waiting until fall when she could get some money from wild rice harvesting and a payment coming from a treaty annuity. So she went to a land speculator named Lucky Waller, and she said, "I need to pay this bill." She asked to borrow fifty bucks from him until the fall, and he said: "Okay, you can do that. Just sign here and I'll loan you that fifty bucks." So she signed with the thumbprint and went back to her house on Many-Point Lake. About three months later she was ready to repay him the fifty bucks, and the loan shark said: "No, you keep that money. I bought your land from you." He had purchased her eighty acres on Many-Point Lake for fifty bucks. Today that location is a Boy Scout camp.

The White Earth Reservation lost two hundred and fifty thousand acres to the state of Minnesota because of unpaid taxes. By 1920, 99 percent of the original White Earth Reservation land was in non-Indian hands. This was done to native peoples across the country.

We have exhausted all legal recourse for getting back our land. The Federal Circuit Court ruled that to regain their land Indian people had to have filed a lawsuit within seven years of the original time of taking. Still, we believe that we must get our land back. We really do not have any other place to go.

That's why we started the White Earth Land Recovery Project. Our project is like several other projects in Indian communities. We are not trying to displace people who have settled there. A third of our land is held by federal, state and country governments. That land should just be returned to us. It certainly would not displace anyone. Some of the privately held land on our reservation is held by absentee landholders — many of whom have never seen that land; they do not even know where it is. It is a commodity to them, not home. We hope to persuade them to return it to us.

Our project also works to reacquire our land. We bought some land as a site for a roundhouse, a building that holds one of our ceremonial drums. We bought back our burial grounds, which were on private land, because we believe that we should hold the land where our ancestors rest. We purchased a former elementary school, which is now the home of our new radio station and a wind turbine. In 2009, which is the 20th anniversary of our project, we had acquired 1400 acres. We use some of this land to grow and gather sustainable products that we sell: wild rice, maple syrup and candy, berry jams, and Birch bark crafts.

Sustainable Communities, Not Sustainable Development

In conclusion, I want to say there is no such thing as sustainable 30
development. Community is the only thing in my experience that is sustainable. We all need to be involved in building communities — not solely focused on developing things. We can each do that in our own way, whether it is European-American communities or indigenous communities, by restoring a way of life that is based on the land.

The only way you can manage a commons is if you share enough cultural experiences and values so that what you take out of nature doesn't upset the natural balance — minobimaatisiiwin, as we call it. The reason native cultures have remained sustainable for all these centuries is that we are cohesive communities. A common set of values is needed to live together on the land.

Finally, I believe industrial societies continue to consume too much of the world's resources. When you need that many resources, it means constant intervention in other peoples' land and other peoples' countries. It is meaningless to talk about human rights unless you talk about consumption. In order for native communities to live and teach the world about sustainability, the dominant society must change. If modern society continues in the direction it is going, indigenous people's way of life will continue to bear the consequences.

The Gettysburg Address

by Abraham Lincoln

Abraham Lincoln (1809–1865) served as the sixteenth President of the United States, from 1861 until his assassination in 1865. "The Gettysburg Address" was delivered on November 19, 1863, at the dedication of the Soldiers National Cemetery at Gettysburg, Pennsylvania. The battle at Gettysburg, which took place July 1–3, 1863, was a major victory for Union soldiers and is considered a turning point in the war. It was also one of the bloodiest battles, seeing upwards of 51,000 casualties in just three days. Although only 272 words, Lincoln's address is among the most famous speeches ever given.

Four score and seven years ago, our fathers brought forth upon this continent a new nation, conceived in liberty, and dedicated to the proposition that all men are created equal.

Now we are engaged in a great civil war, testing whether that nation, or any nation so conceived and so dedicated, can long endure. We are met on a great battlefield of that war. We have come to dedicate a portion of that field as a final resting-place for those who here gave their lives that that nation might live. It is altogether fitting and proper that we should do this.

But in a larger sense we cannot dedicate — we cannot consecrate — we cannot hallow — this ground. The brave men, living and dead, who struggled here, have consecrated it far above our power to add or detract. The world will little note nor long remember what we say here, but it can never forget what they did here. It is for us, the living, rather, to be dedicated here to the unfinished work which they who fought here have thus far so nobly advanced. It is rather for us to be here dedicated to the great task remaining before us — that from these honored dead we take increased devotion to that cause for which they gave the last full measure of devotion; that we here highly resolve that these dead shall not have died in vain; that this nation, under God, shall have a new birth of freedom; and that government of the people, by the people, and for the people, shall not perish from the earth.

Concerning Cruelty and Mercy, and Whether It Is Better to Be Loved than Feared

by Niccolò Machiavelli

Niccolò Machiavelli (1469–1527) was a statesman and political philosopher of the Italian Renaissance. His most well-known work, The Prince, *is an examination of political power that has often been banned and condemned. This is an excerpt from Chapter 17 of* The Prince.

Every prince should desire to be considered merciful and not cruel. Nevertheless, he must take care not to misuse this mercy.

Cesare Borgia was considered cruel. However, his cruelty reconciled the Romagna, unified it, and restored it to peace and loyalty. When we consider this correctly, we see that he was much more merciful than the Florentine people, who — to avoid a reputation for cruelty — allowed Pistoia to be destroyed.

Therefore, as long as he keeps his subjects united and loyal, a prince should not mind a reputation for cruelty. By setting a few examples, he will be more merciful than those who, through too much mercy, allow disorders to arise, which lead to murders or robberies. These disorders are likely to harm the whole people, while the executions of a prince only harm the individual.

And of all types of princes, it is impossible for the new prince to avoid the reputation for cruelty because new states are full of dangers. Thus Virgil, speaking through the mouth of Dido, excuses the inhumanity of her reign because it is a new one:

Against my will, my fate,
A throne unsettled, and an infant state,
Bid me defend my realms with all my powers,
And with these cruelties guard my shores.

Nevertheless, the prince should be slow to believe and act. He should not show any fear but should proceed in a temperate manner, with caution and humanity, so that too much confidence will not make him reckless and too much distrust will not make him intolerable.

This raises the question of whether it is better to be loved than feared or feared than loved? It might be said that one should wish to be both, but because it is difficult to unite the two in one person, it is much safer to be feared than loved if one of the two must be dispensed with. This is because most men are ungrateful, fickle, false, cowardly, and covetous. As long as you are successful, they are yours entirely. When need is distant, they will offer you their blood, property, life, and children. However, when need approaches, they turn against you.

The prince who relies entirely on their promises and has neglected other precautions will be ruined. Friendships that are obtained through payments — and not through greatness or nobility of mind — may be well earned, but they are not secure. In time of need, they cannot be trusted. Men are less worried about offending someone they love than they are of offending someone they fear. Love is preserved through the bond of obligation, and because men are depraved, they break that bond at every opportunity when it's to their advantage. The bond of fear, however, is preserved by the dread of punishment and never fails.

However, a prince should try to inspire fear in such a way that — even if he does not win love — avoids hatred. He will do very well being feared as long as he is not hated, and he will not be hated as long as he abstains from the property of his subjects and from their women. When it is necessary for him to proceed against the life of someone, he must do it on proper justification and for obvious reasons, and above all else, he must keep his hands off the property of others, for men will more quickly forget the death of their father than the loss of their inheritance. Besides, pretexts for taking away the property of others are never lacking. The one who has once begun to live by robbery will always find pretexts for seizing what belongs to others. Reasons for taking life, on the contrary, are more difficult to find and soon fade.

However, when a prince is with his army and has control of a multitude of soldiers, then it is quite necessary for him to ignore the reputation of cruelty. Without cruelty, he would never hold his army united or disposed to its duties.

Among the wonderful deeds of Hannibal, there is this one — that having led an enormous army of many different races of men to fight in foreign lands, no dissensions arose among them, or against the prince, in either his bad or his good fortune. This came about because of his inhuman cruelty, which along with his boundless courage, made him revered and fearful in the sight of his soldiers. Without that cruelty, his other virtues were not sufficient to produce this effect. Shortsighted writers admire his triumphs from one point of view and then condemn the principal cause of those triumphs.

We know that Hannibal's other virtues would not have been sufficient for him because of the case of Scipio, that most excellent man — and excellent not only in his time but in the memory of man. In spite of those virtues, his army rebelled against him in Spain because of nothing other than his great patience, which gave his soldiers more freedom than is consistent with military discipline. For this, he was attacked in the Senate by Fabius Maximus, who called him the corrupter of the Roman army . . . .

Returning to the question of being feared or loved, I come to the conclusion that men love according to their own will and according to the will of the prince. Therefore, a wise prince should establish himself on the thing that is in his own control and not in the control of others. He must try only to avoid hatred, as I have noted.

The Girls in My Town

by Angela Morales

Angela Morales teaches English at Glendale Community College in California. "The Girls in My Town" was originally published in Southwest Review *and then selected to be published in* The Best American Essays 2013.

1.

Here in the middle of California — in this sun-bleached, hard-tack landscape — we have no choice but to search for beauty. The soil, dun-colored and rock-hard, erodes into a soft layer of silt that covers the town every time the wind blows. All across California's farm belt — this land between the Sierras and the Pacific — rows and rows of cotton bolls, apricot and walnut trees, grapevines and tomato plants, roll out for hundreds of miles. But then the rain ceases. Two years pass. Three years. Early morning dew brings the smell of manure that lingers in our neighborhoods, a smell that grows stronger with every passing month. Winter brings no rain but only a thick layer of tule fog that traps us further in a damp white haze. Bitter particles of pesticides hang in the air. We drive on Highway 99 in search of something to look at and find FOR LEASE signs, abandoned western-themed restaurants, and peeling billboards advertising brand-new housing developments that never panned out — a picture of a two-story tract home adorned with a Spanish tile fountain, a father holding a plump toddler, a chemical-green lawn, a happy yellow dog. Between aqueducts and waterways, mazes of irrigation canals and ditches, we try to improve our minds. We enroll in classes at the community college and vow, once and for all, to see it through.

But our library — a big, sad building — houses old, second-rate books, and the librarians seem tired as they thumb through ladies' magazines and gaze wearily over the tops of their reading glasses. This library, unlike some libraries with summer reading programs and cheery children's wings containing beanbags and puzzles, is not a happy place. Here the hours are limited. Erratic. Now think of the brutally hot sun. You worry about dogs not having any shade. That dog chained to some little leafless tree in the back of somebody's junkyard. That dog whose water bowl is covered in green slime and sits about six inches from the end of his leash. You worry about dogs and children. (Cats can generally take care of themselves.)

2.

Francisco, a beautiful boy, sits at the front of the classroom — center stage. When the girls arrive, they circle around him and slip into desks nearest to him, glancing his way and trying not to giggle every time he makes a comment. He leans forward with folded hands, his feet planted solidly on the floor like some goody-goody schoolboy. When he asks a question — usually something ridiculous — the girls turn completely around in their seats to stare at him. I say, "The midterm exam will be next Tuesday at ten — don't be late!" And he raises his hand and asks stupidly, "Uh . . . Miss? Is there a midterm for this class?" Then one of the serious, not-so beautiful boys murmurs, "*Pendejo*! Open up your ears," and beautiful Francisco will wink at me and yawn. His eyes, translucent and emerald green, make me uneasy. He resembles Johnny Depp but speaks with a slow rising cadence that reminds me of my grandfather — my grandfather who ended up with seven kids and a gambling habit. Francisco tries to flirt with me by calling me *profesora* in that lazy melodic lilt, though around here — at age thirty-two — I am old enough to be his mother. I wonder which girl will get to him first and then whether he'll pay child support or if he'll want to get married *ever*, being so beautiful and all.

3.

Our neighbors across the street whom we call the "Meth Joads" remind us of Steinbeck's Joads because they drive around in a patched-together pickup truck that teeters under the weight of a perpetual mass of junk: wooden pallets, broken bicycles, miscellaneous car parts. Unlike Steinbeck's Joads, however, they are most definitely meth addicts, with the telltale tense jaw, the broken shorn-down teeth, the deep bronchial laugh that inevitably turns into a coughing fit. The Meth Joads have a teenage daughter who sits on the front porch and talks on the cordless phone. One day she's out there talking and I notice that Misty Joad's belly has grown big as a watermelon and is now straining against the seams of her tank top. A few days later, Mr. Meth Joad hauls in a yard-sale crib from his pickup truck. *It's all good*, he says, straining under the weight of the crib, a cigarette between his teeth. The girl, Misty Joad — no more than sixteen and heavily pregnant — paces the sidewalk and talks languidly on that phone like she's waiting for somebody to pick her up and take her somewhere. Every few days a red-faced teenage boy shows up and the two of them drive away in his Mustang. Then the boy stops coming. Eventually Misty Joad walks the sidewalk with her newborn baby. But imagine her power. Even with dirty bare feet and no plans, her body has declared a coup: *If you won't love me, here's a person who will.*

4.

We live down the street from the continuation high school. 5
When we first moved to the neighborhood, Patrick and I referred

to it as the "bad-boy school" because that is what my grandpa used to call the school on his street in Boyle Heights. At that bad-boy school in Boyle Heights, enormous pigs lived belly-deep in black muck — muck that emitted an odor so foul that we tied bandanas over our noses and gagged anyway as we rode our bikes past the pigs' enclosures. I'd spy on those bad boys in their rubber boots as they shoveled muck and slops, and I was glad that, being a girl, I would never have to shovel shit or get my ass bit the way that rogue hog had once bitten Grandma's ass (after it had chased her around the neighborhood for a good forty-five minutes). That pig had gone *hog wild.*

The bad-boy school in this town, though, turns out to be a bad-*girl* school, with a special program for pregnant teens. Sometimes I see those girls exercising on the track — twenty or thirty of them — a whole herd of teenage girls walking around in circles, hands supporting their lower backs, bellies sticking out a mile. Merced gets hotter than hell, so usually the girls pant dramatically and fan themselves, periodically squinting and shielding their eyes from the merciless sky. After their babies are born, most of these girls will come back to school for a few months, and then the majority of them will drop out of school altogether.

I push my own baby in her stroller and observe the girls through the chain-link fence as they complete their one-mile forced march. One starts brushing her hair. The teacher cajoles her and momentarily she quickens her pace, but as soon as the teacher turns around, she slows down again. Looking at them, I try to imagine the moment of love or rage or revenge that brought them here. Most of their babies' fathers will not marry them. Most will continue living in poverty as single mothers. The majority of their children will have learning and behavioral problems. Some of those babies will end up right here back on this very same track.

In the Teen Parent Program, girls are taught life skills, like how to eat healthy foods such as carrot sticks and cottage cheese rather than a *machaca* burrito (two out of three girls are Latinas) and the three-pack of Hostess Ho-Hos. (And who knew that a bacon guacamole Whopper had 1,020 milligrams of sodium and 43 grams of fat?) They watch filmstrips in which fetuses unfurl their tiny limbs; black guppy eyes grow human eyelids; a prehistoric fin separates into ten toes. Later the girls learn about scary conditions like preeclampsia and gestational diabetes and suddenly they understand why so-and-so's cousin gave birth to that extraordinary thirteen-pound infant, the one with doughy, waterlogged skin and a protruding tongue.

They learn how to change a diaper and how to hold a baby's head so it won't bob off to one side. They learn about the soft, downy triangle called the fontanel and how their babies' brains, soft as cream cheese, can be felt by gently placing a finger on that eerie soft spot. They learn about shaken baby syndrome and sudden infant death syndrome and then they are given stickers with emergency contact numbers — school counselors, social workers, paramedics. They are told that they will not be alone and that caring for a child requires both strength and humility. *We are your support system*, the girls are told. *We are here for you.*

10 Across the street from the bad girls' school on the corner of 20th and G Streets, Rollins' Donuts emits the thick, cloying scent of golden doughnuts as they bob around in the fryer. After school the girls disregard what they've learned in health class and line up out the door, shifting their pregnant selves from foot to foot while absent-mindedly massaging the undersides of their bellies, bellies now covered by maternity jeans with spandex tummy panels. Some girls, the rebels, forgo the secondhand maternity clothes altogether (too *old-ladyish!*) and let their bellies hang over the elastic bands of their sweatpants.

Just downwind from Rollins, at the government-approved WIC grocery stores, girls can cash their WIC vouchers for Similac, double-wide boxes of Cheerios, and big hunks of cheese.

In the hospital after my daughter was born, the nurse had brought me yet another stack of forms to fill out. "Here," she'd said, handing me a pen. "You'll definitely want to fill these out." I hoisted the baby onto one shoulder, and just as I had begun to write my name in the first box, I saw that I was about to fill out a Women, Infants, and Children Assistance application.

"Oh, I don't need this," I said. I tried to give back the pen, but she wouldn't take it. "Oh, but you *have* to," she said. "You get free food like bread and milk and formula. Formula's expensive! You'll see! You can get WIC vouchers until the baby is five years old! Imagine five whole years of free food!"

"No, that's okay, really . . ." I said again. She pressed on.

"Why the heck *not*?" she said, leaning close, giving me a conspiratorial look. "Almost everyone gets approved. Well, just think about it."

After she left, I crumpled the forms and shoved them into the trash can. Certainly, I thought, WIC is for *very* poor women — single mothers, teenagers, and migrant farm workers. Being of sound mind and body (or so I tell myself) and having a job, I knew I would not need such assistance, and now I admit to being slightly offended that the nurse had automatically assumed that I needed WIC at all. Based on what? Based on my dark hair and my last name? But in her defense, the odds that a Latina with a newborn baby would need government assistance are, in this town, indeed, very high. Here, population 60,000, one in four women and children is enrolled in WIC. That's a lot of formula. A lot of cheese.

Every day on my street little girls push strollers with real babies in them. The girls walk with their friends — other young girls with *their* babies — sometimes three or four of them at a time. They walk shoulder to shoulder in the middle of the street like they belong to a fertility parade. Sometimes we have to drive around them, swerving gently to the opposite side of the road. "Careful," I'll tell Patrick as he turns the corner. "It's a stroller brigade." It's an evangelist's nightmare (or would that be a dream come true?).

Times have changed since my grandmother and great-grandmother (with sixteen children between them) dodged the shame of being dark and young and pregnant. Without reliable birth control, access to good schools (only the inferior "Indian schools"), and decent jobs with decent wages, what choices did my grandmothers have? Even if girls did not have babies of their own, they often became mothers by default — by tending to younger siblings, nieces, and nephews. Babies were a fact of life. The wealthy had nannies and nursemaids at their disposal. My grandmothers *were* these nannies.

Fast-forward a hundred years and observe the very same girls — now unfettered by husbands and tradition — now walking side by side in the middle of the street, chattering away as they adjust their babies' juice bottles, talk on their cell phones, and halfheartedly dangle little rattles above the strollers. Unlike my grandmothers, the girls in this town have access to birth control pills, integrated schools with specialized programs, and guidance counselors who are supposed to tout the merits of college — even to the brown and black kids. The girls in my town have more choices, though some people might argue that when you're young and poor and your own mother lives on welfare, those choices are hard to find. Love, on the other hand, is easier to find. Love (or the promise of it) is free. Love makes you feel good, especially if you've never had a father, even if only for a few minutes. Love is beautiful: think of walking hand in hand with the green-eyed Francisco at sunset along some fictional beach. And if you end up getting pregnant, *we are here to support you.* And here's a fact about babies: babies now come with many cute accessories — headband bows for little bald heads; Lilliputian T-shirts imprinted with hip slogans like *Ladies' Man* or *Change My Diaper, Biaatch!*; knit caps with built-in Mohawks and bunny ears; pacifiers with vampire fangs painted onto the mouthpiece.

5.

The obstetrics nurse at Mercy Hospital dims the lights and draws the threadbare curtain across the center of the room, a flimsy illusion of privacy between me and my fourteen-year-old roommate. Both our babies had been born around midnight, and now, with babies swaddled and sleeping inside plastic, wheeled bassinets, sleep seems like a superb idea.

Everyone has gone home, and I'm alone for the first time with my newborn daughter. I can't stop staring at her. She'd been the loudest, angriest baby in the nursery, apparently furious at having been exiled from the womb. With our bodies now separate entities, the world, to me, seems upside-down. Sharp-edged. Somewhere a car smashes into a tree. Airborne bacteria and spiky pollens float past. And who is this little human, anyway? What about her life comes predestined? I try to see the tiny, scrolled-up map inside her skull — the grid within her brain, the catalogue of her choices and, ultimately, her destiny and desires: an aversion to crowds, a deep compassion for animals, a love of money, a penchant for mathematics, a blind left eye.

Meanwhile, my roommate and her boyfriend are lying side by side in bed and watching back-to-back episodes of *Cops*. Crack addicts make excuses, a homeless woman sobs over a lost dog, a teenage girl's baby-daddy just put a steak knife to her throat. My roommate's baby-daddy adds his own running commentary: *Damn,* look at that dude! He's so fucked-up. *Hey! Remember when the cops beat the shit out of my uncle?* My roommate murmurs something in reply. And what's going through her head? I try to remember being fourteen. I try to imagine being a mother at age fourteen.

Then my roommate's baby starts crying. The crying gets louder. Pretty soon the baby wails like a peacock. Ay-*ya!* Ay-*ya!* Suddenly the sound of a crying baby makes me feel crazed, like an animal with its paw caught in a trap about to gnaw off its own foot. My head throbs. My spine aches. I wonder if these fourteen-year-old children know what do with an infant. Do *I* know what to do with an infant? How will we keep these babies alive? How will these children survive the years ahead? *Jesus, where the hell are the nurses?* I think. I consider saying something, but I'm too exhausted. I've got seventeen years on her, and compared to her, I'm already an old lady.

6.

The Lamaze teacher said, "Visualize that your uterus is a beautiful spring bud, slowly unfurling its leaves, blossoming right before your eyes." This teacher talked so gently about the body and the birth process — how childbirth happens every single day — how women's bodies are designed for birth. Her voice, like a drug, hypnotized me as I sat cross-legged with the other pregnant women — some with husbands, some with boyfriends, some with their moms. We breathed deeply and traced slow circles across our bellies — a technique that supposedly calms the body, calms the mind.

At the onset of my labor, then, I successfully envisioned 25
a Georgia O'Keeffe orchid, a soft swirl of violet petals and leaves. As labor progressed and the pain intensified — surprise, surprise — my orchid melted away and in its place appeared an engulfing blackness. Eventually, as the pain intensified into lightning bolts, a creature took shape — half man, half goat, with horns, red eyes, and lobster claws, the whole bit; he could have leapt right out of a Francisco de Goya painting. By the eighth hour, the beast had burst right through the floor and had me around the waist and was trying to pull me into the hole that had opened up in the middle of the floor.

Lying in my hospital bed in the small-town Catholic hospital, I decided to surrender myself to the image; in other words, I would not swim against the current and try to turn the demon back into an orchid. Instead, I would face my nightmare head-on: I would grab that son of a bitch by the horns and peer directly into his flaming eyes. *Ha! Two can play at this game*, I thought. Here's what the Lamaze teachers don't tell you about childbirth — particularly childbirth without drugs: the goal is not really to stay calm and focused; the goal is to stay *alive!* Once, when I was eighteen, a fortuneteller peered at my palm and said, "Mmm … lucky you live in *these* times. One hundred years ago you would have died giving birth." In this small-town hospital, though, one hundred years does not seem like that long ago.

So with the fortuneteller's words echoing in my head, I told myself to fight like a warrior. Screaming felt good. I screamed until my throat became sandpaper. Suddenly a nurse grabbed me by the wrist and said sternly, "Dear. You are wasting an awful lot of energy on all that screaming. Why don't you get a hold of yourself? Just *calm* down." I jerked my arm away and glared at her. How dare she tell me how to have a baby? How dare she intrude into my hallucination? Anyway, I thought, she had no idea what she was talking about — all those Lamaze lies, all that childbirth propaganda designed to shut us up — to keep the masses *sedated* so that nurses and doctors don't get headaches.

So I decided that with each contraction I would scream every bad word I knew. *Bitch, motherfucker!* I didn't care what anyone said, not Patrick, not my mother, not even the nuns. It felt good to fight, then, to unleash my rebellious tongue.

Later I wondered about my fourteen-year-old roommate, who had been giving birth at the same time. Why had I not heard her voice? Did she not feel such intense pain? Had she been given an epidural? Was *I* too melodramatic — me with my death-defying warrior fantasy? Now I wish I'd talked to her during those two days that we shared a room. We talked a little bit, but she averted her eyes. Painfully shy. Not much of a talker. I wish I'd asked her how she got through it and whether she dreamed up some flower or some other beautiful thing. What thoughts and images travel through the mind of a fourteen-year-old girl as she becomes a mother?

7.

Carl Jung believed that his schizophrenic patients' hallucinations 30
should be treated with the same respect that one might treat any "real" scenario that one can see with one's own eyes. Jung believed that if a person truly believes that he is being chased by wild tigers in a jungle, you should not remind him that he is actually sitting in a comfortable velour armchair and not running for his life through a jungle. Nor should you tell him that the tigers are simply phantoms or figments of his imagination. Instead, you should help him *to survive*. Instead, ask him, "Have you a spear? Have you a rifle?" Urge him to jump into the river or to grab a big stick. In acknowledging the phantom tigers, Jung believed that he could reaffirm and validate the contents of a mind, those contents being significant in their symbolism and necessary to the survival of their host.

8.

Here is a true story that has become part of our local mythology:

Late one night, fifteen-year-old Benita Ramos pounds on the door of a random house. Crying and begging for help, she says that a man has just kidnapped her son — snatched the stroller right out of her hands. When police arrive, Benita explains that she was visiting the baby's father (age seventeen) at his parents' house, and as she was walking home and pushing the baby's stroller down the dark path, a tall, skinny white guy tackled her from behind and then ran off with the stroller, her baby boy still strapped inside.

That night Benita appears on the eleven o'clock news,

slurring her words and begging for the safe return of her baby. Her family — aunts, uncles, parents — all stand behind her with grim expressions on their faces. The girl's story sounds plausible because terrible things happen to children in our town. Imagine a place of planetary misalignment, a celestial crisscross of weird energy. Imagine the Bermuda Triangle on dry land. Our town, home to the Pitchfork Killer and the Yosemite Killer, makes us believe that anything is possible.

Later that night, though, police find the empty, overturned stroller on the muddy embankment of the creek. In the flashlight's white beam, they spot what looks like the baby's body floating face-down in the black, stagnant water. (Bear Creek, a tributary of the Merced River, begins high in Yosemite backcountry; up there, it's gorgeous and rugged and the water rushes across car-sized boulders, all framed by Douglas firs, sugar pines, and sequoias. Look up and see an impossibly blue sky with fast-moving wisps of vaporous clouds.) But here, far away from the creek's source, the baby's hooded sweatshirt is caught on some protruding branches next to an overturned shopping cart. (God only knows what else is down there.)

35 Eventually Benita confesses, though detectives observe that she is not very articulate; moreover, they say, she acts much younger than a girl of fifteen. Later, by piecing together her confession and forensic evidence, they'll determine that Benita tried to drown the baby in the water fountain at Applegate Park. They'll say that she then threw her baby into the creek and faked the kidnapping.

After this happened, we will always think of Benita's dead baby when we go to Applegate Park, which functions as our town center; we go there most Sundays. Fragrant orange and pink rosebushes surround that fountain, and nearby children can visit a half-blind donkey at the petting zoo or an old bear that paces his enclosure for eighteen hours a day. If Benita's baby boy had lived, surely she would have brought him to ride the miniature train that circles the perimeter of the same park in which she killed him.

But Benita won't say more. She appears to be a broken girl. Detectives claim that because she appears to be mentally disturbed and because she functions below the level of an average fifteen-year-old, they might never get inside her head. What's there to say when you have a baby at age fourteen and your seventeen-year-old boyfriend starts dating some other girl, some little slut from another high school, and now your whole life consists of Pampers and plastic baby bottles, milk-encrusted rubber nipples, and maybe once in a while your life gets supplemented by a Jerry Springer episode and an orange Popsicle?

I just went sort of crazy, she might have said. And, *Having a baby is like really, really hard. Nobody understands.* And if you can love babies when there's nobody else to love, sometimes you hurt babies when there's nobody else to hurt. You don't mean to, exactly — you just can't control it. Maybe it's payback for all that's ever been done to you.

9.

Our mothers tell us the story of La Llorona, which means the Wailing Woman. In the story, La Llorona's husband leaves her for another woman. After being rejected and abandoned, La Llorona plots her revenge.

La Llorona decides to take her children on a picnic next to 40
the river. She brings a quilt and a basket filled with strawberries, hard-boiled eggs, heart-shaped cakes, and honey water (because she really loves them). Imagine a spring day resplendent in all ways: the children play in the tall grass, they laugh, they tumble around.

But oh, what bad luck to have been born a child of La Llorona! (How many times, for how many hundreds of years, have these children had to endure the same fate with variations in details?) Soon she lures the children, one by one, through a low tunnel of shrubs to the river — probably across a raccoon or deer trail. The tunnel, enshrouded by eight-foot-tall reeds, leads to a waterside thicket; here frogs lounge on lily pads and dragonflies dive-bomb the water's surface.

Then she drowns her children, one by one, and afterward she arranges their bodies side by side across the family quilt and kisses each of them in the middle of their cold foreheads. Later, when La Llorona's husband finds the children, his screams can be heard for miles. She's dragged away in chains and put into a dungeon, where she wakes up in shock and realizes what she's done.

For all eternity she will cry out for her dead children. After she dies, her ghost will wander the riverbanks in search of new souls. Our mothers tell us that if we look carefully, we can see La Llorona crouching next to the water, furiously rubbing her hands with sand and gravel. They say that if we listen at night, we can hear moaning and rattling chains. If we're not careful, they say, she might mistake us for her dead children.

Our mothers never talk about any moral of the story. They tell it because it's a good story and they can alter the details as they please. But children are presented with the idea of mothers gone crazy, of mothers who use their children for revenge. Many children have nightmares about La Llorona, because all of our basic fears can be traced to our mothers, whether we realize it or not. During the day she combs our hair and kisses us. At night she's the madwoman in the attic. It's this duplicity that scares the hell out of us. All mothers have dual natures, and La Llorona's pale face and leaf-strewn hair reminds us of this. So we dream about children floating beneath gentle currents, their faces obscured by the water, their small, icy hands floating to the surface. The simple lesson: Stay away from water! Don't go out after dark! Be quiet and go to sleep! The deeper message: Do *our* mothers want to kill *us*? Is it not a question of *if*, but a question of *when*? And most importantly: If our fathers abandon our mothers for the "other woman," should we opt out of the picnic next to the river? (We get these thoughts especially when walking next to creeks or canals or irrigation ditches.)

10.

Once a girl brought her infant to the final exam. She arrived 45
late, all sweaty and exasperated, and I don't remember exactly *why* she brought the baby — probably that her mother couldn't babysit, so I said, *Fine, fine, sit down, take the exam, don't want you to fail on account of that,* knowing these girls have enough problems as it is. So I offered to hold the baby throughout the exam; I jostled it about as I walked up and down the aisles patrolling for cheaters. It was weird, because suddenly I became a mother, teacher, grandmother all at once. I lost a little bit of my authority. I became a relative. A regular person.

Midway through the exam, when the baby started to fuss, I poked the baby's mother on the arm and whispered, *Do you have a bottle?* She dug around in her backpack and (thank goodness) found one. I gave the bottle to the baby while students were bent over their exams. The baby sucked down its formula, making that gulping sound that babies make. They study you, their fat little fingers fondling the edges of the bottle, fondling your fingers, reaching for your nose, their bare toes. This one never took his eyes off me. Once he snapped the rubber nipple with his four teeth and then laughed loudly. The class heard this and then laughed too. The baby wanted us to love him, maybe to improve his chances of survival.

How quickly the border between classroom and home, personal and professional can dissolve! But it felt good to hold a baby in a classroom. I could breathe for a minute. A baby provides comic relief. A baby is funny and random and unscripted. But I could not fully enjoy the moment, because the whole time I was wrestling with ideas like *Is this really a good message to be sending to students? Shouldn't I send her away, saying*

"No children allowed," because those are the rules? Will this baby distract the other students? How much do you bend the rules for these girls with their babies, these girls with the odds stacked so high against them?

11.

My teenage students have babies right in the middle of a semester. The San Joaquin Valley has the highest teen pregnancy rate of any region in the United States. My students call me up and say, "Miss, I just wanted to remind you that my baby is due in a couple days . . . so if you don't see me in class . . . that's why." They disappear for a couple days and then reappear, their eyes slightly glazed. *Back already?* I say, because after my baby was born, I'd staggered around for two weeks feeling like I'd just completed the Bataan Death March. But for most teenagers, the body heals itself and springs back into shape almost immediately; life goes on. Evolutionarily speaking, a quick recovery makes sense. Biologically, humans can give birth at a relatively young age; consider that, on average, girls begin to menstruate at age twelve — sometimes as young as age eight. But to what advantage? Do species evolve to produce as many offspring as possible, even at the risk of mothers being socially and mentally immature? Is it better to throw our DNA into the mix as often as possible to improve the odds that at least some of our genetic material will survive? Consider, though, life within a tribe — all those hands, the elders to keep watch, to give advice, to admonish. Perhaps for some humans, the young-mother model works just fine. But without the tribe, without rules, who will watch over the girls in my town — these girls who often need mothering themselves — these girls with their babies in their low-rent apartments with boyfriends who sometimes marry them, most often do not?

After class one girl says proudly, "Look, Miss. I can already button my old jeans!" She holds up her blouse to reveal her small, swollen belly. Any evidence of her pregnancy has all but disappeared. Who would know that an eight-pound baby had recently been expelled from that same body?

50 At times I'm baffled by the lack of impact motherhood seems to have upon many of my students. Many girls don't appear to be visibly moved by the event of childbirth. Or at least they don't know how to express their feelings about it. Afterward they return to class; I search, but cannot discern any real change in their eyes. *So? Well?* I say. *How did it go?* The girls often shrug. "He weighed nine pounds," they might say, or, "He's already sleeping through the night, Miss." They'll tell me details that they've heard other mothers say, common quips that you hear on TV or in doctors' waiting rooms — bland, unrevealing details that seem scripted. Many of these same girls want to write essays about the births of their babies, but they almost always lack the language to express anything more than a basic plot outline. Example:

> My water bag broke right in the middle of the grocery store. It felt so weird. My mom drove me to the hospital. They put me in bed and got me all hooked up to the machines and then the pain got really bad. It went on for hours. They ended up doing a C-section, thank god. The labor lasted over twenty hours but then the baby was born healthy and now I am so happy. I love my baby so much!

In the margins of their papers, I'll press for specific details and analysis: *Describe the pain! Describe the baby! Do you feel any different? What obstacles do you face now?*

12.

My cousin X. and I practically grew up together. Sometimes she'd stay at our house for seven, eight, nine days, and then I'd stop talking to her. I'd give her the cold shoulder. I just wouldn't talk anymore. She'd say, "Are you mad at me?" I'd shrug. "Are you sick of me?" she'd say. "A little," I'd say. I didn't know how to articulate that I needed my bedroom back. I needed to close the door and read and think. I was that kind of kid. I needed solitude to feel normal. Sometimes I would just lock my door and stay in there the whole day. I'd stare at the ceiling. I remember saying, "I just need to think," not really knowing what I needed to think about. Then she'd say, "Okay, I'd better go home then. I guess I'll call my mom." I loved X. the way only cousins can love other cousins, kids who are thrown together in this world by way of shared mothers, mothers who sometimes turn parenting into an informal commune, the philosophy being *You take them today, I'll take them tomorrow*, the mission statement being *Together we will keep these children alive.* X.'s mother had gotten pregnant when she was eighteen. The guy ended up marrying her and then a couple years later he dumped two-year-old X. and my aunt onto Grandma's front lawn. He tossed their clothes out of the car and all over the grass. Then he drove away. End of story.

So we understood why X. got pregnant at age eighteen. She started looking for love in all the wrong places — love with surfer guys with names like Travis and Dave. One day she got herself knocked up and her stepfather kicked her out of the house and she moved in with us. "I just can't have an abortion again," she told me. "I won't do it." The born-again Christians had gotten ahold of her, pressing antiabortion pamphlets into her hands, pamphlets that contained gruesome pictures of dead fetuses, their tiny hands awash in fresh blood. She'd convinced herself that her dead baby was waiting for her in heaven and for the time being the baby was being cared for by angels, who had it gently by the hand, and that one day it would be reunited with its mommy-on-earth, but only if mommy-on-earth was willing to call herself a sinner and change her wanton ways. "I'm having
55 this baby," she said defiantly. It was a common trope back then.

But babies get annoying real fast. They get bigger and then they squirm away from you and then they call you names like *butthead* and they take off their shoes and hurl them at you and as soon as you get the shoes laced up again, they pry them off and toss them behind the dresser, and inevitably you lose that shoe and now you've got four mismatched shoes without mates. Toddlers can be hard to take, especially when they start saying NO all the time and that's the only word they know. They poke you in the eyes when you're sleeping and you're dead tired and they always have runny noses and the snot runs into their mouths and they lick at it with the edge of their tongues or smear it onto damp encrusted sleeves. They jump on you when you don't expect it, knees and elbows jamming into your ribs, into your chest, into your cheekbones, and the more you try to wrench them off, the more they want to jump on you again; sometimes you want to shove them off and maybe pinch their little arms or yank a clump of hair or leave them in the crib even if they're crying and calling you so pitifully, and you know this borders on child abuse, but it's really hard when there's no father and you are *it* — the kid's sun and moon.

13.

My daughter and my fourteen-year-old roommate's daughter — born on the same night, the same hour — are now thirteen years old. When I look at my own daughter I cannot believe that a girl of roughly her age and temperament could be a mother. She slams doors. She stomps around. She throws up her hands and says, "Are you *kidding* me?" She sketches pictures of horses and then crumples them up. She announces, "I'll take animals over people *any* day" (and she means it). And although her fingers are now longer than mine — her hands more graceful — I cannot, no matter how hard I try, imagine those hands changing a diaper.

Would our daughters have anything in common? My roommate's daughter, according to county statistics (based on her mother's age and ethnicity), will very likely have a baby before she turns eighteen. Then the girl will most likely drop out of school and struggle to care for her child in this place of leached soil tuned to clay. My roommate's daughter may never know about the migratory waterfowl such as Canadian geese and whistling swans that once stopped off in our valley marshlands — most of which have been drained to rechannel water for irrigation. And maybe the babies, in some weird way, reflect our need to find beauty once again in this landscape. In any case, I suspect our connection to the land runs deeper than we know.

As for our daughters, the fortuneteller might peer into her crystal ball or examine our girls' palms and see a whole web of alternate realities. *Anything can happen*, she might say. For all of us, the road is wide open.

Remarks by the President at Howard University Commencement Ceremony

by Barack Obama

Barack Obama (b. 1961) was elected President of the United States in 2008 and reelected in 2012. He delivered this commencement address on May 7, 2016, to the graduating class of Howard University, an historically black college. The university is located in Washington, DC, and was founded in 1867.

To President Frederick, the Board of Trustees, faculty and staff, fellow recipients of honorary degrees, thank you for the honor of spending this day with you. And congratulations to the Class of 2016! [*Applause*.] Four years ago, back when you were just freshmen, I understand many of you came by my house the night I was reelected. [*Laughter*.] So I decided to return the favor and come by yours.

To the parents, the grandparents, aunts, uncles, brothers, sisters, all the family and friends who stood by this class, cheered them on, helped them get here today — this is your day, as well. Let's give them a big round of applause, as well. [*Applause*.]

I know you're all excited today. You might be a little tired, as well. Some of you were up all night making sure your credits were in order. [*Laughter*.] Some of you stayed up too late, ended up at HoChi at 2 a.m. [*Laughter*.] Got some mambo sauce on your fingers. [*Laughter*.]

But you got here. And you've all worked hard to reach this day. You've shuttled between challenging classes and Greek life.

You've led clubs, played an instrument or a sport. You volunteered, you interned. You held down one, two, maybe three jobs. You've made lifelong friends and discovered exactly what you're made of. The "Howard Hustle" has strengthened your sense of purpose and ambition.

5 Which means you're part of a long line of Howard graduates. Some are on this stage today. Some are in the audience. That spirit of achievement and special responsibility has defined this campus ever since the Freedman's Bureau established Howard just four years after the Emancipation Proclamation; just two years after the Civil War came to an end. They created this university with a vision — a vision of uplift; a vision for an America where our fates would be determined not by our race, gender, religion, or creed, but where we would be free — in every sense — to pursue our individual and collective dreams.

It is that spirit that's made Howard a centerpiece of African-American intellectual life and a central part of our larger American story. This institution has been the home of many firsts: the first black Nobel Peace Prize winner. The first black Supreme Court justice. But its mission has been to ensure those firsts were not the last. Countless scholars, professionals, artists, and leaders from every field received their training here. The generations of men and women who walked through this yard helped reform our government, cure disease, grow a black middle class, advance civil rights, shape our culture. The seeds of change — for all Americans — were sown here. And that's what I want to talk about today.

As I was preparing these remarks, I realized that when I was first elected President, most of you — the Class of 2016 — were just starting high school. Today, you're graduating college. I used to joke about being old. Now I realize I'm old. [*Laughter.*] It's not a joke anymore. [*Laughter.*]

But seeing all of you here gives me some perspective. It makes me reflect on the changes that I've seen over my own lifetime. So let me begin with what may sound like a controversial statement — a hot take.

Given the current state of our political rhetoric and debate, let me say something that may be controversial, and that is this: America is a better place today than it was when I graduated from college. [*Applause.*] Let me repeat: America is by almost every measure better than it was when I graduated from college. It also happens to be better off than when I took office — [*laughter*] — but that's a longer story. [*Applause.*] That's a different discussion for another speech.

But think about it. I graduated in 1983. New York City, 10
America's largest city, where I lived at the time, had endured a decade marked by crime and deterioration and near bankruptcy. And many cities were in similar shape. Our nation had gone through years of economic stagnation, the stranglehold of foreign oil, a recession where unemployment nearly scraped 11 percent. The auto industry was getting its clock cleaned by foreign competition. And don't even get me started on the clothes and the hairstyles. I've tried to eliminate all photos of me from this period. I thought I looked good. [*Laughter.*] I was wrong.

Since that year — since the year I graduated — the poverty rate is down. Americans with college degrees, that rate is up. Crime rates are down. America's cities have undergone a renaissance. There are more women in the workforce. They're earning more money. We've cut teen pregnancy in half. We've slashed the African-American dropout rate by almost 60 percent, and all of you have a computer in your pocket that gives you the world at the touch of a button. In 1983, I was part of fewer than 10 percent of African-Americans who graduated with a bachelor's degree. Today, you're part of the more than 20 percent who will. And more than half of blacks say we're better off than our parents were at our age and that our kids will be better off, too.

So America is better. And the world is better, too. A wall

came down in Berlin. An Iron Curtain was torn asunder. The obscenity of apartheid came to an end. A young generation in Belfast and London have grown up without ever having to think about IRA bombings. In just the past 16 years, we've come from a world without marriage equality to one where it's a reality in nearly two dozen countries. Around the world, more people live in democracies. We've lifted more than 1 billion people from extreme poverty. We've cut the child mortality rate worldwide by more than half.

America is better. The world is better. And stay with me now — race relations are better since I graduated. That's the truth. No, my election did not create a post-racial society. I don't know who was propagating that notion. That was not mine. But the election itself — and the subsequent one — because the first one, folks might have made a mistake. [*Laughter.*] The second one, they knew what they were getting. The election itself was just one indicator of how attitudes had changed.

In my inaugural address, I remarked that just 60 years earlier, my father might not have been served in a D.C. restaurant — at least not certain of them. There were no black CEOs of Fortune 500 companies. Very few black judges. Shoot, as Larry Wilmore pointed out last week, a lot of folks didn't even think blacks had the tools to be a quarterback. Today, former Bull Michael Jordan isn't just the greatest basketball player of all time — he owns the team. [*Laughter.*] When I was graduating, the main black hero on TV was Mr. T. [*Laughter.*] Rap and hip hop were counterculture, underground. Now, Shonda Rhimes owns Thursday night, and Beyoncé runs the world. [*Laughter.*] We're no longer only entertainers, we're producers, studio executives. No longer small business owners — we're CEOs, we're mayors,
15 representatives, Presidents of the United States. [*Applause.*]

I am not saying gaps do not persist. Obviously, they do. Racism persists. Inequality persists. Don't worry — I'm going to get to that. But I wanted to start, Class of 2016, by opening your eyes to the moment that you are in. If you had to choose one moment in history in which you could be born, and you didn't know ahead of time who you were going to be — what nationality, what gender, what race, whether you'd be rich or poor, gay or straight, what faith you'd be born into — you wouldn't choose 100 years ago. You wouldn't choose the fifties, or the sixties, or the seventies. You'd choose right now. If you had to choose a time to be, in the words of Lorraine Hansberry, "young, gifted, and black" in America, you would choose right now. [*Applause.*]

I tell you all this because it's important to note progress. Because to deny how far we've come would do a disservice to the cause of justice, to the legions of foot soldiers; to not only the incredibly accomplished individuals who have already been mentioned, but your mothers and your dads, and grandparents and great-grandparents, who marched and toiled and suffered and overcame to make this day possible. I tell you this not to lull you into complacency, but to spur you into action — because there's still so much more work to do, so many more miles to travel. And America needs you to gladly, happily take up that work. You all have some work to do. So enjoy the party, because you're going to be busy. [*Laughter.*]

Yes, our economy has recovered from crisis stronger than almost any other in the world. But there are folks of all races who are still hurting — who still can't find work that pays enough to keep the lights on, who still can't save for retirement. We've still got a big racial gap in economic opportunity. The overall unemployment rate is five percent, but the black unemployment rate is almost nine. We've still got an achievement gap when black boys and girls graduate high school and college at lower rates than white boys and white girls. Harriet Tubman may be going on the twenty, but we've still got a gender gap when a black woman working full-time still earns just 66 percent of what a white man gets paid. [*Applause.*]

We've got a justice gap when too many black boys and girls

pass through a pipeline from underfunded schools to overcrowded jails. This is one area where things have gotten worse. When I was in college, about half a million people in America were behind bars. Today, there are about 2.2 million. Black men are about six times likelier to be in prison right now than white men.

Around the world, we've still got challenges to solve that threaten everybody in the 21st century — old scourges like disease and conflict, but also new challenges, from terrorism and climate change.

So make no mistake, Class of 2016 — you've got plenty of work to do. But as complicated and sometimes intractable as these challenges may seem, the truth is that your generation is better positioned than any before you to meet those challenges, to flip the script.

Now, how you do that, how you meet these challenges, how you bring about change will ultimately be up to you. My generation, like all generations, is too confined by our own experience, too invested in our own biases, too stuck in our ways to provide much of the new thinking that will be required. But us old-heads have learned a few things that might be useful in your journey. So with the rest of my time, I'd like to offer some suggestions for how young leaders like you can fulfill your destiny and shape our collective future — bend it in the direction of justice and equality and freedom.

First of all — and this should not be a problem for this group — be confident in your heritage. [*Applause.*] Be confident in your blackness. One of the great changes that's occurred in our country since I was your age is the realization there's no one way to be black. Take it from somebody who's seen both sides of debate about whether I'm black enough. [*Laughter.*] In the past couple months, I've had lunch with the Queen of England and hosted Kendrick Lamar in the Oval Office. There's no straitjacket, there's no constraints, there's no litmus test for authenticity.

Look at Howard. One thing most folks don't know about Howard is how diverse it is. When you arrived here, some of you were like, oh, they've got black people in Iowa? [*Laughter.*] But it's true — this class comes from big cities and rural communities, and some of you crossed oceans to study here. You shatter stereotypes. Some of you come from a long line of Bison. Some of you are the first in your family to graduate from college. [*Applause.*] You all talk different, you all dress different. You're Lakers fans, Celtics fans, maybe even some hockey fans. [*Laughter.*]

And because of those who've come before you, you have models to follow. You can work for a company, or start your own. You can go into politics, or run an organization that holds politicians accountable. You can write a book that wins the National Book Award, or you can write the new run of "Black Panther." Or, like one of your alumni, Ta-Nehisi Coates, you can go ahead and just do both. You can create your own style, set your own standard of beauty, embrace your own sexuality. Think about an icon we just lost — Prince. He blew up categories. People didn't know what Prince was doing. [*Laughter.*] And folks loved him for it.

You need to have the same confidence. Or as my daughters 25
tell me all the time, "You be you, Daddy." [*Laughter.*] Sometimes Sasha puts a variation on it — "You do you, Daddy." [*Laughter.*] And because you're a black person doing whatever it is that you're doing, that makes it a black thing. Feel confident.

Second, even as we each embrace our own beautiful, unique, and valid versions of our blackness, remember the tie that does bind us as African-Americans — and that is our particular awareness of injustice and unfairness and struggle. That means we cannot sleepwalk through life. We cannot be ignorant of history. [*Applause.*] We can't meet the world with a sense of entitlement. We can't walk by a homeless man without asking why a society as wealthy as ours allows that state of affairs to occur. We can't just lock up a low-level dealer without asking why this boy, barely out of childhood, felt he had no other options. We have cousins and uncles and brothers and sisters who we remember were just as smart and just as talented as we were, but somehow got ground down by structures that are unfair and unjust.

And that means we have to not only question the world as it is, and stand up for those African-Americans who haven't been so lucky — because, yes, you've worked hard, but you've also been lucky. That's a pet peeve of mine: people who have been successful and don't realize they've been lucky. That God may have blessed them; it wasn't nothing you did. So don't have an attitude. But we must expand our moral imaginations to understand and empathize with all people who are struggling, not just black folks who are struggling — the refugee, the immigrant, the rural poor, the transgender person, and yes, the middle-aged white guy who you may think has all the advantages, but over the last several decades has seen his world upended by economic and cultural and technological change, and feels powerless to stop it. You got to get in his head, too.

Number three: you have to go through life with more than just passion for change; you need a strategy. I'll repeat that. I want you to have passion, but you have to have a strategy. Not just awareness, but action. Not just hashtags, but votes.

You see, change requires more than righteous anger. It requires a program, and it requires organizing. At the 1964 Democratic Convention, Fannie Lou Hamer — all five-feet-four-inches tall — gave a fiery speech on the national stage. But then she went back home to Mississippi and organized cotton pickers. And she didn't have the tools and technology where you can whip up a movement in minutes. She had to go door to door. And I'm so proud of the new guard of black civil rights leaders who understand this. It's thanks in large part to the activism of young people like many of you, from Black

Twitter to Black Lives Matter, that America's eyes have been opened — white, black, Democrat, Republican — to the real problems, for example, in our criminal justice system.

But to bring about structural change, lasting change, aware- 30
ness is not enough. It requires changes in law, changes in custom. If you care about mass incarceration, let me ask you: how are you pressuring members of Congress to pass the criminal justice reform bill now pending before them? [*Applause.*] If you care about better policing, do you know who your district attorney is? Do you know who your state's attorney general is? Do you know the difference? Do you know who appoints the police chief and who writes the police training manual? Find out who they are, what their responsibilities are. Mobilize the community, present them with a plan, work with them to bring about change, hold them accountable if they do not deliver. Passion is vital, but you've got to have a strategy.

And your plan better include voting — not just some of the time, but all the time. [*Applause.*] It is absolutely true that 50 years after the Voting Rights Act, there are still too many barriers in this country to vote. There are too many people trying to erect new barriers to voting. This is the only advanced democracy on Earth that goes out of its way to make it difficult for people to vote. And there's a reason for that. There's a legacy to that.

But let me say this: even if we dismantled every barrier to voting, that alone would not change the fact that America has some of the lowest voting rates in the free world. In 2014, only 36 percent of Americans turned out to vote in the midterms — the second-lowest participation rate on record. Youth turnout — that would be you — was less than 20 percent. Less than 20 percent. Four out of five did not vote. In 2012, nearly two in three African-Americans turned out. And then, in 2014, only two in five turned out. You don't think that made a difference in terms of the Congress I've got to deal with? And then people are wondering, well, how come Obama hasn't gotten this done?

How come he didn't get that done? You don't think that made a difference? What would have happened if you had turned out at 50, 60, 70 percent, all across this country? People try to make this political thing really complicated. Like, what kind of reforms do we need? And how do we need to do that? You know what, just vote. It's math. If you have more votes than the other guy, you get to do what you want. [*Laughter.*] It's not that complicated.

And you don't have excuses. You don't have to guess the number of jellybeans in a jar or bubbles on a bar of soap to register to vote. You don't have to risk your life to cast a ballot. Other people already did that for you. [*Applause.*] Your grandparents, your great-grandparents might be here today if they were working on it. What's your excuse? When we don't vote, we give away our power, disenfranchise ourselves — right when we need to use the power that we have; right when we need your power to stop others from taking away the vote and rights of those more vulnerable than you are — the elderly and the poor, the formerly incarcerated trying to earn their second chance.

So you got to vote all the time, not just when it's cool, not just when it's time to elect a President, not just when you're inspired. It's your duty. When it's time to elect a member of Congress or a city councilman, or a school board member, or a sheriff. That's how we change our politics — by electing people at every level who are representative of and accountable to us. It is not that complicated. Don't make it complicated.

35 And finally, change requires more than just speaking out — it requires listening, as well. In particular, it requires listening to those with whom you disagree, and being prepared to compromise. When I was a state senator, I helped pass Illinois's first racial profiling law, and one of the first laws in the nation requiring the videotaping of confessions in capital cases. And we were successful because, early on, I engaged law enforcement. I didn't say to them, oh, you guys are so racist, you need

to do something. I understood, as many of you do, that the overwhelming majority of police officers are good, and honest, and courageous, and fair, and love the communities they serve.

And we knew there were some bad apples, and that even the good cops with the best of intentions — including, by the way, African-American police officers — might have unconscious biases, as we all do. So we engaged and we listened, and we kept working until we built consensus. And because we took the time to listen, we crafted legislation that was good for the police — because it improved the trust and cooperation of the community — and it was good for the communities, who were less likely to be treated unfairly. And I can say this unequivocally: without at least the acceptance of the police organizations in Illinois, I could never have gotten those bills passed. Very simple. They would have blocked them.

The point is, you need allies in a democracy. That's just the way it is. It can be frustrating and it can be slow. But history teaches us that the alternative to democracy is always worse. That's not just true in this country. It's not a black or white thing. Go to any country where the give and take of democracy has been repealed by one-party rule, and I will show you a country that does not work.

And democracy requires compromise, even when you are 100 percent right. This is hard to explain sometimes. You can be completely right, and you still are going to have to engage folks who disagree with you. If you think that the only way forward is to be as uncompromising as possible, you will feel good about yourself, you will enjoy a certain moral purity, but you're not going to get what you want. And if you don't get what you want long enough, you will eventually think the whole system is rigged. And that will lead to more cynicism, and less participation, and a downward spiral of more injustice and more anger and more despair. And that's never been the source of our progress. That's how we cheat ourselves of progress.

We remember Dr. King's soaring oratory, the power of his letter from a Birmingham jail, the marches he led. But he also sat down with President Johnson in the Oval Office to try and get a Civil Rights Act and a Voting Rights Act passed. And those two seminal bills were not perfect — just like the Emancipation Proclamation was a war document as much as it was some clarion call for freedom. Those mileposts of our progress were not perfect. They did not make up for centuries of slavery or Jim Crow or eliminate racism or provide for 40 acres and a mule. But they made things better. And you know what, I will take better every time. I always tell my staff — better is good, because you consolidate your gains and then you move on to the next fight from a stronger position.

40 Brittany Packnett, a member of the Black Lives Matter movement and Campaign Zero, one of the Ferguson protest organizers, she joined our Task Force on 21st Century Policing. Some of her fellow activists questioned whether she should participate. She rolled up her sleeves and sat at the same table with big city police chiefs and prosecutors. And because she did, she ended up shaping many of the recommendations of that task force. And those recommendations are now being adopted across the country — changes that many of the protesters called for. If young activists like Brittany had refused to participate out of some sense of ideological purity, then those great ideas would have just remained ideas. But she did participate. And that's how change happens.

America is big and it is boisterous and it is more diverse than ever. The president told me that we've got a significant Nepalese contingent here at Howard. I would not have guessed that. Right on. But it just tells you how interconnected we're becoming. And with so many folks from so many places, converging, we are not always going to agree with each other.

Another Howard alum, Zora Neale Hurston, once said — this is a good quote here: "Nothing that God ever made is the same thing to more than one person." Think about that. That's why our democracy gives us a process designed for us to settle our disputes with argument and ideas and votes instead of violence and simple majority rule.

So don't try to shut folks out, don't try to shut them down, no matter how much you might disagree with them. There's been a trend around the country of trying to get colleges to disinvite speakers with a different point of view, or disrupt a politician's rally. Don't do that — no matter how ridiculous or offensive you might find the things that come out of their mouths. Because as my grandmother used to tell me, every time a fool speaks, they are just advertising their own ignorance. Let them talk. Let them talk. If you don't, you just make them a victim, and then they can avoid accountability.

That doesn't mean you shouldn't challenge them. Have the confidence to challenge them, the confidence in the rightness of your position. There will be times when you shouldn't compromise your core values, your integrity, and you will have the responsibility to speak up in the face of injustice. But listen. Engage. If the other side has a point, learn from them. If they're wrong, rebut them. Teach them. Beat them on the battlefield of ideas. And you might as well start practicing now, because one thing I can guarantee you — you will have to deal with ignorance, hatred, racism, foolishness, trifling folks. [*Laughter.*] I promise you, you will have to deal with all that at every stage of your life. That may not seem fair, but life has never been completely fair. Nobody promised you a crystal stair. And if you want to make life fair, then you've got to start with the world as it is.

So that's my advice. That's how you change things. Change 45
isn't something that happens every four years or eight years; change is not placing your faith in any particular politician and then just putting your feet up and saying, okay, go. Change is the effort of committed citizens who hitch their wagons

to something bigger than themselves and fight for it every single day.

That's what Thurgood Marshall understood — a man who graduated from Howard Law, went home to Baltimore, and started his own law practice. He and his mentor, Charles Hamilton Houston, rolled up their sleeves and they set out to overturn segregation. They worked through the NAACP. Filed dozens of lawsuits, fought dozens of cases. And after nearly twenty years of effort — twenty years — Thurgood Marshall ultimately succeeded in bringing his righteous cause before the Supreme Court, and securing the ruling in Brown v. Board of Education that separate could never be equal. [*Applause.*] Twenty years.

Marshall, Houston — they knew it would not be easy. They knew it would not be quick. They knew all sorts of obstacles would stand in their way. They knew that even if they won, that would just be the beginning of a longer march to equality. But they had discipline. They had persistence. They had faith — and a sense of humor. And they made life better for all Americans.

And I know you graduates share those qualities. I know it because I've learned about some of the young people graduating here today. There's a young woman named Ciearra Jefferson, who's graduating with you. And I'm just going to use her as an example. I hope you don't mind, Ciearra. Ciearra grew up in Detroit and was raised by a poor single mom who worked seven days a week in an auto plant. And for a time, her family found themselves without a place to call home. They bounced around between friends and family who might take them in. By her senior year, Ciearra was up at 5:00 am every day, juggling homework, extracurricular activities, volunteering, all while taking care of her little sister. But she knew that education was her ticket to a better life. So she never gave up. Pushed herself to excel. This daughter of a single mom who works on the assembly line turned down a full scholarship to Harvard to come to Howard. [*Applause.*]

And today, like many of you, Ciearra is the first in her family to graduate from college. And then, she says, she's going to go back to her hometown, just like Thurgood Marshall did, to make sure all the working folks she grew up with have access to the health care they need and deserve. As she puts it, she's going to be a "change agent." She's going to reach back and help folks like her succeed.

And people like Ciearra are why I remain optimistic about 50
America. [*Applause.*] Young people like you are why I never give in to despair.

James Baldwin once wrote, "Not everything that is faced can be changed, but nothing can be changed until it is faced."

Graduates, each of us is only here because someone else faced down challenges for us. We are only who we are because someone else struggled and sacrificed for us. That's not just Thurgood Marshall's story, or Ciearra's story, or my story, or your story — that is the story of America. A story whispered by slaves in the cotton fields, the song of marchers in Selma, the dream of a King in the shadow of Lincoln. The prayer of immigrants who set out for a new world. The roar of women demanding the vote. The rallying cry of workers who built America. And the GIs who bled overseas for our freedom.

Now it's your turn. And the good news is, you're ready. And when your journey seems too hard, and when you run into a chorus of cynics who tell you that you're being foolish to keep believing or that you can't do something, or that you should just give up, or you should just settle — you might say to yourself a little phrase that I've found handy these last eight years: yes, we can.

Congratulations, Class of 2016! [*Applause.*] Good luck! God bless you. God bless the United States of America. I'm proud of you.

The American Crisis
by Thomas Paine

Thomas Paine (1737–1809) was an influential writer and propagandist who assisted in garnering public support for the cause of American independence from England. In 1776, Paine published the pamphlet Common Sense, *which argued that American independence from England was inevitable. In addition to* Common Sense, *Paine assisted in sustaining the morale of the American soldiers and people during the war with a series of sixteen articles written under the title* The American Crisis *and published during the years 1776–1783. The first article, printed here, is arguably the most well known of these articles. It was published on December 19, 1776, during a time when the morale of the Continental Army was incredibly low due to many defeats and no major victories. In hopes that the article would have a similar rallying effect as* Common Sense, *General George Washington ordered it to be read aloud to the soldiers at Valley Forge.*

These are the times that try men's souls. The summer soldier and the sunshine patriot will, in this crisis, shrink from the service of their country; but he that stands it *now*, deserves the love and thanks of man and woman. Tyranny, like hell, is not easily conquered; yet we have this consolation with us, that the harder the conflict, the more glorious the triumph. What we obtain too cheap, we esteem too lightly: it is dearness only that gives every thing its value. Heaven knows how to put a proper price upon its goods; and it would be strange indeed if so celestial an article as FREEDOM should not be highly rated. Britain, with an army to enforce her tyranny, has declared that she has a right (*not only to* TAX) but "to BIND *us in* ALL CASES WHATSOEVER," and if being *bound in that manner*, is not slavery, then is there not such a thing as slavery upon earth.

Even the expression is impious; for so unlimited a power can belong only to God.

Whether the independence of the continent was declared too soon, or delayed too long, I will not now enter into as an argument; my own[1] simple opinion is, that had it been eight months earlier, it would have been much better. We did not make a proper use of last winter, neither could we, while we were in a dependent state. However, the fault, if it were one, was all our own; we have none to blame but ourselves. But no great deal is lost yet. All that Howe has been doing for this month past, is rather a ravage than a conquest, which the spirit of the Jerseys, a year ago, would have quickly repulsed, and which time and a little resolution will soon recover.

I have as little superstition in me as any man living, but my secret opinion has ever been, and still is, that God Almighty will not give up a people to military destruction, or leave them unsupportedly to perish, who have so earnestly and so repeatedly sought to avoid the calamities of war, by every decent method which wisdom could invent.

Neither have I so much of the infidel in me, as to suppose that He has relinquished the government of the world, and given us up to the care of devils; and as I do not, I cannot see on what grounds the king of Britain can look up to heaven for help against us: a common murderer, a highwayman, or a house-breaker, has as good a pretense as he.

'Tis surprising to see how rapidly a panic will sometimes 5
run through a country. All nations and ages have been subject to them: Britain has trembled like an ague at the report of a French fleet of flat bottomed boats; and in the fourteenth [fifteenth] century the whole English army, after ravaging the kingdom of

[1] *The present winter is worth an age, if rightly employed; but, if lost or neglected, the whole continent will partake of the evil; and there is no punishment that man does not deserve, be he who, or what, or where he will, that may be the means of sacrificing a season so precious and useful.*

France, was driven back like men petrified with fear; and this brave exploit was performed by a few broken forces collected and headed by a woman, Joan of Arc. Would that heaven might inspire some Jersey maid to spirit up her countrymen, and save her fair fellow sufferers from ravage and ravishment! Yet panics, in some cases, have their uses; they produce as much good as hurt. Their duration is always short; the mind soon grows through them, and acquires a firmer habit than before. But their peculiar advantage is, that they are the touchstones of sincerity and hypocrisy, and bring things and men to light, which might otherwise have lain forever undiscovered. In fact, they have the same effect on secret traitors, which an imaginary apparition would have upon a private murderer. They sift out the hidden thoughts of man, and hold them up in public to the world. Many a disguised Tory has lately shown his head, that shall penitentially solemnize with curses the day on which Howe arrived upon the Delaware.

As I was with the troops at Fort Lee, and marched with them to the edge of Pennsylvania, I am well acquainted with many circumstances, which those who live at a distance know but little or nothing of. Our situation there was exceedingly cramped, the place being a narrow neck of land between the North River and the Hackensack. Our force was inconsiderable, being not one fourth so great as Howe could bring against us. We had no army at hand to have relieved the garrison, had we shut ourselves up and stood on our defense. Our ammunition, light artillery, and the best part of our stores, had been removed, on the apprehension that Howe would endeavor to penetrate the Jerseys, in which case fort Lee could be of no use to us; for it must occur to every thinking man, whether in the army or not, that these kind of field forts are only for temporary purposes, and last in use no longer than the enemy directs his force against the particular object, which such forts are raised to defend. Such was our situation and condition at fort Lee on the morning of the 20th of November, when an officer arrived with information that the enemy with 200 boats had landed about seven miles above: Major General [Nathaniel] Green, who commanded the garrison, immediately ordered them under arms, and sent express to General Washington at the town of Hackensack, distant by the way of the ferry = six miles. Our first object was to secure the bridge over the Hackensack, which laid up the river between the enemy and us, about six miles from us, and three from them. General Washington arrived in about three quarters of an hour, and marched at the head of the troops towards the bridge, which place I expected we should have a brush for; however, they did not choose to dispute it with us, and the greatest part of our troops went over the bridge, the rest over the ferry, except some which passed at a mill on a small creek, between the bridge and the ferry, and made their way through some marshy grounds up to the town of Hackensack, and there passed the river. We brought off as much baggage as the wagons could contain, the rest was lost. The simple object was to bring off the garrison, and march them on till they could be strengthened by the Jersey or Pennsylvania militia, so as to be enabled to make a stand. We staid four days at Newark, collected our out-posts with some of the Jersey militia, and marched out twice to meet the enemy, on being informed that they were advancing, though our numbers were greatly inferior to theirs. Howe, in my little opinion, committed a great error in generalship in not throwing a body of forces off from Staten Island through Amboy, by which means he might have seized all our stores at Brunswick, and intercepted our march into Pennsylvania; but if we believe the power of hell to be limited, we must likewise believe that their agents are under some providential control.

I shall not now attempt to give all the particulars of our retreat to the Delaware; suffice it for the present to say, that both officers and men, though greatly harassed and fatigued, frequently without rest, covering, or provision, the inevitable consequences of a long retreat, bore it with a manly and martial spirit. All their wishes centered in one, which was, that the country would turn out and help them to drive the enemy back. Voltaire has remarked that king William never appeared to full advantage but in difficulties and in action; the same remark may be made on General Washington, for the character fits him. There is a natural firmness in some minds which cannot be unlocked by trifles, but which, when unlocked, discovers a cabinet of fortitude; and I reckon it among those kind of public blessings, which we do not immediately see, that God hath blessed him with uninterrupted health, and given him a mind that can even flourish upon care.

I shall conclude this paper with some miscellaneous remarks on the state of our affairs; and shall begin with asking the following question, Why is it that the enemy have left the New-England provinces, and made these middle ones the seat of war? The answer is easy: New-England is not infested with Tories, and we are. I have been tender in raising the cry against these men, and used numberless arguments to show them their danger, but it will not do to sacrifice a world either to their folly or their baseness. The period is now arrived, in which either they or we must change our sentiments, or one or both must fall. And what is a Tory? Good God! what is he? I should not be afraid to go with a hundred Whigs against a thousand Tories, were they to attempt to get into arms. Every Tory is a coward; for servile, slavish, self-interested fear is the foundation of Toryism; and a man under such influence, though he may be cruel, never can be brave.

But, before the line of irrecoverable separation be drawn between us, let us reason the matter together: Your conduct is an invitation to the enemy, yet not one in a thousand of you has heart enough to join him. Howe is as much deceived by you as the American cause is injured by you. He expects you will all take up arms, and flock to his standard, with muskets on your shoulders. Your opinions are of no use to him, unless you support him personally, for 'tis soldiers, and not Tories, that he wants.

I once felt all that kind of anger, which a man ought to feel, against the mean principles that are held by the Tories: a noted one, who kept a tavern at Amboy, was standing at his door, with as pretty a child in his hand, about eight or nine years old, as I ever saw, and after speaking his mind as freely as he thought was prudent, finished with this unfatherly expression, "*Well! give me peace in my day.*" Not a man lives on the continent but fully believes that a separation must some time or other finally take place, and a generous parent should have said, "*If there must be trouble, let it be in my day, that my child may have peace*"; and this single reflection, well applied, is sufficient to awaken every man to duty. Not a place upon earth might be so happy as America. Her situation is remote from all the wrangling world, and she has nothing to do but to trade with them. A man can distinguish himself between temper and principle, and I am as confident, as I am that God governs the world, that America will never be happy till she gets clear of foreign dominion. Wars, without ceasing, will break out till that period arrives, and the continent must in the end be conqueror; for though the flame of liberty may sometimes cease to shine, the coal can never expire.

America did not, nor does not want force; but she wanted a proper application of that force. Wisdom is not the purchase of a day, and it is no wonder that we should err at the first setting off. From an excess of tenderness, we were unwilling to raise an army, and trusted our cause to the temporary defence of a well-meaning militia. A summer's experience has now taught us better; yet with those troops, while they were collected, we were able to set bounds to the progress of the enemy, and, thank God! they are again assembling. I always considered militia as the best troops in the world for a sudden exertion, but they will not do for a long campaign. Howe, it is probable, will make an attempt on this city; should he fail on this side the Delaware, he is ruined: if he succeeds, our cause is not ruined. He stakes all on his side against a part on ours; admitting he succeeds, the consequence will be, that armies from both ends of the continent will march to assist their suffering friends in the middle states; for he cannot go everywhere, it is impossible. I consider Howe as the greatest enemy the Tories have; he is bringing a war into their country, which, had it not been for him and partly for themselves, they had been clear of. Should he now be expelled, I wish with all the devotion of a Christian, that the names of Whig and Tory may never more be mentioned; but should the Tories give him encouragement to come, or assistance if he come, I as sincerely wish that our next year's arms may expel them from the continent, and the congress appropriate their possessions to the relief of those who have suffered in well-doing. A single successful battle next year will settle the whole. America could carry on a two years war by the confiscation of the property of disaffected persons, and be made happy by their expulsion. Say not that this is revenge, call it rather the soft resentment of a suffering people, who, having no object in view but the *good of all*, have staked their *own all* upon a seemingly doubtful event. Yet it is folly to argue against determined hardness; eloquence may strike the ear, and the language of sorrow draw forth the tear of compassion, but nothing can reach the heart that is steeled with prejudice.

Quitting this class of men, I turn with the warm ardor of a friend to those who have nobly stood, and are yet determined to stand the matter out: I call not upon a few, but upon all: not on *this* state or *that* state, but on *every* state: up and help us; lay your shoulders to the wheel; better have too much force than too little, when so great an object is at stake. Let it be told to the future world, that in the depth of winter, when nothing but hope and virtue could survive, that the city and the country, alarmed at one common danger, came forth to meet and to repulse it. Say not that thousands are gone, turn out your tens of thousands; throw not the burden of the day upon Providence, but "*show your faith by your works,*" that God may bless you. It matters not where you live, or what rank of life you hold, the evil or the blessing will reach you all. The far and the near, the home counties and the back, the rich and the poor, will suffer or rejoice alike. The heart that feels not now, is dead: the blood of his children will curse his cowardice, who shrinks back at a time when a little might have saved the whole, and made *them* happy. I love the man that can smile in trouble, that can gather strength from distress, and grow brave by reflection. 'Tis the business of little minds to shrink; but he whose heart is firm, and whose conscience approves his conduct, will pursue his principles unto death. My own line of reasoning is to myself as straight and clear as a ray of light. Not all the treasures of the world, so far as I believe, could have induced me to support an offensive war, for I think it murder; but if a thief breaks into my house, burns and destroys my property, and kills or threatens to kill me, or those that are in it, and to "*bind me in all cases whatsoever*" to his absolute will, am I to suffer it? What signifies it to me, whether he who does it is a king or a common man; my countryman or not my countryman; whether it be done by an individual villain, or an army of them? If we reason to the root of things we shall find no difference; neither can any just cause be assigned why we should punish in the one case and pardon in the other. Let them call me rebel, and welcome, I feel no concern from it; but I should suffer the misery of devils, were I to make a whore of my soul by swearing allegiance to one whose character is that of a sottish, stupid, stubborn, worthless, brutish man. I conceive likewise a horrid idea in receiving mercy from a being, who at the last day shall be shrieking to the rocks and mountains to cover him, and fleeing with terror from the orphan, the widow, and the slain of America.

There are cases which cannot be overdone by language, and this is one. There are persons, too, who see not the full extent of the evil which threatens them; they solace themselves with hopes that the enemy, if he succeed, will be merciful. It is the madness of folly, to expect mercy from those who have refused to do justice; and even mercy, where conquest is the object, is only a trick of war; the cunning of the fox is as murderous as the violence of the wolf, and we ought to guard equally against both. Howe's first object is, partly by threats and partly by promises, to terrify or seduce the people to deliver up their arms and receive mercy. The ministry recommended the same plan to Gage, and this is what the Tories call making their peace, "*a peace which passeth all understanding" indeed!* A peace which would be the immediate forerunner of a worse ruin than any we have yet thought of. Ye men of Pennsylvania, do reason upon these things! Were the back counties to give up their arms, they would fall an easy prey to the Indians, who are all armed: this perhaps is what some Tories would not be sorry for. Were the home counties to deliver up their arms, they would be exposed to the resentment of the back counties, who would then have it in their power to chastise their defection at pleasure. And were any one state to give up its arms, *that* state must be garrisoned by all Howe's army of Britons and Hessians to preserve it from the anger of the rest. Mutual fear is the principal link in the chain of mutual love, and woe be to that state that breaks the compact. Howe is mercifully inviting you to barbarous destruction, and men must be either rogues or fools that will not see it. I dwell not upon the vapors of imagination: I bring reason to your ears, and, in language as plain as A, B, C, hold up truth to your eyes.

I thank God, that I fear not. I see no real cause for fear. I know our situation well, and can see the way out of it. While our army was collected, Howe dared not risk a battle; and it is no credit to him that he decamped from the White Plains, and waited a mean opportunity to ravage the defenseless Jerseys; but it is great credit to us, that, with a handful of men, we sustained an orderly retreat for near an hundred miles, brought off our ammunition, all our field pieces, the greatest part of our stores, and had four rivers to pass. None can say that our retreat was precipitate, for we were near three weeks in performing it, that the country might have time to come in. Twice we marched back to meet the enemy, and remained out till dark. The sign of fear was not seen in our camp, and had not some of the cowardly and disaffected inhabitants spread false alarms through the country, the Jerseys had never been ravaged. Once more we are again collected and collecting; our new army at both ends of the continent is recruiting fast, and we shall be able to open the next campaign with sixty thousand men, well armed and clothed. This is our situation, and who will may know it. By perseverance and fortitude we have the prospect of a glorious issue; by cowardice and submission, the sad choice of a variety of evils — a ravaged country — a depopulated city — habitations without safety, and slavery without hope — our homes turned into barracks and bawdyhouses for Hessians, and a future race to provide for, whose fathers we shall doubt of. Look on this picture and weep over it! and if there yet remains one thoughtless wretch who believes it not, let him suffer it unlamented.

Does America Still Exist?

by Richard Rodriguez

Richard Rodriguez (b.1944), the child of Spanish-speaking Mexican immigrants, grew up in California. Entering school with little knowledge of English, he studied at Stanford University, Columbia University, and earned his Ph.D. in literature from the University of California at Berkeley, where he now teaches. In addition to writing essays, he has published the autobiographical Hunger of Memory: The Education of Richard Rodriguez *(1982), which received critical acclaim, and* Days of Obligation: An Argument with My Mexican Father *(1992). The following essay first appeared in* Harper's *(March 1984) as part of a group of essays written in response to the question "Does America Still Exist?"*

For the children of immigrant parents the knowledge comes easier. America exists everywhere in the city — on billboards, frankly in the smell of French fries and popcorn. It exists in the pace: traffic lights, the assertions of neon, the mysterious bong-bong-bong through the atriums of department stores. America exists as the voice of the crowd, a menacing sound — the high nasal accent of American English.

When I was a boy in Sacramento (California, the fifties), people would ask me, "Where you from?" I was born in this country, but I knew the question meant to decipher my darkness, my looks.

My mother once instructed me to say, "I am an American of Mexican descent." By the time I was nine or ten, I wanted to say, but dared not reply, "I am an American."

Immigrants come to America and, against hostility or mere loneliness, they recreate a homeland in the parlor, tacking up postcards or calendars of some impossible blue — lake or sea or sky. Children of immigrant parents are supposed to perch on a hyphen between two countries. Relatives assume the achievement as much as anyone. Relatives are, in any case, surprised when the child begins losing old ways. One day at the family picnic the boy wanders away from their spiced food and faceless stories to watch other boys play baseball in the distance.

5 There is sorrow in the American memory, guilty sorrow for having left something behind — Portugal, China, Norway. The American story is the story of immigrant children and of their children — children no longer able to speak to grandparents. The memory of exile becomes inarticulate as it passes from generation to generation, along with wedding rings and pocket watches — like some mute stone in a wad of old lace. Europe. Asia. Eden.

But, it needs to be said, if this is a country where one stops being Vietnamese or Italian, this is a country where one begins to be an American. America exists as a culture and a grin, a faith and a shrug. It is clasped in a handshake, called by a first name.

As much as the country is joined in a common culture, however, Americans are reluctant to celebrate the process of assimilation. We pledge allegiance to diversity. America was born Protestant and bred Puritan, and the notion of community we share is derived from a seventeenth-century faith. Presidents and the pages of ninth-grade civics readers yet proclaim the orthodoxy: We are gathered together — but as individuals, with separate pasts, distinct destinies. Our society is as paradoxical as a Puritan congregation: We stand together, alone.

Americans have traditionally defined themselves by what they refused to include. As often, however, Americans have struggled, turned in good conscience at last to assert the great

Protestant virtue of tolerance. Despite outbreaks of nativist frenzy, America has remained an immigrant county, open and true to itself.

Against pious emblems of rural America — soda fountain, Elks hall, Protestant church, and now shopping mall — stands the cold-hearted city, crowded with races and ambition, curious laughter, much that is odd. Nevertheless, it is the city that has most truly represented America. In the city, however, the millions of singular lives have had no richer notion of wholeness to describe them than the idea of pluralism.

"Where you from?" the American asks the immigrant child. "Mexico," the boy learns to say.

Mexico, the country to my blood ancestors, offers formal contrast to the American achievement. If the United States was formed by Protestant individualism, Mexico was shaped by a medieval Catholic dream of one world. The Spanish journeyed to Mexico to plunder, and they may have gone, in God's name, with an arrogance peculiar to those who intend to convert. But through the conversion, the Indian converted the Spaniard. A new race was born, the mestizo, wedding European to Indian. José Vasconcelos, the Mexican philosopher, has celebrated this New World creation, proclaiming it the "cosmic race."

Centuries later, in a San Francisco restaurant, a Mexican-American lawyer of my acquaintance says, in English, over *salade niçoise*, that he does not intend to assimilate into gringo society. His claim is echoed by a chorus of others (Italian-Americans, Greeks, Asians) in this era of ethnic pride. The melting pot has been retired, clanking into the museum of quaint disgrace, alongside Aunt Jemima and the Katzenjammer Kids. But resistance to assimilation is characteristically American. It only makes clear how inevitable the process of assimilation actually is.

For generations, this has been the pattern. Immigrant parents have sent their children to school (simply, they thought) to acquire the "skills" to survive in the city. The child returned home with a voice his parents barely recognized or understood, couldn't trust, and didn't like.

In Eastern cities — Philadelphia, New York, Boston, Baltimore — class after class gathered immigrant children to women (usually women) who stood in front of rooms full of children, changing children. So also for me in the 1950s. Irish-Catholic nuns. California. The old story. The hyphen tipped to the right, away from Mexico and toward a confusing but true American identity.

I speak now in the chromium American accent of my gram- 15
mar school classmates — Billy Reckers, Mike Bradley, Carol Schmidt, Kathy O'Grady. . . . I believe I became like my classmates, became German, Polish, and (like my teachers) Irish. And because assimilation is always reciprocal, my classmates got something of me. (I mean sad eyes; belief in the Indian Virgin; a taste for sugar skulls on the Feast of the Dead.) In the blending, we became what our parents could never have been, and we carried America one revolution further.

"Does America still exist?" Americans have been asking the question for so long that to ask it again only proves our continuous link. But perhaps the question deserves to be asked with urgency now. Since the black civil rights movement of the 1960s, our tenuous notion of a shared public life has deteriorated notably.

The struggle of black men and women did not eradicate racism, but it became the great moment in the life of America's conscience. Water hoses, bulldogs, blood — the images, rendered black, white, rectangular, passed into living rooms.

It is hard to look at a photograph of a crowd taken, say, in 1890 or in 1930 and not notice the absence of blacks. (It becomes an impertinence to wonder if America *still* exists.)

In the sixties, other groups of Americans learned to champion their rights by analogy to the black civil rights movement.

But the heroic vision faded. Dr. Martin Luther King, Jr., had spoken with Pauline eloquence of a nation that would unite Christian and Jew, old and young, rich and poor. Within a decade, the struggles of the 1960s were reduced to a bureaucratic competition for little more than pieces of a representational pie. The quest for a portion of power became an end in itself. The metaphor for the American city of the 1970s was a committee: one black, one woman, one person under thirty…

If the small town had sinned against America by too neatly defining who could be an American, the city's sin was a romantic secession. One noticed the romanticism in the antiwar movement — certain demonstrators who demonstrated a lack of tact or desire to persuade and seemed content to play secular protestants. One noticed the romanticism in the competition among members of "minority groups" to claim the status of Primary Victim. To Americans unconfident of their common identity, minority standing became a way of asserting individuality. Middle-class Americans — men and women clearly not the primary victims of social oppression — brandished their suffering with exuberance.

The dream of a single society probably died with *The Ed Sullivan Show*. The reality of America persists. Teenagers pass through big-city high schools banded in racial groups, their collars turned up to a uniform shrug. But then they graduate to jobs at the phone company or in banks, where they end up working alongside people unlike themselves. Typists and tellers walk out together at lunchtime.

It is easier for us as Americans to believe the obvious fact of our separateness — easier to imagine the black and white Americans prophesied by the Kerner report (broken class, street fires) — than to recognize the reality of a city street at lunchtime. Americans are wedded by proximity to a common culture. The panhandler at one corner is related to the pamphleteer at the next who is related to the banker who is kin to the Chinese old man wearing an MIT sweatshirt. In any true national history, Thomas Jefferson begets Martin Luther King, Jr., who begets the Gray Panthers. It is because we lack a vision of ourselves entire — the city street is crowded and we are each preoccupied with finding our own way home — that we lack an appropriate hymn.

Under my window now passes a little white girl softly rehearsing to herself a Motown obbligato.

Four Freedoms

by Franklin Delano Roosevelt

Franklin Delano Roosevelt (1882–1945) was the thirty-second President of the United States from 1933–1945, elected to a total of four terms. He delivered the following speech on January 6, 1941, as part of his State of the Union address. At the time of this speech's delivery, Germany and its allies had already invaded and conquered Poland, Finland, Norway, Denmark, Lithuania, Estonia, Latvia, and France. Germany had also begun a bombing campaign on London that would last for 57 straight nights.

Mr. President, Mr. Speaker, Members of the Seventy-seventh Congress: I address you, the Members of the Seventy-seventh Congress, at a moment unprecedented in the history of the Union. I use the word "unprecedented," because at no previous time has American security been as seriously threatened from without as it is today.

Since the permanent formation of our Government under the Constitution, in 1789, most of the periods of crisis in our history have related to our domestic affairs. Fortunately, only one of these — the four-year War Between the States — ever threatened our national unity. Today, thank God, one hundred and thirty million Americans, in forty-eight States, have forgotten points of the compass in our national unity.

It is true that prior to 1914 the United States often had been disturbed by events in other Continents. We had even engaged in two wars with European nations and in a number of undeclared wars in the West Indies, in the Mediterranean and in the Pacific for the maintenance of American rights and for the principles of peaceful commerce. But in no case had a serious threat been raised against our national safety or our continued independence.

What I seek to convey is the historic truth that the United States as a nation has at all times maintained clear, definite opposition, to any attempt to lock us in behind an ancient Chinese wall while the procession of civilization went past. Today, thinking of our children and of their children, we oppose enforced isolation for ourselves or for any other part of the Americas.

That determination of ours, extending over all these years, 5
was proved, for example, during the quarter century of wars following the French Revolution.

While the Napoleonic struggles did threaten interests of the United States because of the French foothold in the West Indies and in Louisiana, and while we engaged in the War of 1812 to vindicate our right to peaceful trade, it is nevertheless clear that neither France nor Great Britain, nor any other nation, was aiming at domination of the whole world.

In like fashion from 1815 to 1914 — ninety-nine years — no single war in Europe or in Asia constituted a real threat against our future or against the future of any other American nation.

Except in the Maximilian interlude in Mexico, no foreign power sought to establish itself in this Hemisphere; and the strength of the British fleet in the Atlantic has been a friendly strength. It is still a friendly strength.

Even when the World War broke out in 1914, it seemed to contain only small threat of danger to our own American future. But, as time went on, the American people began to visualize what the downfall of democratic nations might mean to our own democracy.

We need not overemphasize imperfections in the Peace of 10
Versailles. We need not harp on failure of the democracies to deal with problems of world reconstruction. We should remember

that the Peace of 1919 was far less unjust than the kind of "pacification" which began even before Munich, and which is being carried on under the new order of tyranny that seeks to spread over every continent today. The American people have unalterably set their faces against that tyranny.

Every realist knows that the democratic way of life is at this moment being directly assailed in every part of the world — assailed either by arms, or by secret spreading of poisonous propaganda by those who seek to destroy unity and promote discord in nations that are still at peace.

During sixteen long months this assault has blotted out the whole pattern of democratic life in an appalling number of independent nations, great and small. The assailants are still on the march, threatening other nations, great and small.

Therefore, as your President, performing my constitutional duty to "give to the Congress information of the state of the Union," I find it, unhappily, necessary to report that the future and the safety of our country and of our democracy are overwhelmingly involved in events far beyond our borders.

Armed defense of democratic existence is now being gallantly waged in four continents. If that defense fails, all the population and all the resources of Europe, Asia, Africa and Australasia will be dominated by the conquerors. Let us remember that the total of those populations and their resources in those four continents greatly exceeds the sum total of the population and the resources of the whole of the Western Hemisphere — many times over.

15 In times like these it is immature — and incidentally, untrue — for anybody to brag that an unprepared America, single-handed, and with one hand tied behind its back, can hold off the whole world.

No realistic American can expect from a dictator's peace international generosity, or return of true independence, or world disarmament, or freedom of expression, or freedom of religion — or even good business.

Such a peace would bring no security for us or for our neighbors. "Those, who would give up essential liberty to purchase a little temporary safety, deserve neither liberty nor safety."

As a nation, we may take pride in the fact that we are soft-hearted; but we cannot afford to be soft-headed.

We must always be wary of those who with sounding brass and a tinkling cymbal preach the "ism" of appeasement.

We must especially beware of that small group of selfish 20
men who would clip the wings of the American eagle in order to feather their own nests.

I have recently pointed out how quickly the tempo of modern warfare could bring into our very midst the physical attack which we must eventually expect if the dictator nations win this war.

There is much loose talk of our immunity from immediate and direct invasion from across the seas. Obviously, as long as the British Navy retains its power, no such danger exists. Even if there were no British Navy, it is not probable that any enemy would be stupid enough to attack us by landing troops in the United States from across thousands of miles of ocean, until it had acquired strategic bases from which to operate.

But we learn much from the lessons of the past years in Europe — particularly the lesson of Norway, whose essential seaports were captured by treachery and surprise built up over a series of years.

The first phase of the invasion of this Hemisphere would not be the landing of regular troops. The necessary strategic points would be occupied by secret agents and their dupes — and great numbers of them are already here, and in Latin America.

As long as the aggressor nations maintain the offensive, 25
they — not we — will choose the time and the place and the method of their attack.

That is why the future of all the American Republics is today in serious danger.

That is why this Annual Message to the Congress is unique in our history.

That is why every member of the Executive Branch of the Government and every member of the Congress faces great responsibility and great accountability.

The need of the moment is that our actions and our policy should be devoted primarily — almost exclusively — to meeting this foreign peril. For all our domestic problems are now a part of the great emergency.

30 Just as our national policy in internal affairs has been based upon a decent respect for the rights and the dignity of all our fellow men within our gates, so our national policy in foreign affairs has been based on a decent respect for the rights and dignity of all nations, large and small. And the justice of morality must and will win in the end.

Our national policy is this:

First, by an impressive expression of the public will and without regard to partisanship, we are committed to all-inclusive national defense.

Second, by an impressive expression of the public will and without regard to partisanship, we are committed to full support of all those resolute peoples, everywhere, who are resisting aggression and are thereby keeping war away from our Hemisphere. By this support, we express our determination that the democratic cause shall prevail; and we strengthen the defense and the security of our own nation.

Third, by an impressive expression of the public will and without regard to partisanship, we are committed to the proposition that principles of morality and considerations for our own security will never permit us to acquiesce in a peace dictated by aggressors and sponsored by appeasers. We know that enduring peace cannot be bought at the cost of other people's freedom.

In the recent national election there was no substantial dif- 35
ference between the two great parties in respect to that national policy. No issue was fought out on this line before the American electorate. Today it is abundantly evident that American citizens everywhere are demanding and supporting speedy and complete action in recognition of obvious danger.

Therefore, the immediate need is a swift and driving increase in our armament production.

Leaders of industry and labor have responded to our summons. Goals of speed have been set. In some cases these goals are being reached ahead of time; in some cases we are on schedule; in other cases there are slight but not serious delays; and in some cases — and I am sorry to say very important cases — we are all concerned by the slowness of the accomplishment of our plans.

The Army and Navy, however, have made substantial progress during the past year. Actual experience is improving and speeding up our methods of production with every passing day. And today's best is not good enough for tomorrow.

I am not satisfied with the progress thus far made. The men in charge of the program represent the best in training, in ability, and in patriotism. They are not satisfied with the progress thus far made. None of us will be satisfied until the job is done.

No matter whether the original goal was set too high or 40
too low, our objective is quicker and better results. To give you two illustrations:

We are behind schedule in turning out finished airplanes; we are working day and night to solve the innumerable problems and to catch up.

We are ahead of schedule in building warships but we are working to get even further ahead of that schedule.

To change a whole nation from a basis of peacetime production of implements of peace to a basis of wartime production of implements of war is no small task. And the greatest difficulty comes at the beginning of the program, when new tools, new plant facilities, new assembly lines, and new ship ways must first be constructed before the actual material begins to flow steadily and speedily from them.

The Congress, of course, must rightly keep itself informed at all times of the progress of the program. However, there is certain information, as the Congress itself will readily recognize, which, in the interests of our own security and those of the nations that we are supporting, must of needs be kept in confidence.

45 New circumstances are constantly begetting new needs for our safety. I shall ask this Congress for greatly increased new appropriations and authorizations to carry on what we have begun.

I also ask this Congress for authority and for funds sufficient to manufacture additional munitions and war supplies of many kinds, to be turned over to those nations which are now in actual war with aggressor nations.

Our most useful and immediate role is to act as an arsenal for them as well as for ourselves. They do not need man power, but they do need billions of dollars worth of the weapons of defense.

The time is near when they will not be able to pay for them all in ready cash. We cannot, and we will not, tell them that they must surrender, merely because of present inability to pay for the weapons which we know they must have.

I do not recommend that we make them a loan of dollars with which to pay for these weapons — a loan to be repaid in dollars.

50 I recommend that we make it possible for those nations to continue to obtain war materials in the United States, fitting their orders into our own program. Nearly all their materiel would, if the time ever came, be useful for our own defense.

Taking counsel of expert military and naval authorities, considering what is best for our own security, we are free to decide how much should be kept here and how much should be sent abroad to our friends who by their determined and heroic resistance are giving us time in which to make ready our own defense.

For what we send abroad, we shall be repaid within a reasonable time following the close of hostilities, in similar materials, or, at our option, in other goods of many kinds, which they can produce and which we need.

Let us say to the democracies: "We Americans are vitally concerned in your defense of freedom. We are putting forth our energies, our resources and our organizing powers to give you the strength to regain and maintain a free world. We shall send you, in ever-increasing numbers, ships, planes, tanks, guns. This is our purpose and our pledge."

In fulfillment of this purpose we will not be intimidated by the threats of dictators that they will regard as a breach of international law or as an act of war our aid to the democracies which dare to resist their aggression. Such aid is not an act of war, even if a dictator should unilaterally proclaim it so to be.

When the dictators, if the dictators, are ready to make 55
war upon us, they will not wait for an act of war on our part. They did not wait for Norway or Belgium or the Netherlands to commit an act of war.

Their only interest is in a new one-way international law, which lacks mutuality in its observance, and, therefore, becomes an instrument of oppression.

The happiness of future generations of Americans may well depend upon how effective and how immediate we can make our aid felt. No one can tell the exact character of the emergency situations that we may be called upon to meet. The Nation's hands must not be tied when the Nation's life is in danger.

We must all prepare to make the sacrifices that the emergency — almost as serious as war itself — demands. Whatever stands in the way of speed and efficiency in defense preparations must give way to the national need.

A free nation has the right to expect full cooperation from all groups. A free nation has the right to look to the leaders of business, of labor, and of agriculture to take the lead in stimulating effort, not among other groups but within their own groups.

60 The best way of dealing with the few slackers or trouble makers in our midst is, first, to shame them by patriotic example, and, if that fails, to use the sovereignty of Government to save Government.

As men do not live by bread alone, they do not fight by armaments alone. Those who man our defenses, and those behind them who build our defenses, must have the stamina and the courage which come from unshakable belief in the manner of life which they are defending. The mighty action that we are calling for cannot be based on a disregard of all things worth fighting for.

The Nation takes great satisfaction and much strength from the things which have been done to make its people conscious of their individual stake in the preservation of democratic life in America. Those things have toughened the fiber of our people, have renewed their faith and strengthened their devotion to the institutions we make ready to protect.

Certainly this is no time for any of us to stop thinking about the social and economic problems which are the root cause of the social revolution which is today a supreme factor in the world.

For there is nothing mysterious about the foundations of a healthy and strong democracy. The basic things expected by our people of their political and economic systems are simple.

65 They are:

- Equality of opportunity for youth and for others.
- Jobs for those who can work.
- Security for those who need it.
- The ending of special privilege for the few.

- The preservation of civil liberties for all.
- The enjoyment of the fruits of scientific progress in a wider and constantly rising standard of living.

These are the simple, basic things that must never be lost sight of in the turmoil and unbelievable complexity of our modern world. The inner and abiding strength of our economic and political systems is dependent upon the degree to which they fulfill these expectations.

Many subjects connected with our social economy call for immediate improvement.

As examples:

We should bring more citizens under the coverage of old-age pensions and unemployment insurance.

We should widen the opportunities for adequate medical care.

We should plan a better system by which persons deserving or needing gainful employment may obtain it.

I have called for personal sacrifice. I am assured of the willingness of almost all Americans to respond to that call.

A part of the sacrifice means the payment of more money in taxes. In my Budget Message I shall recommend that a greater portion of this great defense program be paid for from taxation than we are paying today. No person should try, or be allowed, to get rich out of this program; and the principle of tax payments in accordance with ability to pay should be constantly before our eyes to guide our legislation.

If the Congress maintains these principles, the voters, putting patriotism ahead of pocketbooks, will give you their applause.

In the future days, which we seek to make secure, we look forward to a world founded upon four essential human freedoms.

The first is freedom of speech and expression — everywhere in the world.

The second is freedom of every person to worship God in his own way — everywhere in the world.

85 The third is freedom from want — which, translated into world terms, means economic understandings which will secure to every nation a healthy peacetime life for its inhabitants — everywhere in the world.

The fourth is freedom from fear — which, translated into world terms, means a world-wide reduction of armaments to such a point and in such a thorough fashion that no nation will be in a position to commit an act of physical aggression against any neighbor — anywhere in the world.

That is no vision of a distant millennium. It is a definite basis for a kind of world attainable in our own time and generation. That kind of world is the very antithesis of the so-called new order of tyranny which the dictators seek to create with the crash of a bomb.

To that new order we oppose the greater conception — the moral order. A good society is able to face schemes of world domination and foreign revolutions alike without fear.

Since the beginning of our American history, we have been engaged in change — in a perpetual peaceful revolution — a revolution which goes on steadily, quietly adjusting itself to changing conditions — without the concentration camp or the quick-lime in the ditch. The world order which we seek is the cooperation of free countries, working together in a friendly, civilized society.

90 This nation has placed its destiny in the hands and heads and hearts of its millions of free men and women; and its faith in freedom under the guidance of God. Freedom means the supremacy of human rights everywhere. Our support goes to those who struggle to gain those rights or keep them. Our strength is our unity of purpose. To that high concept there can be no end save victory.

The Social Contract

by Jean-Jacques Rousseau

Jean-Jacques Rousseau (1712–1778) was a Geneva-born philosopher during the period of the Enlightenment. This period emphasized societal progress through reason and analysis, including sciences and the arts. While Rousseau was a philosopher during the Enlightenment, some of his ideas ran counter to this movement. Rousseau's The Social Contract, *published in 1762, examines the concepts of equality and freedom within the confines of modern society. The following excerpt comprises Book I of* The Social Contract.

I mean to inquire if, in the civil order, there can be any sure and legitimate rule of administration, men being taken as they are and laws as they might be. In this inquiry I shall endeavor always to unite what right sanctions with what is prescribed by interest, in order that justice and utility may in no case be divided.

I enter upon my task without proving the importance of the subject. I shall be asked if I am a prince or a legislator, to write on politics. I answer that I am neither, and that is why I do so. If I were a prince or a legislator, I should not waste time in saying what wants doing; I should do it, or hold my peace.

As I was born a citizen of a free State, and a member of the Sovereign, I feel that, however feeble the influence my voice can have on public affairs, the right of voting on them makes it my duty to study them: and I am happy, when I reflect upon governments, to find my inquiries always furnish me with new reasons for loving that of my own country.

1. Subject of the First Book

Man is born free; and everywhere he is in chains. One thinks himself the master of others, and still remains a greater slave than they. How did this change come about? I do not know. What can make it legitimate? That question I think I can answer.

If I took into account only force, and the effects derived from it, I should say: "As long as a people is compelled to obey, and obeys, it does well; as soon as it can shake off the yoke, and shakes it off, it does still better; for, regaining its liberty by the same right as took it away, either it is justified in resuming it, or there was no justification for those who took it away." But the social order is a sacred right which is the basis of all other rights. Nevertheless, this right does not come from nature, and must therefore be founded on conventions. Before coming to that, I have to prove what I have just asserted.

2. The First Societies

The most ancient of all societies, and the only one that is natural, is the family: and even so the children remain attached to the father only so long as they need him for their preservation. As soon as this need ceases, the natural bond is dissolved. The children, released from the obedience they owed to the father, and the father, released from the care he owed his children, return equally to independence. If they remain united, they continue so no longer naturally, but voluntarily; and the family itself is then maintained only by convention.

This common liberty results from the nature of man. His first law is to provide for his own preservation, his first cares are those which he owes to himself; and, as soon as he reaches years of discretion, he is the sole judge of the proper means of preserving himself, and consequently becomes his own master.

The family then may be called the first model of political societies: the ruler corresponds to the father, and the people to the children; and all, being born free and equal, alienate their liberty only for their own advantage. The whole difference is that, in the family, the love of the father for his children repays him for the care he takes of them, while, in the State, the pleasure of commanding takes the place of the love which the chief cannot have for the peoples under him.

Grotius denies that all human power is established in favor of the governed, and quotes slavery as an example. His usual method of reasoning is constantly to establish right by fact.[1] It would be possible to employ a more logical method, but none could be more favorable to tyrants.

It is then, according to Grotius, doubtful whether the human race belongs to a hundred men, or that hundred men to the human race: and, throughout his book, he seems to incline to the former alternative, which is also the view of Hobbes. On this showing, the human species is divided into so many herds of cattle, each with its ruler, who keeps guard over them for the purpose of devouring them.

As a shepherd is of a nature superior to that of his flock, the shepherds of men, i.e., their rulers, are of a nature superior to that of the peoples under them. Thus, Philo tells us, the Emperor Caligula reasoned, concluding equally well either that kings were gods, or that men were beasts.

The reasoning of Caligula agrees with that of Hobbes and Grotius. Aristotle, before any of them, had said that men are by no means equal naturally, but that some are born for slavery, and others for dominion.

Aristotle was right; but he took the effect for the cause. Nothing can be more certain than that every man born in slavery is born for slavery. Slaves lose everything in their chains, even

[1] *Learned inquiries into public right are often only the history of past abuses; and troubling to study them too deeply is a profitless infatuation"* (Essay on the Interests of France in Relation to its Neighbors, *by the Marquis d'Argenson). This is exactly what Grotius has done.*

the desire of escaping from them: they love their servitude, as the comrades of Ulysses loved their brutish condition.[2] If then there are slaves by nature, it is because there have been slaves against nature. Force made the first slaves, and their cowardice perpetuated the condition.

I have said nothing of King Adam, or Emperor Noah, father of the three great monarchs who shared out the universe, like the children of Saturn, whom some scholars have recognized in them. I trust to getting due thanks for my moderation; for, being a direct descendant of one of these princes, perhaps of the eldest branch, how do I know that a verification of titles might not leave me the legitimate king of the human race? In any case, there can be no doubt that Adam was sovereign of the world, as Robinson Crusoe was of his island, as long as he was its only inhabitant; and this empire had the advantage that the monarch, safe on his throne, had no rebellions, wars, or conspirators to fear.

3. The Right of the Strongest

15 The strongest is never strong enough to be always the master, unless he transforms strength into right, and obedience into duty. Hence the right of the strongest, which, though to all seeming meant ironically, is really laid down as a fundamental principle. But are we never to have an explanation of this phrase? Force is a physical power, and I fail to see what moral effect it can have. To yield to force is an act of necessity, not of will — at the most, an act of prudence. In what sense can it be a duty?

Suppose for a moment that this so-called "right" exists. I maintain that the sole result is a mass of inexplicable nonsense. For, if force creates right, the effect changes with the cause: every force that is greater than the first succeeds to its right. As soon as it is possible to disobey with impunity, disobedience is

[2] *See a short treatise of Plutarch's entitled* That Animals Reason.

legitimate; and, the strongest being always in the right, the only thing that matters is to act so as to become the strongest. But what kind of right is that which perishes when force fails? If we must obey perforce, there is no need to obey because we ought; and if we are not forced to obey, we are under no obligation to do so. Clearly, the word "right" adds nothing to force: in this connection, it means absolutely nothing.

Obey the powers that be. If this means yield to force, it is a good precept, but superfluous: I can answer for its never being violated. All power comes from God, I admit; but so does all sickness: does that mean that we are forbidden to call in the doctor? A brigand surprises me at the edge of a wood: must I not merely surrender my purse on compulsion; but, even if I could withhold it, am I in conscience bound to give it up? For certainly the pistol he holds is also a power.

Let us then admit that force does not create right, and that we are obliged to obey only legitimate powers. In that case, my original question recurs.

4. Slavery

Since no man has a natural authority over his fellow, and force creates no right, we must conclude that conventions form the basis of all legitimate authority among men.

If an individual, says Grotius, can alienate his liberty and 20
make himself the slave of a master, why could not a whole people do the same and make itself subject to a king? There are in this passage plenty of ambiguous words which would need explaining; but let us confine ourselves to the word *alienate*. To alienate is to give or to sell. Now, a man who becomes the slave of another does not give himself; he sells himself, at the least for his subsistence: but for what does a people sell itself? A king is so far from furnishing his subjects with their subsistence that he gets his own only from them; and, according to Rabelais, kings

do not live on nothing. Do subjects then give their persons on condition that the king takes their goods also? I fail to see what they have left to preserve.

It will be said that the despot assures his subjects civil tranquility. Granted; but what do they gain, if the wars his ambition brings down upon them, his insatiable avidity, and the vexatious conduct of his ministers press harder on them than their own dissensions would have done? What do they gain, if the very tranquility they enjoy is one of their miseries? Tranquility is found also in dungeons; but is that enough to make them desirable places to live in? The Greeks imprisoned in the cave of the Cyclops lived there very tranquilly, while they were awaiting their turn to be devoured.

To say that a man gives himself gratuitously is to say what is absurd and inconceivable; such an act is null and illegitimate, from the mere fact that he who does it is out of his mind. To say the same of a whole people is to suppose a people of madmen; and madness creates no right.

Even if each man could alienate himself, he could not alienate his children: they are born men and free; their liberty belongs to them, and no one but they has the right to dispose of it. Before they come to years of discretion, the father can, in their name, lay down conditions for their preservation and well-being, but he cannot give them irrevocably and without conditions: such a gift is contrary to the ends of nature, and exceeds the rights of paternity. It would therefore be necessary, in order to legitimize an arbitrary government, that in every generation the people should be in a position to accept or reject it; but, were this so, the government would be no longer arbitrary.

To renounce liberty is to renounce being a man, to surrender the rights of humanity and even its duties. For him who renounces everything no indemnity is possible. Such a renunciation is incompatible with man's nature; to remove all liberty from his will is to remove all morality from his acts. Finally, it is an empty and contradictory convention that sets up, on the one side, absolute authority, and, on the other, unlimited obedience. Is it not clear that we can be under no obligation to a person from whom we have the right to exact everything? Does not this condition alone, in the absence of equivalence or exchange, in itself involve the nullity of the act? For what right can my slave have against me, when all that he has belongs to me, and, his right being mine, this right of mine against myself is a phrase devoid of meaning?

Grotius and the rest find in war another origin for the so- 25
called right of slavery. The victor having, as they hold, the right of killing the vanquished, the latter can buy back his life at the price of his liberty; and this convention is the more legitimate because it is to the advantage of both parties.

But it is clear that this supposed right to kill the conquered is by no means deducible from the state of war. Men, from the mere fact that, while they are living in their primitive independence, they have no mutual relations stable enough to constitute either the state of peace or the state of war, cannot be naturally enemies. War is constituted by a relation between things, and not between persons; and, as the state of war cannot arise out of simple personal relations, but only out of real relations, private war, or war of man with man, can exist neither in the state of nature, where there is no constant property, nor in the social state, where everything is under the authority of the laws.

Individual combats, duels and encounters, are acts which cannot constitute a state; while the private wars, authorized by the Establishments of Louis IX, King of France, and suspended by the Peace of God, are abuses of feudalism, in itself an absurd system if ever there was one, and contrary to the principles of natural right and to all good polity.

War then is a relation, not between man and man, but between State and State, and individuals are enemies only accidentally, not as men, nor even as citizens,[3] but as soldiers; not as members of their country, but as its defenders. Finally, each State can have for enemies only other States, and not men; for between things disparate in nature there can be no real relation.

Furthermore, this principle is in conformity with the established rules of all times and the constant practice of all civilized peoples. Declarations of war are intimations less to powers than to their subjects. The foreigner, whether king, individual, or people, who robs, kills or detains the subjects, without declaring war on the prince, is not an enemy, but a brigand. Even in real war, a just prince, while laying hands, in the enemy's country, on all that belongs to the public, respects the lives and goods of individuals: he respects rights on which his own are founded. The object of the war being the destruction of the hostile State, the other side has a right to kill its defenders, while they are bearing arms; but as soon as they lay them down and surrender, they cease to be enemies or instruments of the enemy, and become once more merely men, whose life no one has any right to take. Sometimes it is possible to kill the State without killing a single one of its members; and war gives no right which is not necessary to the gaining of its object. These principles are not those of Grotius: they are not based on the authority of poets, but derived from the nature of reality and based on reason.

[3] *The Romans, who understood and respected the right of war more than any other nation on earth, carried their scruples on this head so far that a citizen was not allowed to serve as a volunteer without engaging himself expressly against the enemy, and against such and such an enemy by name. A legion in which the younger Cato was seeing his first service under Popilius having been reconstructed, the elder Cato wrote to Popilius that, if he wished his son to continue serving under him, he must administer to him a new military oath, because, the first having been annulled, he was no longer able to bear arms against the enemy. The same Cato wrote to his son telling him to take great care not to go into battle before taking this new oath. I know that the siege of Clusium and other isolated events can be quoted against me; but I am citing laws and customs. The Romans are the people that least often transgressed its laws; and no other people has had such good ones.*

The right of conquest has no foundation other than the 30
right of the strongest. If war does not give the conqueror the right to massacre the conquered peoples, the right to enslave them cannot be based upon a right which does not exist. No one has a right to kill an enemy except when he cannot make him a slave, and the right to enslave him cannot therefore be derived from the right to kill him. It is accordingly an unfair exchange to make him buy at the price of his liberty his life, over which the victor holds no right. Is it not clear that there is a vicious circle in founding the right of life and death on the right of slavery, and the right of slavery on the right of life and death?

Even if we assume this terrible right to kill everybody, I maintain that a slave made in war, or a conquered people, is under no obligation to a master, except to obey him as far as he is compelled to do so. By taking an equivalent for his life, the victor has not done him a favor; instead of killing him without profit, he has killed him usefully. So far then is he from acquiring over him any authority in addition to that of force, that the state of war continues to subsist between them: their mutual relation is the effect of it, and the usage of the right of war does not imply a treaty of peace. A convention has indeed been made; but this convention, so far from destroying the state of war, presupposes its continuance.

So, from whatever aspect we regard the question, the right of slavery is null and void, not only as being illegitimate, but also because it is absurd and meaningless. The words *slave* and *right* contradict each other, and are mutually exclusive. It will always be equally foolish for a man to say to a man or to a people: "I make with you a convention wholly at your expense and wholly to my advantage; I shall keep it as long as I like, and you will keep it as long as I like."

5. That We Must Always Go Back to a First Convention

Even if I granted all that I have been refuting, the friends of despotism would be no better off. There will always be a great difference between subduing a multitude and ruling a society. Even if scattered individuals were successively enslaved by one man, however numerous they might be, I still see no more than a master and his slaves, and certainly not a people and its ruler; I see what may be termed an aggregation, but not an association; there is as yet neither public good nor body politic. The man in question, even if he has enslaved half the world, is still only an individual; his interest, apart from that of others, is still a purely private interest. If this same man comes to die, his empire, after him, remains scattered and without unity, as an oak falls and dissolves into a heap of ashes when the fire has consumed it.

A people, says Grotius, can give itself to a king. Then, according to Grotius, a people is a people before it gives itself. The gift is itself a civil act, and implies public deliberation. It would be better, before examining the act by which a people gives itself to a king, to examine that by which it has become a people; for this act, being necessarily prior to the other, is the true foundation of society.

Indeed, if there were no prior convention, where, unless the election were unanimous, would be the obligation on the minority to submit to the choice of the majority? How have a hundred men who wish for a master the right to vote on behalf of ten who do not? The law of majority voting is itself something established by convention, and presupposes unanimity, on one occasion at least.

6. The Social Compact

I suppose men to have reached the point at which the obstacles in the way of their preservation in the state of nature show their power of resistance to be greater than the resources at the disposal of each individual for his maintenance in that state. That primitive condition can then subsist no longer; and the human race would perish unless it changed its manner of existence.

But, as men cannot engender new forces, but only unite and direct existing ones, they have no other means of preserving themselves than the formation, by aggregation, of a sum of forces great enough to overcome the resistance. These they have to bring into play by means of a single motive power, and cause to act in concert.

This sum of forces can arise only where several persons come together: but, as the force and liberty of each man are the chief instruments of his self-preservation, how can he pledge them without harming his own interests, and neglecting the care he owes to himself? This difficulty, in its bearing on my present subject, may be stated in the following terms:

> "The problem is to find a form of association which will defend and protect with the whole common force the person and goods of each associate, and in which each, while uniting himself with all, may still obey himself alone, and remain as free as before."

This is the fundamental problem of which the Social Contract provides the solution.

The clauses of this contract are so determined by the nature of the act that the slightest modification would make them vain and ineffective; so that, although they have perhaps never been formally set forth, they are everywhere the same and everywhere tacitly admitted and recognized, until, on the violation of the social compact, each regains his original rights and resumes his natural liberty, while losing the conventional liberty in favor of which he renounced it.

These clauses, properly understood, may be reduced to one — the total alienation of each associate, together with all his rights, to the whole community; for, in the first place, as each gives himself absolutely, the conditions are the same for all; and, this being so, no one has any interest in making them burdensome to others.

Moreover, the alienation being without reserve, the union is as perfect as it can be, and no associate has anything more to demand: for, if the individuals retained certain rights, as there would be no common superior to decide between them and the public, each, being on one point his own judge, would ask to be so on all; the state of nature would thus continue, and the association would necessarily become inoperative or tyrannical.

Finally, each man, in giving himself to all, gives himself to nobody; and as there is no associate over whom he does not acquire the same right as he yields others over himself, he gains an equivalent for everything he loses, and an increase of force for the preservation of what he has.

If then we discard from the social compact what is not of its essence, we shall find that it reduces itself to the following terms:

> "Each of us puts his person and all his power in common under the supreme direction of the general will, and, in our corporate capacity, we receive each member as an indivisible part of the whole."

45 At once, in place of the individual personality of each contracting party, this act of association creates a moral and collective body, composed of as many members as the assembly contains votes, and receiving from this act its unity, its common identity, its life and its will. This public person, so formed by the union of all other persons formerly took the name of *city*,[4]

[4] *The real meaning of this word has been almost wholly lost in modern times; most people mistake a town for a city, and a townsman for a citizen. They do not know that houses make a town, but citizens a city. The same mistake long ago cost the Carthaginians dear. I have never read of the title of citizens being*

and now takes that of *Republic* or *body politic;* it is called by its members *State* when passive. *Sovereign* when active, and *Power* when compared with others like itself. Those who are associated in it take collectively the name of *people*, and severally are called *citizens,* as sharing in the sovereign power, and subjects, as being under the laws of the State. But these terms are often confused and taken one for another: it is enough to know how to distinguish them when they are being used with precision.

7. The Sovereign

This formula shows us that the act of association comprises a mutual undertaking between the public and the individuals, and that each individual, in making a contract, as we may say, with himself, is bound in a double capacity; as a member of the Sovereign he is bound to the individuals, and as a member of the State to the Sovereign. But the maxim of civil right, that no one is bound by undertakings made to himself, does not apply in this case; for there is a great difference between incurring an obligation to yourself and incurring one to a whole of which you form a part.

Attention must further be called to the fact that public deliberation, while competent to bind all the subjects to the Sovereign, because of the two different capacities in which each of them may be regarded, cannot, for the opposite reason, bind the Sovereign to itself; and that it is consequently against the nature of the body politic for the Sovereign to impose on itself a

given to the subjects of any prince, not even the ancient Macedonians or the English of today, though they are nearer liberty than any one else. The French alone everywhere familiarly adopt the name of citizens, because, as can be seen from their dictionaries, they have no idea of its meaning; otherwise they would be guilty in usurping it, of the crime of lèse-majesté: *among them, the name expresses a virtue, and not a right. When Bodin spoke of our citizens and townsmen, he fell into a bad blunder in taking the one class for the other. M. d'Alembert has avoided the error, and, in his article on Geneva, has clearly distinguished the four orders of men (or even five, counting mere foreigners) who dwell in our town, of which two only compose the Republic. No other French writer, to my knowledge, has understood the real meaning of the word citizen.*

law which it cannot infringe. Being able to regard itself in only one capacity, it is in the position of an individual who makes a contract with himself; and this makes it clear that there neither is nor can be any kind of fundamental law binding on the body of the people — not even the social contract itself. This does not mean that the body politic cannot enter into undertakings with others, provided the contract is not infringed by them; for in relation to what is external to it, it becomes a simple being, an individual.

But the body politic or the Sovereign, drawing its being wholly from the sanctity of the contract, can never bind itself, even to an outsider, to do anything derogatory to the original act, for instance, to alienate any part of itself, or to submit to another Sovereign. Violation of the act by which it exists would be self-annihilation; and that which is itself nothing can create nothing.

As soon as this multitude is so united in one body, it is impossible to offend against one of the members without attacking the body, and still more to offend against the body without the members resenting it. Duty and interest therefore equally oblige the two contracting parties to give each other help; and the same men should seek to combine, in their double capacity, all the advantages dependent upon that capacity.

50 Again, the Sovereign, being formed wholly of the individuals who compose it, neither has nor can have any interest contrary to theirs; and consequently the sovereign power need give no guarantee to its subjects, because it is impossible for the body to wish to hurt all its members. We shall also see later on that it cannot hurt any in particular. The Sovereign, merely by virtue of what it is, is always what it should be.

This, however, is not the case with the relation of the subjects to the Sovereign, which, despite the common interest, would have no security that they would fulfill their undertakings, unless it found means to assure itself of their fidelity.

In fact, each individual, as a man, may have a particular will contrary or dissimilar to the general will which he has as a citizen. His particular interest may speak to him quite differently from the common interest: his absolute and naturally independent existence may make him look upon what he owes to the common cause as a gratuitzous contribution, the loss of which will do less harm to others than the payment of it is burdensome to himself; and, regarding the moral person which constitutes the State as a *persona ficta*, because not a man, he may wish to enjoy the rights of citizenship without being ready to fulfill the duties of a subject. The continuance of such an injustice could not but prove the undoing of the body politic.

In order then that the social compact may not be an empty formula, it tacitly includes the undertaking, which alone can give force to the rest, that whoever refuses to obey the general will shall be compelled to do so by the whole body. This means nothing less than that he will be forced to be free; for this is the condition which, by giving each citizen to his country, secures him against all personal dependence. In this lies the key to the working of the political machine; this alone legitimizes civil undertakings, which, without it, would be absurd, tyrannical, and liable to the most frightful abuses.

8. The Civil State

The passage from the state of nature to the civil state produces a very remarkable change in man, by substituting justice for instinct in his conduct, and giving his actions the morality they had formerly lacked. Then only, when the voice of duty takes the place of physical impulses and right of appetite, does man, who so far had considered only himself, find that he is forced to act on different principles, and to consult his reason before listening to his inclinations. Although, in this state, he deprives himself of some advantages which he got from nature, he gains in return others so great, his faculties are so stimulated and developed, his ideas so extended, his feelings so ennobled, and his whole soul so uplifted, that, did not the abuses of this new condition often degrade him below that which he left, he would be bound to bless continually the happy moment which took him from it for ever, and, instead of a stupid and unimaginative animal, made him an intelligent being and a man.

55 Let us draw up the whole account in terms easily commensurable. What man loses by the social contract is his natural liberty and an unlimited right to everything he tries to get and succeeds in getting; what he gains is civil liberty and the proprietorship of all he possesses. If we are to avoid mistake in weighing one against the other, we must clearly distinguish natural liberty, which is bounded only by the strength of the individual, from civil liberty, which is limited by the general will; and possession, which is merely the effect of force or the right of the first occupier, from property, which can be founded only on a positive title.

We might, over and above all this, add, to what man acquires in the civil state, moral liberty, which alone makes him truly master of himself; for the mere impulse of appetite is slavery, while obedience to a law which we prescribe to ourselves is liberty. But I have already said too much on this head, and the philosophical meaning of the word liberty does not now concern us.

9. Real Property

Each member of the community gives himself to it, at the moment of its foundation, just as he is, with all the resources at his command, including the goods he possesses. This act does not make possession, in changing hands, change its nature, and become property in the hands of the Sovereign; but, as the forces of the city are incomparably greater than those of an individual, public possession is also, in fact, stronger and more irrevocable, without being any more legitimate, at any rate from the point of view of foreigners. For the State, in relation to its members, is master of all their goods by the social contract, which, within the State, is the basis of all rights; but, in relation to other powers, it is so only by the right of the first occupier, which it holds from its members.

The right of the first occupier, though more real than the right of the strongest, becomes a real right only when the right of property has already been established. Every man has naturally a right to everything he needs; but the positive act which makes him proprietor of one thing excludes him from everything else. Having his share, he ought to keep to it, and can have no further right against the community. This is why the right of the first occupier, which in the state of nature is so weak, claims the respect of every man in civil society. In this right we are respecting not so much what belongs to another as what does not belong to ourselves.

In general, to establish the right of the first occupier over a plot of ground, the following conditions are necessary: first, the land must not yet be inhabited; secondly, a man must occupy only the amount he needs for his subsistence; and, in the third place, possession must be taken, not by an empty ceremony, but by labor and cultivation, the only sign of proprietorship that should be respected by others, in default of a legal title.

In granting the right of first occupancy to necessity and 60
labor, are we not really stretching it as far as it can go? Is it possible to leave such a right unlimited? Is it to be enough to set foot on a plot of common ground, in order to be able to call yourself at once the master of it? Is it to be enough that a man has the strength to expel others for a moment, in order to establish his right to prevent them from ever returning? How can a man or a people seize an immense territory and keep it from the rest of the world except by a punishable usurpation,

since all others are being robbed, by such an act, of the place of habitation and the means of subsistence which nature gave them in common? When Nunez Balboa, standing on the seashore, took possession of the South Seas and the whole of South America in the name of the crown of Castile, was that enough to dispossess all their actual inhabitants, and to shut out from them all the princes of the world? On such a showing, these ceremonies are idly multiplied, and the Catholic King need only take possession all at once, from his apartment, of the whole universe, merely making a subsequent reservation about what was already in the possession of other princes.

We can imagine how the lands of individuals, where they were contiguous and came to be united, became the public territory, and how the right of Sovereignty, extending from the subjects over the lands they held, became at once real and personal. The possessors were thus made more dependent, and the forces at their command used to guarantee their fidelity. The advantage of this does not seem to have been felt by ancient monarchs, who called themselves Kings of the Persians, Scythians, or Macedonians, and seemed to regard themselves more as rulers of men than as masters of a country. Those of the present day more cleverly call themselves Kings of France, Spain, England, etc.: thus holding the land, they are quite confident of holding the inhabitants.

The peculiar fact about this alienation is that, in taking over the goods of individuals, the community, so far from despoiling them, only assures them legitimate possession, and changes usurpation into a true right and enjoyment into proprietorship. Thus the possessors, being regarded as depositaries of the public good, and having their rights respected by all the members of the State and maintained against foreign aggression by all its forces, have, by a cession which benefits both the public and still more themselves, acquired, so to speak, all that they gave up. This paradox may easily be explained by the distinction between the rights which the Sovereign and the proprietor have over the same estate, as we shall see later on.

It may also happen that men begin to unite one with another before they possess anything, and that, subsequently occupying a tract of country which is enough for all, they enjoy it in common, or share it out among themselves, either equally or according to a scale fixed by the Sovereign. However the acquisition be made, the right which each individual has to his own estate is always subordinate to the right which the community has over all: without this, there would be neither stability in the social tie, nor real force in the exercise of Sovereignty.

I shall end this chapter and this book by remarking on a fact on which the whole social system should rest: i.e., that, instead of destroying natural inequality, the fundamental compact substitutes, for such physical inequality as nature may have set up between men, an equality that is moral and legitimate, and that men, who may be unequal in strength or intelligence, become every one equal by convention and legal right.[5]

[5] *Under bad governments, this equality is only apparent and illusory: it serves only to keep the pauper in his poverty and the rich man in the position he has usurped. In fact, laws are always of use to those who possess and harmful to those who have nothing: from which it follows that the social state is advantageous to men only when all have something and none too much.*

Morality and Birth Control

by Margaret Sanger

Margaret Sanger (1879–1966) is one of the defining figures of the birth control movement, and she is credited for coining the term "birth control" in 1914. In 1921, Sanger founded the American Birth Control League, which later became the Planned Parenthood Federation. Sanger fought to bring birth control information and contraceptives to women, a direct challenge to the Comstock Act of 1873, which made it a federal offense to distribute contraceptives in the mail or across state lines. Sanger's advocacy also challenged the many state laws that made it a crime to distribute birth control or information concerning birth control. This essay was originally published in February 1918.

Throughout the ages, every attempt woman has made to strike off the shackles of slavery has been met with the argument that such an act would result in the downfall of her morality. Suffrage was going to "break up the home." Higher education would unfit her for motherhood, and co-education would surely result in making her immoral. Even today, in some of the more backward countries reading and writing is stoutly discouraged by the clerical powers because "women may read about things they should not know."

We now know that there never can be a free humanity until woman is freed from ignorance, and we know, too, that woman can never call herself free until she is mistress of her own body. Just so long as man dictates and controls the standards of sex morality, just so long will man control the world.

Birth control is the first important step woman must take toward the goal of her freedom. It is the first step she must take to be man's equal. It is the first step they must both take toward human emancipation.

The Twentieth Century can make progress only by fighting the superstitions and prejudices created in the Nineteenth Century — fighting them in the open with the public searchlight upon them.

The first questions we must ask ourselves are: Are we satisfied 5
with present day morality? Are we satisfied with the results of present day standards of morality? Are these so satisfying that they need no improvement?

For fourteen years I worked as a nurse in the factory and tenement districts of New York City. Eight years ago I was called into a home where the father, a machinist by trade, was earning eighteen dollars a week. He was at the time the father of six living children, to all appearances a sober, serious and hard working man. His wife, a woman in her thirties, toiled early and late helping him to keep the home together and the little ones out of the sweatshops, for they were both anxious to give their children a little schooling.

Two years ago I came across this same family, and found that five more children had been added in the meantime to their household. The three youngest were considered by medical authorities to be hopelessly feeble-minded, two of the older girls were prostitutes; three of the boys were serving long term sentences in penitentiaries, while another of the children had been injured by a fall and so badly crippled that she will not be able to help herself for years to come.

Out of this family of eleven children only two are now of any use to society, a little girl of seven, who stays at home and cares for her crippled sister during the day while the mother scrubs office floors, and a boy of nine who sells chewing gum after school hours at a subway exit. The father has become a hopeless drunkard, of whom the mother and children live in terror.

This is but one illustration of the results of our present day morality. Here was an opportunity for society to develop and preserve six children for human service; but prudery and ignorance added five more to this group, with the result that two out of eleven are left to fit the struggle against pauperism and charity. Will they succumb?

Another case I should like to cite shows how shallow is the concern of society in regard to the over-crowded tenements, where thousands of little children occupy sleeping quarters with parents and boarders whose every act is visible to all. Morality indeed! Society is much like the ostrich with its head in the sand. It will not look at facts and face the responsibility of its own stupidity.

I recall the death-bed scene, when the patient, a woman of twenty-six, passed away during the birth of her seventh child. Five out of the seven were girls, the eldest being about ten years old. Upon the death of this woman, this girl began to assume the duties of her mother and continued to keep the four men roomers who had lodged in their home for years. A few years later, I found this girl suffering from the ravages of syphilis, although she had only just entered the period of puberty. She told me she could not remember when she had not dressed before the roomers, and on winter nights she often slept in their beds. She was already old — old in ignorance, in vulgarity, in degeneracy.

Another womanhood blighted in the bud, battered by ignorance, another soul sunk in despair.

These five girl-women did not ask society to fill their minds, as it was willing to do, with a useless knowledge of Greek, Latin or the Sciences. But they did need and unconsciously demand the knowledge of life, of hygiene and sex psychology which is so prudishly and shamefully denied them. No doubt these five sisters will soon represent the ruins of an ancient prejudice, and five more derelicts will be added to that particular relic heap of humanity.

Again, is there anything more sickening to truth than the attitude of society toward that catch phrase "Sacred Motherhood"? Take another illustration and lay bare the living facts and view them for awhile.

Two sisters lived in an upstate town, members of a large 15
family, where the older daughters worked in factories, in order that the younger girls might have educational advantages. The youngest fell in love with a good-for-nothing fellow, with the result that she had an illegal child. Disgrace, ostracism and remorse drove her out into the world, and together with her baby she drifted from house to house in the capacity of a servant, until finally the baby died, leaving the mother free to enter upon another vocation.

During this time, however, due to the condescending treatment accorded to her by the women who employed her, she had become so accustomed to look upon herself as an outcast that soon, with other companions of her frame of mind, she began trafficking. . . on the streets of New York.

Now the second sister, a few years older, also fell in love with one of the "town heroes," and came to grief; but owing to the "disgrace" of the youngest sister and sympathy for the elder members of the family, who were completely anguish-stricken over this second mishap, the old family physician took her in charge and sent to her a place where an illegal operation was performed upon her. She returned, a sadder but wiser girl, to her home, finished the high school course, and several years later she became the principal of a school.

Today she is one of the most respected women in that county. She devotes her life outside school hours to a sympathetic understanding of the needs of young boys and girls, and her sordid early experience, put to good use, has helped many boys and girls to lead clean lives.

These cases represent actual modern conditions. Our laws force women into celibacy on the one hand, or abortion on the other.

20 Both conditions are declared by eminent medical authorities to be injurious to health.

The ever-ascending standard and cost of living, combined with the low wage of the young men of today, tend toward the postponement of marriage.

Has knowledge of birth control, so carefully guarded and so secretly practiced by the women of the wealthy class — and so tenaciously withheld from the working women — brought them misery? Rather, has it not promoted greater happiness, greater freedom, greater prosperity and more harmony among them? The women who have this knowledge are the women who have been free to develop, free to enjoy in its best sense, and free to advance the interests of the community. And their men are the ones who motor, who sail yachts, who legislate, who lead and control. The men, women and children of this class do not form any part whatever in the social problems of our times.

Had this class continued to reproduce in the prolific manner of the working people in the past twenty-five years, can human imagination picture what conditions would be today? All of our problems are the result of overbreeding among the working class, and if morality is to mean anything at all to us, we must regard all the changes which tend toward the uplift and survival of the human race as moral.

Knowledge of birth control is essentially moral. Its general, though prudent, practice must lead to a higher individuality and ultimately to a cleaner race.

Declaration of Sentiments and Resolutions

by Elizabeth Cady Stanton

Elizabeth Cady Stanton (1815–1902) was an abolitionist and early leader of the women's rights movement. In July of 1848, Stanton and others held the first national women's rights convention at Seneca Falls, New York. At this convention, 68 women and 32 men signed this declaration, of which Stanton was the primary author.

When, in the course of human events, it becomes necessary for one portion of the family of man to assume among the people of the earth a position different from that which they have hitherto occupied, but one to which the laws of nature and of nature's God entitle them, a decent respect to the opinions of mankind requires that they should declare the causes that impel them to such a course.

We hold these truths to be self-evident: that all men and women are created equal; that they are endowed by their Creator with certain inalienable rights; that among these are life, liberty, and the pursuit of happiness; that to secure these rights governments are instituted, deriving their just powers from the consent of the governed. Whenever any form of government becomes destructive of these ends, it is the right of those who suffer from it to refuse allegiance to it, and to insist upon the institution of a new government, laying its foundation on such principles, and organizing its powers in such form, as to them shall seem most likely to effect their safety and happiness. Prudence, indeed, will dictate that governments long established should not be changed for light and transient causes; and accordingly all experience hath shown that mankind are more disposed to suffer, while evils are sufferable, than to right themselves by abolishing the forms to which they were accustomed. But when a long train of abuses and usurpations, pursuing invariably the same object evinces a design to reduce them under absolute despotism, it is their duty to throw off such government, and to provide new guards for their future security. Such has been the patient sufferance of the women under this government, and such is now the necessity which constrains them to demand the equal station to which they are entitled.The history of mankind is a history of repeated injuries and usurpations on the part of man toward woman, having in direct object the establishment of an absolute tyranny over her. To prove this, let facts be submitted to a candid world.

He has never permitted her to exercise her inalienable right to the elective franchise.

He has compelled her to submit to laws, in the formation of which she had no voice.

He has withheld from her rights which are given to the most ignorant and degraded men — both natives and foreigners.

Having deprived her of this first right of a citizen, the elective franchise, thereby leaving her without representation in the halls of legislation, he has oppressed her on all sides.

He has made her, if married, in the eye of the law, civilly dead.

He has taken from her all right in property, even to the wages she earns.

He has made her, morally, an irresponsible being, as she can commit many crimes with impunity, provided they be done in the presence of her husband. In the covenant of marriage, she is compelled to promise obedience to her husband, he becoming, to all intents and purposes, her master — the law giving him power to deprive her of her liberty, and to administer chastisement.

He has so framed the laws of divorce, as to what shall be the proper causes, and in case of separation, to whom the guardianship of the children shall be given, as to be wholly regardless of the happiness of women — the law, in all cases, going upon a false supposition of the supremacy of man, and giving all power into his hands. 10

After depriving her of all rights as a married woman, if single, and the owner of property, he has taxed her to support a government which recognizes her only when her property can be made profitable to it.

He has monopolized nearly all the profitable employments, and from those she is permitted to follow, she receives but a scanty remuneration. He closes against her all the avenues to wealth and distinction which he considers most honorable to himself. As a teacher of theology, medicine, or law, she is not known.

He has denied her the facilities for obtaining a thorough education, all colleges being closed against her.

He allows her in Church, as well as State, but a subordinate position, claiming Apostolic authority for her exclusion from the ministry, and, with some exceptions, from any public participation in the affairs of the Church.

He has created a false public sentiment by giving to the world a different code of morals for men and women, by which moral delinquencies which exclude women from society, are not only tolerated, but deemed of little account in man. 15

He has usurped the prerogative of Jehovah himself, claiming it as his right to assign for her a sphere of action, when that belongs to her conscience and to her God.

He has endeavored, in every way that he could, to destroy her confidence in her own powers, to lessen her self-respect, and to make her willing to lead a dependent and abject life.

Now, in view of this entire disfranchisement of one-half the people of this country, their social and religious degradation — in view of the unjust laws above mentioned, and because women do feel themselves aggrieved, oppressed, and fraudulently deprived of their most sacred rights, we insist that they have immediate admission to all the rights and privileges which belong to them as citizens of the United States.

In entering upon the great work before us, we anticipate no small amount of misconception, misrepresentation, and ridicule; but we shall use every instrumentality within our power to effect our object. We shall employ agents, circulate tracts, petition the State and National legislatures, and endeavor to enlist the pulpit and the press in our behalf. We hope this Convention will be followed by a series of Conventions embracing every part of the country.

20 WHEREAS, The great precept of nature is conceded to be, that "man shall pursue his own true and substantial happiness." Blackstone in his Commentaries remarks, that this law of Nature being coeval with mankind, and dictated by God himself, is of course superior in obligation to any other. It is binding over all the globe, in all countries and at all times; no human laws are of any validity if contrary to this, and such of them as are valid, derive all their force, and all their validity, and all their authority, mediately and immediately, from this original; therefore,

Resolved, That such laws as conflict, in any way, with the true and substantial happiness of woman, are contrary to the great precept of nature and of no validity, for this is "superior in obligation to any other."

Resolved, That all laws which prevent woman from occupying such a station in society as her conscience shall dictate, or which place her in a position inferior to that of man, are contrary to the great precept of nature, and therefore of no force or authority.

Resolved, That woman is man's equal — was intended to be so by the Creator, and the highest good of the race demands that she should be recognized as such.

Resolved, That the women of this country ought to be enlightened in regard to the laws under which they live, that they may no longer publish their degradation by declaring themselves satisfied with their present position, nor their ignorance, by asserting that they have all the rights they want.

Resolved, That inasmuch as man, while claiming for himself intellectual superiority, does accord to woman moral superiority, it is pre-eminently his duty to encourage her to speak and teach, as she has an opportunity, in all religious assemblies.

Resolved, That the same amount of virtue, delicacy, and refinement of behavior that is required of woman in the social state, should also be required of man, and the same transgressions should be visited with equal severity on both man and woman.

Resolved, That the objection of indelicacy and impropriety, which is so often brought against woman when she addresses a public audience, comes with a very ill-grace from those who encourage, by their attendance, her appearance on the stage, in the concert, or in feats of the circus.

Resolved, That woman has too long rested satisfied in the circumscribed limits which corrupt customs and a perverted application of the Scriptures have marked out for her, and that it is time she should move in the enlarged sphere which her great Creator has assigned her.

Resolved, That it is the duty of the women of this country to secure to themselves their sacred right to the elective franchise.

Resolved, That the equality of human rights results necessarily from the fact of the identity of the race in capabilities and responsibilities.

Resolved, therefore, That, being invested by the Creator with the same capabilities, and the same consciousness of responsibility for their exercise, it is demonstrably the right and duty of woman, equally with man, to promote every righteous cause by every righteous means; and especially in regard to the great subjects of morals and religion, it is self-evidently her right to participate with her brother in teaching them, both in private and in public, by writing and by speaking, by any instrumentalities proper to be used, and in any assemblies proper to be held; and this being a self-evident truth growing out of the divinely implanted principles of human nature, any custom or authority adverse to it, whether modern or wearing the hoary sanction of antiquity, is to be regarded as a self-evident falsehood, and at war with mankind.

Resolved, That the speedy success of our cause depends upon the zealous and untiring efforts of both men and women, for the overthrow of the monopoly of the pulpit, and for the securing to woman an equal participation with men in the various trades, professions, and commerce.

The Solitude of Self

by Elizabeth Cady Stanton

Elizabeth Cady Stanton (1815–1902) was an abolitionist and early leader of the women's rights movement. She served as the first president of the National American Women Suffrage Association. In 1892, she resigned from the organization, and "The Solitude of Self" was the speech she gave upon her resignation.

The point I wish plainly to bring before you on this occasion is the individuality of each human soul; our Protestant idea, the right of individual conscience and judgment; our republican idea, individual citizenship. In discussing the rights of woman, we are to consider, first, what belongs to her as an individual, in a world of her own, the arbiter of her own destiny, an imaginary Robinson Crusoe, with her woman, Friday, on a solitary island. Her rights under such circumstances are to use all her faculties for her own safety and happiness.

Secondly, if we consider her as a citizen, as a member of a great nation, she must have the same rights as all others members, according to the fundamental principles of our Government.

Thirdly, viewed as a woman, an equal factor in civilization, her rights and duties are still the same — individual happiness and development.

Fourthly, it is only the incidental relations of life, such as mother, wife, sister, daughter, which may involve some special duties and training. . . .

The strongest reason for giving woman all the opportunities 5
for higher education, for the full development of her faculties, her forces of mind and body; for giving her the most enlarged

freedom of thought and action; a complete emancipation from all forms of bondage, of custom, dependence, superstition; from all the crippling influences of fear — is the solitude and personal responsibility of her own individual life. The strongest reason why we ask for woman a voice in the government under which she lives; in the religion she is asked to believe; equality in social life, where she is the chief factor; a place in the trades and professions, where she may earn her bread, is because of her birthright to self-sovereignty; because, as an individual, she must rely on herself. No matter how much women prefer to lean, to be protected and supported, nor how much men desire to have them do so, they must make the voyage of life alone, and for safety in an emergency, they must know something of the laws of navigation. To guide our own craft, we must be captain, pilot, engineer; with chart and compass to stand at the wheel; to watch the winds and waves, and know when to take in the sail, and to read the signs in the firmament over all. It matters not whether the solitary voyager is man or woman; nature, having endowed them equally, leaves them to their own skill and judgment in the hour of danger, and, if not equal to the occasion, alike they perish.

To appreciate the importance of fitting every human soul for independent action, think for a moment of the immeasurable solitude of self. We come into the world alone, unlike all who have gone before us, we leave it alone, under circumstances peculiar to ourselves. No mortal ever has been, no mortal ever will be like the soul just launched on the sea of life. There can never again be just such a combination of prenatal influences; never again just such environments as make up the infancy, youth and manhood of this one. Nature never repeats herself, and the possibilities of one human soul will never be found in another. No one has ever found two blades of ribbon grass alike, and no one will ever find two human beings alike. Seeing, then, what must be the infinite diversity in human character, we can in a measure appreciate the loss to a nation when any class of the people is uneducated and unrepresented in the government.

We ask for the complete development of every individual, first, for his own benefit and happiness. In fitting out an army, we give each soldier his own knapsack, arms, powder, his blanket, cup, knife, fork and spoon. We provide alike for all their individual necessities; then each man bears his own burden.

Again, we ask complete individual development for the general good; for the consensus of the competent on the whole round of human interests, on all questions of national life; and here each man must bear his share of the general burden. It is sad to see how soon friendless children are left to bear their own burdens, before they can analyze their feelings; before they can even tell their joys and sorrows, they are thrown on their own resources. The great lesson that nature seems to teach us at all ages in self-dependence, self-protection, self-support. . . .

In youth our most bitter disappointments, our brightest hopes and ambitions, are known only to ourselves. Even our friendship and love we never fully share with another; there is something of every passion, in every situation, we conceal. Even so in our triumphs and our defeats. . . .

We ask no sympathy from others in the anxiety and agony 10
of a broken friendship or shattered love. When death sunders our nearest ties, alone we sit in the shadow of our affliction. Alike amid the greatest triumphs and darkest tragedies of life, we walk alone. On the divine heights of human attainment, eulogized and worshiped as a hero or saint, we stand alone. In ignorance, poverty and vice, as a pauper or criminal, alone we starve or steal; alone we suffer the sneers and rebuffs of our fellows; alone we are hunted and hounded through dark courts and alleys, in by-ways and high-ways; alone we stand in the judgment seat; alone in the prison cell we lament our crimes

and misfortunes; alone we expiate them on the gallows. In hours like these we realize the awful solitude of individual life, its pains, its penalties, its responsibilities, hours in which the youngest and most helpless are thrown on their own resources for guidance and consolation. Seeing, then, that life must ever be a march and a battle that each soldier must be equipped for his own protection, it is the height of cruelty to rob the individual of a single natural right.

To throw obstacles in the way of a complete education is like putting out the eyes; to deny the rights of property is like cutting off the hands. To refuse political equality is to rob the ostracized of all self-respect; of credit in the market place; of recompense in the world of work, of a voice in choosing those who make and administer the law, a choice in the jury before whom they are tried, and in the judge who decides their punishment. Think of . . . woman's position! Robbed of her natural rights, handicapped by law and custom at every turn, yet compelled to fight her own battles, and in the emergencies of life to fall back on herself for protection. . . .

The young wife and mother, at the head of some establishment, with a kind husband to shield her from the adverse winds of life, with wealth, fortune and position, has a certain harbor of safety, secure against the ordinary ills of life. But to manage a household, have a desirable influence in society, keep her friends and the affections of her husband, train her children and servants well, she must have rare common sense, wisdom, diplomacy, and a knowledge of human nature. To do all this, she needs the cardinal virtues and the strong points of character that the most successful statesman possesses. An uneducated woman trained to dependence, with no resources in herself, must make a failure of any position in life. But society says women do not need a knowledge of the world, the liberal training that experience in public life must give, all the advantages of collegiate education; but when for the lack of all this, the woman's happiness is wrecked, alone she bears her humiliation; and the solitude of the weak and the ignorant is indeed pitiable. In the wild chase for the prizes of life, they are ground to powder.

In age, when the pleasures of youth are passed, children grown up, married and gone, the hurry and bustle of life in a measure over, when the hands are weary of active service, when the old arm chair and the fireside are the chosen resorts, then men and women alike must fall hack on their own resources. If they cannot find companionship in books, if they have no interest in the vital questions of the hour, no interest in watching the consummation of reforms with which they might have been identified, they soon pass into their dotage. The more fully the faculties of the mind are developed and kept in use, the longer the period of vigor and active interest in all around us continues. If, from a life-long participation in public affairs, a woman feels responsible for the laws regulating our system of education, the discipline of our jails and prisons, the sanitary condition of our private homes, public buildings and thoroughfares, an interest in commerce, finance, our foreign relations, in any or all these questions, her solitude will at least be respectable, and she will not be driven to gossip or scandal for entertainment.

The chief reason for opening to every soul the doors to the whole round of human duties and pleasures is the individual development thus attained, the resources thus provided under all circumstances to mitigate the solitude that at times must come to everyone. . . .

Inasmuch, then, as woman shares equally the joys and sor- 15
rows of time and eternity, is it not the height of presumption in man to propose to represent her at the ballot box and the throne of grace, to do her voting in the state, her praying in the church, and to assume the position of high priest at the family altar?

Nothing strengthens the judgment and quickens the conscience like individual responsibility. Nothing adds such dignity to character as the recognition of one's self-sovereignty; the right to an equal place, everywhere conceded — a place earned by personal merit, not an artificial attainment by inheritance, wealth, family and position. Conceding, then, that the responsibilities of life rest equally on man and woman, that their destiny is the same, they need the same preparation for time and eternity. The talk of sheltering woman from the fierce storms of life is the sheerest mockery, for they beat on her from every point of the compass, just as they do on man, and with more fatal results, for he has been trained to protect himself, to resist, and to conquer. Such are the facts in human experience, the responsibilities of individual sovereignty. Rich and poor, intelligent and ignorant, wise and foolish, virtuous and vicious, man and woman; it is ever the same, each soul must depend wholly on itself.

Whatever the theories may be of woman's dependence on man, in the supreme moments of her life, he cannot bear her burdens. Alone she goes to the gates of death to give life to every man that is born into the world; no one can share her fears, no one can mitigate her pangs; and if her sorrow is greater than she can bear, alone she passes beyond the gates into the vast unknown.

From the mountain-tops of Judea long ago, a heavenly voice bade his disciples, "Bear ye one another's burdens"; but humanity has not yet risen to that point of self-sacrifice; and if ever so willing, how few the burdens are that one soul can bear for another! . . .

So it ever must be in the conflicting scenes of life, in the long, weary march, each one walks alone. We may have many friends, love, kindness, sympathy and charity, to smooth our pathway in everyday life, but in the tragedies and triumphs of human experience, each mortal stands alone.

But when all artificial trammels are removed, and women 20
are recognized as individuals, responsible for their own environments, thoroughly educated for all positions in life they may be called to fill; with all the resources in themselves that liberal thought and broad culture can give; guided by their own conscience and judgment, trained to self-protection, by a healthy development of the muscular system, and skill in the use of weapons and defense; and stimulated to self-support by a knowledge of the business world and the pleasure that pecuniary independence must ever give; when women are trained in this way, they will in a measure be fitted for those hours of solitude that come alike to all, whether prepared or otherwise. As in our extremity we must depend on ourselves, the dictates of wisdom point to complete individual development.

In talking of education, how shallow the argument that each class must be educated for the special work it proposes to do, and that all those faculties not needed in this special work must lie dormant and utterly wither for want of use, when, perhaps, these will be the very faculties needed in life's greatest emergencies! Some say, "Where is the use of drilling girls in the languages, the sciences, in law, medicine, theology. As wives, mothers, housekeepers, cooks, they need a different curriculum from boys who are to fill all positions. The chief cooks in our great hotels and ocean steamers are men. In our large cities, men run the bakeries; they make our bread, cake and pies. They manage the laundries; they are now considered our best milliners and dressmakers. Because some men fill these departments of usefulness, shall we regulate the curriculum in Harvard and Yale to their present necessities? If not, why this talk in our best colleges of a curriculum for girls who are crowding into the trades and professions, teachers in all our public schools, rapidly filling many lucrative and honorable positions in life?". . .

Women are already the equals of men in the whole realm of thought, in art, science, literature and government. . . . The poetry and novels of the century are theirs, and they have touched the keynote of reform, in religion, politics and social life. They fill the editor's and professor's chair, plead at the bar of justice, walk the wards of the hospital, speak from the pulpit and the platform. Such is the type of womanhood that an enlightened public sentiment welcomes today, and such the triumph of the facts of life over the false theories of the past.

Is it, then, consistent to hold the developed woman of this day within the same narrow political limits as the dame with the spinning wheel and knitting needle occupied in the past? No, no! Machinery has taken the labors of woman as well as man on its tireless shoulders; the loom and the spinning wheel are but dreams of the past; the pen, the brush, the easel, the chisel, have taken their places, while the hopes and ambitions of women are essentially changed.

We see reason sufficient in the outer conditions of human beings for individual liberty and development, but when we consider the self-dependence of every human soul, we see the need of courage, judgment and the exercise of every faculty of mind and body, strengthened and developed by use, in woman as well as man.

Whatever may be said of man's protecting power in ordinary conditions, amid all the terrible disasters by land and sea, in the supreme moments of danger, alone woman must ever meet the horrors of the situation. The Angel of Death even makes no royal pathway for her. Man's love and sympathy enter only into the sunshine of our lives. In that solemn solitude of self, that links us with the immeasurable and the eternal, each soul lives alone forever. A recent writer says: "I remember once, in crossing the Atlantic, to have gone upon the deck of the ship at midnight, when a dense black cloud enveloped the sky, and the great deep was roaring madly under the lashes of demoniac winds. My feeling was not of danger or fear (which is a base surrender of the immortal soul) but of utter desolation and loneliness; a little speck of life shut in by a tremendous darkness. . . ."

And yet, there is a solitude which each and every one of us has always carried with him, more inaccessible than the ice-cold mountains, more profound than the midnight sea; the solitude of self. Our inner being which we call ourself, no eye nor touch of man or angel has ever pierced. It is more hidden than the caves of the gnome; the sacred adytum of the oracle; the hidden chamber of Eleusinian mystery, for to it only omniscience is permitted to enter.

Such is individual life. Who, I ask you, can take, dare take on himself the rights, the duties, the responsibilities of another human soul?

Civil Disobedience

by Henry David Thoreau

Henry David Thoreau (1817–1862) was a writer and leader of the transcendentalist movement. Transcendentalists believed that all individuals' souls were connected to one another, as well as with God and nature. In 1848, Thoreau presented a lecture at the Concord Lyceum entitled "The Rights and Duties of the Individual in Relation to Government," which formed the basis for this essay.

I heartily accept the motto, "That government is best which governs least"; and I should like to see it acted up to more rapidly and systematically. Carried out, it finally amounts to this, which also I believe — "That government is best which governs not at all"; and when men are prepared for it, that will be the kind of government which they will have. Government is at best but an expedient; but most governments are usually, and all governments are sometimes, inexpedient. The objections which have been brought against a standing army, and they are many and weighty, and deserve to prevail, may also at last be brought against a standing government. The standing army is only an arm of the standing government. The government itself, which is only the mode which the people have chosen to execute their will, is equally liable to be abused and perverted before the people can act through it. Witness the present Mexican war, the work of comparatively a few individuals using the standing government as their tool; for, in the outset, the people would not have consented to this measure.

This American government — what is it but a tradition, though a recent one, endeavoring to transmit itself unimpaired to posterity, but each instant losing some of its integrity? It has not the vitality and force of a single living man; for a single man can bend it to his will. It is a sort of wooden gun to the people themselves. But it is not the less necessary for this; for the people must have some complicated machinery or other, and hear its din, to satisfy that idea of government which they have. Governments show thus how successfully men can be imposed on, even impose on themselves, for their own advantage. It is excellent, we must all allow. Yet this government never of itself furthered any enterprise, but by the alacrity with which it got out of its way. *It* does not keep the country free. *It* does not settle the West. *It* does not educate. The character inherent in the American people has done all that has been accomplished; and it would have done somewhat more, if the government had not sometimes got in its way. For government is an expedient by which men would fain succeed in letting one another alone; and, as has been said, when it is most expedient, the governed are most let alone by it. Trade and commerce, if they were not made of india-rubber, would never manage to bounce over the obstacles which legislators are continually putting in their way; and, if one were to judge these men wholly by the effects of their actions and not partly by their intentions, they would deserve to be classed and punished with those mischievous persons who put obstructions on the railroads.

But, to speak practically and as a citizen, unlike those who call themselves no-government men, I ask for, not *at once* no government, but at once a better government. Let every man make known what kind of government would command his respect, and that will be one step toward obtaining it.

After all, the practical reason why, when the power is once in the hands of the people, a majority are permitted, and for a long period continue, to rule is not because they are most likely to be in the right, nor because this seems fairest to the minority, but because they are physically the strongest. But a government in which the majority rule in all cases cannot be based on justice, even as far as men understand it. Can there not be a government in which majorities do not virtually decide right and wrong, but conscience? — in which majorities decide only those questions to which the rule of expediency is applicable? Must the citizen ever for a moment, or in the least degree, resign his conscience to the legislation? Why has every man a conscience, then? I think that we should be men first, and subjects afterward. It is not desirable to cultivate a respect for the law, so much as for the right. The only obligation which I have a right to assume is to do at any time what I think right. It is truly enough said that a corporation has no conscience; but a corporation of conscientious men is a corporation *with* a conscience. Law never made men a whit more just; and, by means of their respect for it, even the well-disposed are daily made the agents of injustice. A common and natural result of an undue respect for law is, that you may see a file of soldiers, colonel, captain, corporal, privates, powder-monkeys, and all, marching in admirable order over hill and dale to the wars, against their wills, ay, against their common sense and consciences, which makes it very steep marching indeed, and produces a palpitation of the heart. They have no doubt that it is a damnable business in which they are concerned; they are all peaceably inclined. Now, what are they? Men at all? or small movable forts and magazines, at the service of some unscrupulous man in power? Visit the Navy-Yard, and behold a marine, such a man as an American government can make, or such as it can make a man with its black arts — a mere shadow and reminiscence of humanity, a man laid out alive and standing, and already, as one may say, buried under arms with funeral accompaniments, though it may be, —

"Not a drum was heard, not a funeral note,
As his corse to the rampart we hurried;
Not a soldier discharged his farewell shot
O'er the grave where our hero we buried."

The mass of men serve the state thus, not as men mainly, 5
but as machines, with their bodies. They are the standing army, and the militia, jailers, constables, posse comitatus, etc. In most cases there is no free exercise whatever of the judgment or of the moral sense; but they put themselves on a level with wood and earth and stones; and wooden men can perhaps be manufactured that will serve the purpose as well. Such command no more respect than men of straw or a lump of dirt. They have the same sort of worth only as horses and dogs. Yet such as these even are commonly esteemed good citizens. Others — as most legislators, politicians, lawyers, ministers, and office-holders — serve the state chiefly with their heads; and, as they rarely make any moral distinctions, they are as likely to serve the devil, without *intending* it, as God. A very few — as heroes, patriots, martyrs, reformers in the great sense, and men — serve the state with their consciences also, and so necessarily resist it for the most part; and they are commonly treated as enemies by it. A wise man will only be useful as a man, and will not submit to be "clay," and "stop a hole to keep the wind away," but leave that office to his dust at least: —

"I am too high-born to be propertied,
To be a secondary at control,
Or useful serving-man and instrument
To any sovereign state throughout the world."

He who gives himself entirely to his fellow-men appears to them useless and selfish; but he who gives himself partially to them is pronounced a benefactor and philanthropist.

How does it become a man to behave toward this American government today? I answer, that he cannot without disgrace be associated with it. I cannot for an instant recognize that political organization as *my* government which is the *slave's* government also.

All men recognize the right of revolution; that is, the right to refuse allegiance to, and to resist, the government, when its tyranny or its inefficiency are great and unendurable. But almost all say that such is not the case now. But such was the case, they think, in the Revolution Of '75. If one were to tell me that this was a bad government because it taxed certain foreign commodities brought to its ports, it is most probable that I should not make an ado about it, for I can do without them. All machines have their friction; and possibly this does enough good to counterbalance the evil. At any rate, it is a great evil to make a stir about it. But when the friction comes to have its machine, and oppression and robbery are organized, I say, let us not have such a machine any longer. In other words, when a sixth of the population of a nation which has undertaken to be the refuge of liberty are slaves, and a whole country is unjustly overrun and conquered by a foreign army, and subjected to military law, I think that it is not too soon for honest men to rebel and revolutionize. What makes this duty the more urgent is the fact that the country so overrun is not our own, but ours is the invading army.

Paley, a common authority with many on moral questions, in his chapter on the "Duty of Submission to Civil Government," resolves all civil obligation into expediency; and he proceeds to say that "so long as the interest of the whole society requires it, that is, so long as the established government cannot be resisted or changed without public inconveniency, it is the will of God that the established government be obeyed, and no longer. . . . This principle being admitted, the justice of every particular case of resistance is reduced to a computation of the quantity of the danger and grievance on the one side, and of the probability and expense of redressing it on the other." Of this, he says, every man shall judge for himself. But Paley appears never to have contemplated those cases to which the rule of expediency does not apply, in which a people, as well as an individual, must do justice, cost what it may. If I have unjustly wrested a plank from a drowning man, I must restore it to him though I drown myself. This, according to Paley, would be inconvenient. But he that would save his life, in such a case, shall lose it. This people must cease to hold slaves, and to make war on Mexico, though it cost them their existence as a people.

In their practice, nations agree with Paley; but does any 10
one think that Massachusetts does exactly what is right at the present crisis?

> "A drab of state, a cloth-o'-silver slut,
> To have her train borne up,
> and her soul trail in the dirt."

Practically speaking, the opponents to a reform in Massachusetts are not a hundred thousand politicians at the South, but a hundred thousand merchants and farmers here, who are more interested in commerce and agriculture than they are in humanity, and are not prepared to do justice to the slave and to Mexico, *cost what it may.* I quarrel not with far-off foes, but with those who, near at home, cooperate with, and do the bidding of those far away, and without whom the latter would be harmless. We are accustomed to say, that the mass of men are unprepared; but improvement is slow, because the few are not materially wiser or better than the many. It is not so important that many should be as good as you, as that there be some absolute goodness somewhere; for that will leaven the whole lump. There are thousands who are in *opinion* opposed to slavery and to the war, who yet in effect do nothing to put an end to them; who, esteeming themselves children of Washington and Franklin, sit down with their hands in their pockets, and say that they know not what to do, and do nothing; who even postpone the question of freedom to the question of free trade, and quietly read the prices-current along with the latest advices from Mexico, after dinner, and, it may be, fall asleep over them both. What is the price-current of an honest man and patriot today? They hesitate, and they regret, and sometimes they petition; but they do nothing in earnest and with effect. They will wait, well disposed, for others to remedy the evil, that they may no longer have it to regret. At most, they give only a cheap vote, and a feeble countenance and God-speed, to the right, as it goes by them. There are nine hundred and ninety-nine patrons of virtue to one virtuous man. But it is easier to deal with the real possessor of a thing than with the temporary guardian of it.

All voting is a sort of gaming, like checkers or backgammon, with a slight moral tinge to it, a playing with right and wrong, with moral questions; and betting naturally accompanies it. The character of the voters is not staked. I cast my vote, perchance, as I think right; but I am not vitally concerned that that right should prevail. I am willing to leave it to the majority. Its obligation, therefore, never exceeds that of expediency. Even voting *for the right is doing* nothing for it. It is only expressing to men feebly your desire that it should prevail. A wise man will not leave the right to the mercy of chance, nor wish it to prevail through the power of the majority. There is but little virtue in the action of masses of men. When the majority shall at length vote for the abolition of slavery, it will be because they are indifferent to slavery, or because there is but little slavery left to be abolished by their vote. *They* will then be the only slaves. Only *his* vote can hasten the abolition of slavery who asserts his own freedom by his vote.

I hear of a convention to be held at Baltimore, or elsewhere, for the selection of a candidate for the Presidency, made up chiefly of editors, and men who are politicians by profession; but I think, what is it to any independent, intelligent, and respectable man what decision they may come to? Shall we not have the advantage of his wisdom and honesty, nevertheless? Can we not count upon some independent votes? Are there not many individuals in the country who do not attend conventions? But no: I find that the respectable man, so called, has immediately drifted from his position, and despairs of his country, when his country has more reason to despair of him. He forthwith adopts one of the candidates thus selected as the only *available* one, thus proving that he is himself *available* for any purposes of the demagogue. His vote is of no more worth than that of any unprincipled foreigner or hireling native, who may have been bought. O for a *man* who is a man, and, as my neighbor says, has a bone in his back which you cannot pass your hand through! Our statistics are at fault: the population has been returned too large. How many *men* are there to a square thousand miles in this country? Hardly one. Does not America offer any inducement for men to settle here? The American has dwindled into an Odd Fellow — one who may be known by the development of his organ of gregariousness, and a manifest lack of intellect and cheerful self-reliance; whose first and chief concern, on coming into the world, is to see that the almshouses are in good repair; and, before yet he has lawfully donned the virile garb, to collect a fund for the support of the widows and orphans that may be; who, in short, ventures to live only by the aid of the Mutual Insurance company, which has promised to bury him decently.

It is not a man's duty, as a matter of course, to devote himself to the eradication of any, even the most enormous, wrong; he may still properly have other concerns to engage him; but it is his duty, at least, to wash his hands of it, and, if he gives it no thought longer, not to give it practically his support. If I devote myself to other pursuits and contemplations, I must first see, at least, that I do not pursue them sitting upon another man's shoulders. I must get off him first, that he may pursue his contemplations too. See what gross inconsistency is tolerated. I have heard some of my townsmen say, "I should like to have them order me out to help put down an insurrection of the slaves, or to march to Mexico; — see if I would go"; and yet these very men have each, directly by their allegiance, and so indirectly, at least, by their money, furnished a substitute. The soldier is applauded who refuses to serve in an unjust war by those who do not refuse to sustain the unjust government which makes the war; is applauded by those whose own act and authority he disregards and sets at naught; as if the state were penitent to that degree that it differed one to scourge it while it sinned, but not to that degree that it left off sinning for a moment. Thus, under the name of Order and Civil Government, we are all made at last to pay homage to and support our own meanness. After the first blush of sin comes its indifference; and from immoral it becomes, as it were, unmoral, and not quite unnecessary to that life which we have made.

15 The broadest and most prevalent error requires the most disinterested virtue to sustain it. The slight reproach to which the virtue of patriotism is commonly liable, the noble are most likely to incur. Those who, while they disapprove of the character and measures of a government, yield to it their allegiance and support are undoubtedly its most conscientious supporters, and so frequently the most serious obstacles to reform. Some are petitioning the State to dissolve the Union, to disregard the requisitions of the President. Why do they not dissolve it themselves — the union between themselves and the State — and refuse to pay their quota into its treasury? Do not they

stand in the same relation to the State that the State does to the Union? And have not the same reasons prevented the State from resisting the Union which have prevented them from resisting the State?

How can a man be satisfied to entertain an opinion merely, and enjoy *it*? Is there any enjoyment in it, if his opinion is that he is aggrieved? If you are cheated out of a single dollar by your neighbor, you do not rest satisfied with knowing that you are cheated, or with saying that you are cheated, or even with petitioning him to pay you your due; but you take effectual steps at once to obtain the full amount, and see that you are never cheated again. Action from principle, the perception and the performance of right, changes things and relations; it is essentially revolutionary, and does not consist wholly with anything which was. It not only divides States and churches, it divides families; ay, it divides the *individual*, separating the diabolical in him from the divine.

Unjust laws exist: shall we be content to obey them, or shall we endeavor to amend them, and obey them until we have succeeded, or shall we transgress them at once? Men generally, under such a government as this, think that they ought to wait until they have persuaded the majority to alter them. They think that, if they should resist, the remedy would be worse than the evil. But it is the fault of the government itself that the remedy *is* worse than the evil. *It* makes it worse. Why is it not more apt to anticipate and provide for reform? Why does it not cherish its wise minority? Why does it cry and resist before it is hurt? Why does it not encourage its citizens to be on the alert to point out its faults, and *do* better than it would have them? Why does it always crucify Christ, and excommunicate Copernicus and Luther, and pronounce Washington and Franklin rebels?

One would think, that a deliberate and practical denial of its authority was the only offence never contemplated by government; else, why has it not assigned its definite, its suitable and proportionate, penalty? If a man who has no property refuses but once to earn nine shillings for the State, he is put in prison for a period unlimited by any law that I know, and determined only by the discretion of those who placed him there; but if he should steal ninety times nine shillings from the State, he is soon permitted to go at large again.

If the injustice is part of the necessary friction of the machine of government, let it go, let it go: perchance it will wear smooth — certainly the machine will wear out. If the injustice has a spring, or a pulley, or a rope, or a crank, exclusively for itself, then perhaps you may consider whether the remedy will not be worse than the evil; but if it is of such a nature that it requires you to be the agent of injustice to another, then, I say, break the law. Let your life be a counter-friction to stop the machine. What I have to do is to see, at any rate, that I do not lend myself to the wrong which I condemn.

As for adopting the ways which the State has provided for remedying the evil, I know not of such ways. They take too much time, and a man's life will be gone. I have other affairs to attend to. I came into this world, not chiefly to make this a good place to live in, but to live in it, be it good or bad. A man has not everything to do, but something; and because he cannot do *everything,* it is not necessary that he should do *something* wrong. It is not my business to be petitioning the Governor or the Legislature any more than it is theirs to petition me; and if they should not bear my petition, what should I do then? But in this case the State has provided no way: its very Constitution is the evil. This may seem to be harsh and stubborn and unconciliatory; but it is to treat with the utmost kindness and consideration the only spirit that can appreciate or deserves it. So is an change for the better, like birth and death, which convulse the body.

I do not hesitate to say, that those who call themselves Abolitionists should at once effectually withdraw their support, both in person and property, from the government of Massachusetts, and not wait till they constitute a majority of one, before they suffer the right to prevail through them. I think that it is enough if they have God on their side, without waiting for that other one. Moreover, any man more right than his neighbors constitutes a majority of one already.

I meet this American government, or its representative, the State government, directly, and face to face, once a year — no more — in the person of its tax-gatherer; this is the only mode in which a man situated as I am necessarily meets it; and it then says distinctly, Recognize me; and the simplest, the most effectual, and, in the present posture of affairs, the indispensablest mode of treating with it on this head, of expressing your little satisfaction with and love for it, is to deny it then. My civil neighbor, the tax-gatherer, is the very man I have to deal with — for it is, after all, with men and not with parchment that I quarrel — and he has voluntarily chosen to be an agent of the government. How shall he ever know well what he is and does as an officer of the government, or as a man, until he is obliged to consider whether he shall treat me, his neighbor, for whom he has respect, as a neighbor and well-disposed man, or as a maniac and disturber of the peace, and see if he can get over this obstruction to his neighborliness without a ruder and more impetuous thought or speech corresponding with his action. I know this well, that if one thousand, if one hundred, if ten men whom I could name — if ten honest men only — ay, if *one* HONEST man, in this State of Massachusetts, *ceasing to hold slaves*, were actually to withdraw from this co-partnership, and be locked up in the county jail therefor, it would be the abolition of slavery in America. For it matters not how small the beginning may seem to be: what is once well done is done forever. But we love better to talk about it: that we say is our mission, Reform keeps many scores of newspapers in its service, but not one man. If my esteemed neighbor, the State's ambassador, who will devote his days to the settlement of the question of human rights in the Council Chamber, instead of being threatened with the prisons of Carolina, were to sit down the prisoner of Massachusetts, that State which is so anxious to foist the sin of slavery upon her sister — though at present she can discover only an act of inhospitality to be the ground of a quarrel with her — the Legislature would not wholly waive the subject the following winter.

Under a government which imprisons any unjustly, the true place for a just man is also a prison. The proper place today, the only place which Massachusetts has provided for her freer and less desponding spirits, is in her prisons, to be put out and locked out of the State by her own act, as they have already put themselves out by their principles. It is there that the fugitive slave, and the Mexican prisoner on parole, and the Indian come to plead the wrongs of his race should find them; on that separate, but more free and honorable, ground, where the State places those who are not *with* her, but *against* her — the only house in a slave State in which a free man can abide with honor. If any think that their influence would be lost there, and their voices no longer afflict the ear of the State, that they would not be as an enemy within its walls, they do not know by how much truth is stronger than error, nor how much more eloquently and effectively he can combat injustice who has experienced a little in his own person. Cast your whole vote, not a strip of paper merely, but your whole influence. A minority is powerless while it conforms to the majority; it is not even a minority then; but it is irresistible when it clogs by its whole weight. If the alternative is to keep all just men in prison, or give up war and slavery, the State will not hesitate which to choose. If a thousand men were not to pay their tax-bills this year, that would not be a violent and bloody measure, as it would be to pay them, and enable the State to commit violence and shed innocent blood. This is, in fact, the definition of a peaceable revolution, if any such is possible. If the tax-gatherer, or any other public officer, asks me, as one has done, "But what shall I do?" my answer is, "If you really wish to do anything, resign your office." When the subject has refused allegiance, and the officer has resigned his office, then the revolution is accomplished. But even suppose blood should flow. Is there not a sort of blood shed when the conscience is wounded? Through this wound a man's real manhood and immortality flow out, and he bleeds to an everlasting death. I see this blood flowing now.

I have contemplated the imprisonment of the offender, rather than the seizure of his goods — though both will serve the same purpose — because they who assert the purest right, and consequently are most dangerous to a corrupt State, commonly have not spent much time in accumulating property. To such the State renders comparatively small service, and a slight tax is wont to appear exorbitant, particularly if they are obliged to earn it by special labor with their hands. If there were one who lived wholly without the use of money, the State itself would hesitate to demand it of him. But the rich man — not to make any invidious comparison — is always sold to the institution which makes him rich. Absolutely speaking, the more money, the less virtue; for money comes between a man and his objects, and obtains them for him; and it was certainly no great virtue to obtain it. It puts to rest many questions which he would otherwise be taxed to answer; while the only new question which it puts is the hard but superfluous one, how to spend it. Thus his moral ground is taken from under his feet. The opportunities of living are diminished in proportion as what are called the "means" are increased. The best thing a man can do for his culture when he is rich is to endeavor to carry out those schemes which he entertained when he was poor. Christ answered the Herodians according to their condition. "Show me the tribute-money," said he; — and one took a penny out of his pocket; — if you use money which has the image of Caesar on it, and which he has made current and valuable, that is, *if you are men of the State,* and gladly enjoy the advantages of Caesar's government, then pay him back some of his own when he demands it. "Render therefore to Caesar that which is Caesar's, and to God those things which are God's" — leaving them no wiser than before as to which was which; for they did not wish to know.

When I converse with the freest of my neighbors, I perceive that, whatever they may say about the magnitude and seriousness of the question, and their regard for the public tranquility, the long and the short of the matter is, that they cannot spare the protection of the existing government, and they dread the consequences to their property and families of disobedience to it. For my own part, I should not like to think that I ever rely on the protection of the State. But, if I deny the authority of the State when it presents its tax-bill, it will soon take and waste all my property, and so harass me and my children without end. This is hard. This makes it impossible for a man to live honestly, and at the same time comfortably, in outward respects. It will not be worth the while to accumulate property; that would be sure to go again. You must hire or squat somewhere, and raise but a small crop, and eat that soon. You must live within yourself, and depend upon yourself always tucked up and ready for a start, and not have many affairs. A man may grow rich in Turkey even, if he will be in all respects a good subject of the Turkish government. Confucius said: "If a state is governed by the principles of reason, poverty and misery are subjects of shame; if a state is not governed by the principles of reason, riches and honors are the subjects of shame." No: until I want the protection of Massachusetts to be extended to me in some distant Southern port, where my liberty is endangered, or until I am bent solely on building up an estate at home by peaceful enterprise, I can afford to refuse allegiance to Massachusetts, and her right to my property and life. It costs me less in every sense to incur the penalty of disobedience to the State than it would to obey. I should feel as if I were worth less in that case.

Some years ago, the State met me in behalf of the Church, and commanded me to pay a certain sum toward the support of a clergyman whose preaching my father attended, but never I myself. "Pay," it said, "or be locked up in the jail." I declined to pay. But, unfortunately, another man saw fit to pay it. I did not see why the schoolmaster should be taxed to support the priest, and not the priest the schoolmaster; for I was not the State's schoolmaster, but I supported myself by voluntary subscription. I did not see why the lyceum should not present its tax-bill, and have the State to back its demand, as well as the Church. However, at the request of the selectmen, I condescended to make some such statement as this in writing: — "Know all men by these presents, that I, Henry Thoreau, do not wish to be regarded as a member of any incorporated society which I have not joined." This I gave to the town clerk; and he has it. The State, having thus learned that I did not wish to be regarded as a member of that church, has never made a like demand on me since; though it said that it must adhere to its original presumption that time. If I had known how to name them, I should then have signed off in detail from all the societies which I never signed on to; but I did not know where to find a complete list.

I have paid no poll-tax for six years. I was put into a jail once on this account, for one night; and, as I stood considering the walls of solid stone, two or three feet thick, the door of wood and iron, a foot thick, and the iron grating which strained the light, I could not help being struck with the foolishness of that institution which treated me as if I were mere flesh and blood and bones, to be locked up. I wondered that it should have concluded at length that this was the best use it could put me to, and had never thought to avail itself of my services in some way. I saw that, if there was a wall of stone between me and my townsmen, there was a still more difficult one to climb or break through before they could get to be as free as I was. I did not for a moment feel confined, and the walls seemed a great waste of stone and mortar. I felt as if I alone of all my townsmen had paid my tax. They plainly did not know how to treat me, but behaved like persons who are underbred. In every threat and in every compliment there was a blunder; for they thought that my chief desire was to stand the other side of that stone wall. I could not but smile to see how industriously they locked the door on my meditations, which followed them out again without let or hindrance, and *they* were really all that was dangerous. As they could not reach me, they had resolved to punish my body; just as boys, if they cannot come at some person against whom they have a spite, will abuse his dog. I saw that the State was half-witted, that it was timid as a lone woman with her silver spoons, and that it did not know its friends from its foes, and I lost all my remaining respect for it, and pitied it.

Thus the State never intentionally confronts a man's sense, intellectual or moral, but only his body, his senses. It is not armed with superior wit or honesty, but with superior physical strength. I was not born to be forced. I will breathe after my own fashion. Let us see who is the strongest. What force has a multitude? They only can force me who obey a higher law than I. They force me to become like themselves. I do not hear of *men* being *forced* to have this way or that by masses of men. What sort of life were that to live? When I meet a government which says to me, "Your money or your life," why should I be in haste to give it my money? It may be in a great strait, and not know what to do: I cannot help that. It must help itself;

do as I do. It is not worth the while to snivel about it. I am not responsible for the successful working of the machinery of society. I am not the son of the engineer. I perceive that, when an acorn and a chestnut fall side by side, the one does not remain inert to make way for the other, but both obey their own laws, and spring and grow and flourish as best they can, till one, perchance, overshadows and destroys the other. If a plant cannot live according to its nature, it dies; and so a man.

The night in prison was novel and interesting enough. The prisoners in their shirt-sleeves were enjoying a chat and the evening air in the doorway, when I entered. But the jailer said, "Come, boys, it is time to lock up"; and so they dispersed, and I heard the sound of their steps returning into the hollow apartments. My room-mate was introduced to me by the jailer as "a first-rate fellow and a clever man." When the door was locked, he showed me where to hang my hat, and how he managed matters there. The rooms were whitewashed once a month; and this one, at least, was the whitest, most simply furnished, and probably the neatest apartment in the town. He naturally wanted to know where I came from, and what brought me there; and, when I had told him, I asked him in my turn how he came there, presuming him to be an honest man, of course; and, as the world goes, I believe he was. "Why," said he, "they accuse me of burning a barn; but I never did it." As near as I could discover, he had probably gone to bed in a barn when drunk, and smoked his pipe there; and so a barn was burnt. He had the reputation of being a clever man, had been there some three months waiting for his trial to come on, and would have to wait as much longer; but he was quite domesticated and contented, since he got his board for nothing, and thought that he was well treated.

He occupied one window, and I the other; and I saw that 30
if one stayed there long, his principal business would be to look

out the window. I had soon read all the tracts that were left there, and examined where former prisoners had broken out, and where a grate had been sawed off, and heard the history of the various occupants of that room; for I found that even here there was a history and a gossip which never circulated beyond the walls of the jail. Probably this is the only house in the town where verses are composed, which are afterward printed in a circular form, but not published. I was shown quite a long list of verses which were composed by some young men who had been detected in an attempt to escape, who avenged themselves by singing them.

I pumped my fellow-prisoner as dry as I could, for fear I should never see him again; but at length he showed me which was my bed, and left me to blow out the lamp.

It was like travelling into a far country, such as I had never expected to behold, to lie there for one night. It seemed to me that I never had heard the town clock strike before, nor the evening sounds of the village; for we slept with the windows open, which were inside the grating. It was to see my native village in the light of the Middle Ages, and our Concord was turned into a Rhine stream, and visions of knights and castles passed before me. They were the voices of old burghers that I heard in the streets. I was an involuntary spectator and auditor of whatever was done and said in the kitchen of the adjacent village inn — a wholly new and rare experience to me. It was a closer view of my native town. I was fairly inside of it. I never had seen its institutions before. This is one of its peculiar institutions; for it is a shire town. I began to comprehend what its inhabitants were about.

In the morning, our breakfasts were put through the hole in the door, in small oblong-square tin pans, made to fit, and holding a pint of chocolate, with brown bread, and an iron spoon. When they called for the vessels again, I was green enough to return what bread I had left; but my comrade seized it, and said that I should lay that up for lunch or dinner. Soon after he was let out to work at haying in a neighboring field, whither he went every day, and would not be back till noon; so he bade me good-day, saying that he doubted if he should see me again.

When I came out of prison — for some one interfered, and paid that tax — I did not perceive that great changes had taken place on the common, such as he observed who went in a youth and emerged a tottering and gray-headed man; and yet a change had to my eyes come over the scene — the town, and State, and country — greater than any that mere time could effect. I saw yet more distinctly the State in which I lived. I saw to what extent the people among whom I lived could be trusted as good neighbors and friends; that their friendship was for summer weather only; that they did not greatly propose to do right; that they were a distinct race from me by their prejudices and superstitions, as the Chinamen and Malays are; that in their sacrifices to humanity they ran no risks, not even to their property; that after all they were not so noble but they treated the thief as he had treated them, and hoped, by a certain outward observance and a few prayers, and by walking in a particular straight though useless path from time to time, to save their souls. This may be to judge my neighbors harshly; for I believe that many of them are not aware that they have such an institution as the jail in their village.

It was formerly the custom in our village, when a poor debtor came out of jail, for his acquaintances to salute him, looking through their fingers, which were crossed to represent the grating of a jail window, "How do ye do?" My neighbors did not thus salute me, but first looked at me, and then at one another, as if I had returned from a long journey. I was put into jail as I was going to the shoemaker's to get a shoe which was mended. When I was let out the next morning, I proceeded to finish my errand,

and, having put on my mended shoe, joined a huckleberry party, who were impatient to put themselves under my conduct; and in half an hour — for the horse was soon tackled — was in the midst of a huckleberry field, on one of our highest hills, two miles off, and then the State was nowhere to be seen.

This is the whole history of "My Prisons."

I have never declined paying the highway tax, because I am as desirous of being a good neighbor as I am of being a bad subject; and as for supporting schools, I am doing my part to educate my fellow-countrymen now. It is for no particular item in the tax-bill that I refuse to pay it. I simply wish to refuse allegiance to the State, to withdraw and stand aloof from it effectually. I do not care to trace the course of my dollar, if I could, till it buys a man or a musket to shoot one with — the dollar is innocent — but I am concerned to trace the effects of my allegiance. In fact, I quietly declare war with the State, after my fashion, though I will still make what use and get what advantage of her I can, as is usual in such cases.

If others pay the tax which is demanded of me, from a sympathy with the State, they do but what they have already done in their own case, or rather they abet injustice to a greater extent than the State requires. If they pay the tax from a mistaken interest in the individual taxed, to save his property, or prevent his going to jail, it is because they have not considered wisely how far they let their private feelings interfere with the public good.

This, then, is my position at present. But one cannot be too much on his guard in such a case, lest his action be biased by obstinacy or an undue regard for the opinions of men. Let him see that he does only what belongs to himself and to the hour.

40 I think sometimes, Why, this people mean well, they are only ignorant; they would do better if they knew how: why give

your neighbors this pain to treat you as they are not inclined to? But I think again, This is no reason why I should do as they do, or permit others to suffer much greater pain of a different kind. Again, I sometimes say to myself, When many millions of men, without heat, without ill will, without personal feeling of any kind, demand of you a few shillings only, without the possibility, such is their constitution, of retracting or altering their present demand, and without the possibility, on your side, of appeal to any other millions, why expose yourself to this overwhelming brute force? You do not resist cold and hunger, the winds and the waves, thus obstinately; you quietly submit to a thousand similar necessities. You do not put your head into the fire. But just in proportion as I regard this as not wholly a brute force, but partly a human force, and consider that I have relations to those millions as to so many millions of men, and not of mere brute or inanimate things, I see that appeal is possible, first and instantaneously, from them to the Maker of them, and, secondly, from them to themselves. But if I put my head deliberately into the fire, there is no appeal to fire or to the Maker of fire, and I have only myself to blame. If I could convince myself that I have any right to be satisfied with men as they are, and to treat them accordingly, and not according, in some respects, to my requisitions and expectations of what they and I ought to be, then, like a good Mussulman and fatalist, I should endeavor to be satisfied with things as they are, and say it is the will of God. And, above all, there is this difference between resisting this and a purely brute or natural force, that I can resist this with some effect; but I cannot expect, like Orpheus, to change the nature of the rocks and trees and beasts.

I do not wish to quarrel with any man or nation. I do not wish to split hairs, to make fine distinctions, or set myself up as better than my neighbors. I seek rather, I may say, even an excuse for conforming to the laws of the land. I am but too ready to conform to them. Indeed, I have reason to suspect myself on this head; and each year, as the tax-gatherer comes round, I find myself disposed to review the acts and position of the general and State governments, and the spirit of the people, to discover a pretext for conformity.

> "We must affect our country as our parents,
> And if at any time we alienate
> Our love or industry from doing it honor,
> We must respect effects and teach the soul
> Matter of conscience and religion,
> And not desire of rule or benefit."

I believe that the State will soon be able to take all my work of this sort out of my hands, and then I shall be no better a patriot than my fellow-countrymen. Seen from a lower point of view, the Constitution, with all its faults, is very good; the law and the courts are very respectable; even this State and this American government are, in many respects, very admirable, and rare things, to be thankful for, such as a great many have described them; but seen from a point of view a little higher, they are what I have described them; seen from a higher still, and the highest, who shall say what they are, or that they are worth looking at or thinking of at all?

However, the government does not concern me much, and I shall bestow the fewest possible thoughts on it. It is not many moments that I live under a government, even in this world. If a man is thought-free, fancy-free, imagination-free, that which *is not* never for a long time appearing *to be* to him, unwise rulers or reformers cannot fatally interrupt him.

I know that most men think differently from myself; but those whose lives are by profession devoted to the study of these or kindred subjects content me as little as any. Statesmen and legislators, standing so completely within the institution, never distinctly and nakedly behold it. They speak of moving society, but have no resting-place without it. They may be men of a certain experience and discrimination, and have no doubt invented ingenious and even useful systems, for which we sincerely thank them; but all their wit and usefulness lie within certain not very wide limits. They are wont to forget that the world is not governed by policy and expediency. Webster never goes behind government, and so cannot speak with authority about it. His words are wisdom to those legislators who contemplate no essential reform in the existing government; but for thinkers, and those who legislate for all time, he never once glances at the subject. I know of those whose serene and wise speculations on this theme would soon reveal the limits of his mind's range and hospitality. Yet, compared with the cheap professions of most reformers, and the still cheaper wisdom and eloquence of politicians in general, his are almost the only sensible and valuable words, and we thank Heaven for him. Comparatively, he is always strong, original, and, above all, practical. Still, his quality is not wisdom, but prudence. The lawyer's truth is not Truth, but consistency or a consistent expediency. Truth is always in harmony with herself, and is not concerned chiefly to reveal the justice that may consist with wrong-doing. He well deserves to be called, as he has been called, the Defender of the Constitution. There are really no blows to be given by him but defensive ones. He is not a leader, but a follower. His leaders are the men of '87 — "I have never made an effort," he says, "and never propose to make an effort; I have never countenanced an effort, and never mean to countenance an effort, to disturb the arrangement as originally made, by which the various States came into the Union." Still thinking of the sanction which the Constitution gives to slavery, he says, "Because it was a part of the original compact — let it stand." Notwithstanding his special acuteness and ability, he is unable to take a fact out of its merely political relations, and behold it as it lies absolutely to be disposed of by the intellect — what, for instance, it behooves a man to do here in America today with regard to slavery — but ventures, or is driven, to make some such desperate answer as the following, while professing to speak absolutely, and as a private man — from which what new and singular code of social duties might be inferred? "The manner," says he, "in which the governments of those States where slavery exists are to regulate it is for their own consideration, under their responsibility to their constituents, to the general laws of propriety, humanity, and justice, and to God. Associations formed elsewhere, springing from a feeling of humanity, or any other cause, have nothing whatever to do with it. They have never received any encouragement from me, and they never will."

45 They who know of no purer sources of truth, who have traced up its stream no higher, stand, and wisely stand, by the Bible and the Constitution, and drink at it there with reverence and humility; but they who behold where it comes trickling into this lake or that pool, gird up their loins once more, and continue their pilgrimage toward its fountain-head.

No man with a genius for legislation has appeared in America. They are rare in the history of the world. There are orators, politicians, and eloquent men, by the thousand; but the speaker has not yet opened his mouth to speak who is capable of settling the much-vexed questions of the day. We love eloquence for its own sake, and not for any truth which it may utter, or any heroism it may inspire. Our legislators have not yet learned the comparative value of free trade and of freedom, of union, and of rectitude, to a nation. They have no genius or talent for comparatively humble questions of taxation and finance, commerce and manufactures and agriculture. If we were left solely to the wordy wit of legislators in Congress for our guidance, uncorrected by the seasonable experience and the effectual complaints of the people, America would not long retain her rank among the nations. For eighteen hundred years, though perchance I have no right to say it, the New Testament has been written; yet where is the legislator who has wisdom and practical talent enough to avail himself of the light which it sheds on the science of legislation?

The authority of government, even such as I am willing to submit to — for I will cheerfully obey those who know and can do better than I, and in many things even those who neither know nor can do so well — is still an impure one: to be strictly just, it must have the sanction and consent of the governed. It can have no pure right over my person and property but what I concede to it. The progress from an absolute to a limited monarchy, from a limited monarchy to a democracy, is a progress toward a true respect for the individual. Even the Chinese philosopher was wise enough to regard the individual as the basis of the empire. Is a democracy, such as we know it, the last improvement possible in government? Is it not possible to take a step further towards recognizing and organizing the rights of man? There will never be a really free and enlightened State until the State comes to recognize the individual as a higher and independent power, from which all its own power and authority are derived, and treats him accordingly. I please myself with imagining a State at least which can afford to be just to all men, and to treat the individual with respect as a neighbor; which even would not think it inconsistent with its own repose if a few were to live aloof from it, not meddling with it, nor embraced by it, who fulfilled all the duties of neighbors and fellow-men. A State which bore this kind of fruit, and suffered it to drop off as fast as it ripened, would prepare the way for a still more perfect and glorious State, which also I have imagined, but not yet anywhere seen.

Simplify, Simplify

by Henry David Thoreau

Henry David Thoreau (1817–1862) was a writer and leader of the transcendentalist movement. Transcendentalists believed that all individuals' souls were connected to one another, as well as with God and nature. In 1845, Thoreau built a small cabin near Walden Pond on a piece of wilderness owned by fellow transcendentalist Ralph Waldo Emerson near Concord, Massachusetts. Thoreau's reflections and ideas during his two-year stay at the cabin are captured in his book Walden. *This excerpt comes from Chapter 2 of that book, "Where I Lived, and What I Lived For."*

I went to the woods because I wished to live deliberately, to front only the essential facts of life, and see if I could not learn what it had to teach, and not, when I came to die, discover that I had not lived. I did not wish to live what was not life, living is so dear; nor did I wish to practice resignation, unless it was quite necessary. I wanted to live deep and suck out all the marrow of life, to live so sturdily and Spartan-like as to put to rout all that was not life, to cut a broad swath and shave close, to drive life into a corner, and reduce it to its lowest terms, and, if it proved to be mean, why then to get the whole and genuine meanness of it, and publish its meanness to the world; or if it were sublime, to know it by experience, and be able to give a true account of it in my next excursion. For most men, it appears to me, are in a strange uncertainty about it, whether it is of the devil or of God, and have *somewhat hastily* concluded that it is the chief end of man here to "glorify God and enjoy him forever."

Still we live meanly, like ants; though the fable tells us that we were long ago changed into men; like pygmies we fight with cranes; it is error upon error, and clout upon clout, and our best virtue has for its occasion a superfluous and evitable wretchedness. Our life is frittered away by detail. An honest man has hardly need to count more than his ten fingers, or in extreme cases he may add his ten toes, and lump the rest. Simplicity, simplicity, simplicity! I say, let your affairs be as two or three, and not a hundred or a thousand; instead of a million count half a dozen, and keep your accounts on your thumbnail. In the midst of this chopping sea of civilized life, such are the clouds and storms and quicksands and thousand-and-one items to be allowed for, that a man has to live, if he would not founder and go to the bottom and not make his port at all, by dead reckoning, and he must be a great calculator indeed who succeeds. Simplify, simplify. Instead of three meals a day, if it be necessary eat but one; instead of a hundred dishes, five; and reduce other things in proportion. Our life is like a German Confederacy, made up of petty states, with its boundary forever fluctuating, so that even a German cannot tell you how it is bounded at any moment. The nation itself, with all its so-called internal improvements, which, by the way are all external and superficial, is just such an unwieldy and overgrown establishment, cluttered with furniture and tripped up by its own traps, ruined by luxury and heedless expense, by want of calculation and a worthy aim, as the million households in the land; and the only cure for it, as for them, is in a rigid economy, a stern and more than Spartan simplicity of life and elevation of purpose. It lives too fast. Men think that it is essential that the *Nation* have commerce, and export ice, and talk through a telegraph, and ride thirty miles an hour, without a doubt, whether *they* do or not; but whether we should live like baboons or like men, is a little uncertain. If we do not get out sleepers, and forge rails, and devote days and nights to the work, but go to tinkering upon our lives to improve *them*, who will build railroads? And if railroads are not built, how shall we get to heaven in season? But if we stay at home and mind our business, who will want railroads? We do not ride on the railroad; it rides upon us. Did you ever think what those sleepers are that underlie the railroad? Each one is a man, an Irishman, or a Yankee man. The rails are laid on them, and they are covered with sand, and the cars run smoothly over them. They are sound sleepers, I assure you. And every few years a new lot is laid down and run over; so that, if some have the pleasure of riding on a rail, others have the misfortune to be ridden upon. And when they run over a man that is walking in his sleep, a supernumerary sleeper in the wrong position, and wake him up, they suddenly stop the cars, and make a hue and cry about it, as if this were an exception. I am glad to know that it takes a gang of men for every five miles to keep the sleepers down and level in their beds as it is, for this is a sign that they may sometime get up again.

Why should we live with such hurry and waste of life? We are determined to be starved before we are hungry. Men say that a stitch in time saves nine, and so they take a thousand stitches today to save nine tomorrow. As for *work*, we haven't any of any consequence. We have the Saint Vitus' dance, and cannot possibly keep our heads still. If I should only give a few pulls at the parish bell-rope, as for a fire, that is, without setting the bell, there is hardly a man on his farm in the outskirts of Concord, notwithstanding that press of engagements which was his excuse so many times this morning, nor a boy, nor a woman, I might almost say, but would forsake all and follow that sound, not mainly to save property from the flames, but, if we will confess the truth, much more to see it burn, since burn it must, and we, be it known, did not set it on fire, — or to see it put out, and have a hand in it, if that is done as handsomely; yes, even if it were the parish church itself. Hardly a man takes a half-hour's nap after dinner, but when he wakes he holds up his head and asks, "What's the news?" as if the rest of mankind had stood his sentinels. Some give directions to be waked every half-hour, doubtless for no other purpose; and then, to pay for it, they tell what they have dreamed. After a night's sleep the news is as indispensable as the breakfast. "Pray tell me anything new that has happened to a man anywhere on this globe," — and he reads it over his coffee and rolls, that a man has had his eyes gouged out this morning on the Wachito River; never dreaming the while that he lives in the dark unfathomed mammoth cave of this world, and has but the rudiment of an eye himself.

The Tyranny of the Majority

by Alexis de Tocqueville

Alexis de Tocqueville (1805–1859) was a French aristocrat who journeyed to America on behalf of the French government with the intent of studying America's prison system in the year 1831. Tocqueville spent nine months in America, and while he did write an essay analyzing America's prisons, his most enduring work is a detailed analysis of American culture and politics titled Democracy in America. *This is an excerpt from Chapter 15 of Volume 1, "Unlimited Power Of The Majority in the United States, and Its Consequences."*

I hold it to be an impious and detestable maxim that, politically speaking, the people have a right to do anything; and yet I have asserted that all authority originates in the will of the majority. Am I, then, in contradiction with myself?

A general law, which bears the name of justice, has been made and sanctioned, not only by a majority of this or that people, but by a majority of mankind. The rights of every people are therefore confined within the limits of what is just. A nation may be considered as a jury which is empowered to represent society at large and to apply justice, which is its law. Ought such a jury, which represents society, to have more power than the society itself whose laws it executes?

When I refuse to obey an unjust law, I do not contest the right of the majority to command, but I simply appeal from the sovereignty of the people to the sovereignty of mankind. Some have not feared to assert that a people can never outstep the boundaries of justice and reason in those affairs which are peculiarly its own; and that consequently full power may be given to the majority by which it is represented. But this is the language of a slave.

A majority taken collectively is only an individual, whose opinions, and frequently whose interests, are opposed to those of another individual, who is styled a minority. If it be admitted that a man possessing absolute power may misuse that power by wronging his adversaries, why should not a majority be liable to the same reproach? Men do not change their characters by uniting with one another; nor does their patience in the presence of obstacles increase with their strength. For my own part, I cannot believe it; the power to do everything, which I should refuse to one of my equals, I will never grant to any number of them. I do not think that, for the sake of preserving liberty, it is possible to combine several principles in the same government so as really to oppose them to one another. The form of government that is usually termed mixed has always appeared to me a mere chimera. Accurately speaking, there is no such thing as a mixed government in the sense usually given to that word, because in all communities some one principle of action may be discovered which preponderates over the others. England in the last century, which has been especially cited as an example of this sort of government, was essentially an aristocratic state, although it comprised some great elements of democracy; for the laws and customs of the country were such that the aristocracy could not but preponderate in the long run and direct public affairs according to its own will. The error arose from seeing the interests of the nobles perpetually contending with those of the people, without considering the issue of the contest, which was really the important point. When a community actually has a mixed government — that is to say, when it is equally divided between adverse principles — it must either experience a revolution or fall into anarchy.

I am therefore of the opinion that social power superior 5
to all others must always be placed somewhere; but I think

that liberty is endangered when this power finds no obstacle which can retard its course and give it time to moderate its own vehemence.

Unlimited power is in itself a bad and dangerous thing. Human beings are not competent to exercise it with discretion. God alone can be omnipotent, because his wisdom and his justice are always equal to his power. There is no power on earth so worthy of honor in itself or clothed with rights so sacred that I would admit its uncontrolled and all-predominant authority. When I see that the right and the means of absolute command are conferred on any power whatever, be it called a people or a king, an aristocracy or a democracy, a monarchy or a republic, I say there is the germ of tyranny, and I seek to live elsewhere, under other laws.

In my opinion, the main evil of the present democratic institutions of the United States does not arise, as is often asserted in Europe, from their weakness, but from their irresistible strength. I am not so much alarmed at the excessive liberty which reigns in that country as at the inadequate securities which one finds there against tyranny. An individual or a party is wronged in the United States, to whom can he apply for redress? If to public opinion, public opinion constitutes the majority; if to the legislature, it represents the majority and implicitly obeys it; if to the executive power, it is appointed by the majority and serves as a passive tool in its hands. The public force consists of the majority under arms; the jury is the majority invested with the right of hearing judicial cases; and in certain states even the judges are elected by the majority. However iniquitous or absurd the measure of which you complain, you must submit to it as well as you can.

If, on the other hand, a legislative power could be so constituted as to represent the majority without necessarily being the slave of its passions, an executive so as to retain a proper share of authority, and a judiciary so as to remain independent of the other two powers, a government would be formed which would still be democratic while incurring scarcely any risk of tyranny.

I do not say that there is a frequent use of tyranny in America at the present day; but I maintain that there is no sure barrier against it, and that the causes which mitigate the government there are to be found in the circumstances and the manners of the country more than in its laws.

Ain't I a Woman?

by Sojourner Truth

Born into slavery in New York as Isabella Baumfree, Sojourner Truth (1797–1883) escaped in 1826, twenty-five years before giving this famous speech to the Akron Convention in 1851. This text is a variation of Truth's original speech, which was originally transcribed using a stereotypical Southern dialect. There is considerable controversy over the content and reception of the original speech, including over basic facts and the crowd's response. This version of the text became widely distributed during the American Civil War, and was reprinted in A History of Women's Suffrage *alongside several other essays and speeches concerning suffrage.*

Well, children, where there is so much racket, there must be something out of kilter. I think that between the niggers of the South and the women at the North, all talking about rights, the white men will be in a fix pretty soon. But what's all this here talking about?

That man over there say that women needs to be helped into carriages, lifted over ditches, and to have the best place everywhere. Nobody ever helps me into carriages, or over mud-puddles, or gives me any best place! And ain't I a woman?

Look at me! Look at my arm! I have ploughed, and planted, and gathered into barns, and no man could head me! And ain't I a woman? I could work as much and eat as much as a man-when I could get it — and bear the lash as well! And ain't I a woman? And when I cried out with my mother's grief, none but Jesus heard me. And ain't I a woman?

Then they talk about this thing in the head; what's this they call it? ["Intellect," someone whispers near.] That's right, honey.

What's that got to do with women's rights or nigger's rights? If my cup won't hold but a pint, and yours holds a quart, wouldn't you be mean not to let me have my little half-measure full?

Then that little man in black there, he says women can't have as much rights as men, because Christ wasn't a woman! Where did your Christ come from? Where did your Christ come from? From God and a woman! Men had nothing to do with Him.

If the first woman God ever made was strong enough to turn the world upside down all alone, these women together ought to be able to turn it back, and get it right side up again! And now that they are asking to do it, the men better let them! Obliged to you for hearing me, and now old Sojourner has got nothing more to say.

Corn-pone Opinions

by Mark Twain

Mark Twain (1835–1910) is the pen-name of Samuel Clemens, a well-known American author who was most famous for his novels The Adventures of Tom Sawyer *and* The Adventures of Huckleberry Finn. *"Corn-pone Opinions" was written in 1901 but not published until after Clemens's death.*

Fifty years ago, when I was a boy of fifteen and helping to inhabit a Missourian village on the banks of the Mississippi, I had a friend whose society was very dear to me because I was forbidden by my mother to partake of it. He was a gay and impudent and satirical and delightful young black man — a slave — who daily preached sermons from the top of his master's woodpile, with me for sole audience. He imitated the pulpit style of the several clergymen of the village, and did it well, and with fine passion and energy. To me he was a wonder. I believed he was the greatest orator in the United States and would some day be heard from. But it did not happen; in the distribution of rewards he was overlooked. It is the way, in this world.

He interrupted his preaching, now and then, to saw a stick of wood; but the sawing was a pretense — he did it with his mouth; exactly imitating the sound the bucksaw makes in shrieking its way through the wood. But it served its purpose; it kept his master from coming out to see how the work was getting along. I listened to the sermons from the open window of a lumber room at the back of the house. One of his texts was this:

"You tell me whar a man gits his corn pone, en I'll tell you what his 'pinions is."

I can never forget it. It was deeply impressed upon me. By my mother. Not upon my memory, but elsewhere. She had slipped in upon me while I was absorbed and not watching. The black philosopher's idea was that a man is not independent, and cannot afford views which might interfere with his bread and butter. If he would prosper, he must train with the majority; in matters of large moment, like politics and religion, he must think and feel with the bulk of his neighbors, or suffer damage in his social standing and in his business prosperities. He must restrict himself to corn-pone opinions — at least on the surface. He must get his opinions from other people; he must reason out none for himself; he must have no first-hand views.

I think Jerry was right, in the main, but I think he did not 5
go far enough:

1. It was his idea that a man conforms to the majority view of his locality by calculation and intention. This happens, but I think it is not the rule.

2. It was his idea that there is such a thing as a first-hand opinion; an original opinion; an opinion which is coldly reasoned out in a man's head, by a searching analysis of the facts involved, with the heart unconsulted, and the jury room closed against outside influences. It may be that such an opinion has been born somewhere, at some time or other, but I suppose it got away before they could catch it and stuff it and put it in the museum.

I am persuaded that a coldly-thought-out and independent verdict upon a fashion in clothes, or manners, or literature, or politics, or religion, or any other matter that is projected into the field of our notice and interest, is a most rare thing — if it has indeed ever existed.

A new thing in costume appears — the flaring hoopskirt, for example — and the passers-by are shocked, and the irreverent laugh. Six months later everybody is reconciled; the fashion has established itself; it is admired, now, and no one laughs. Public opinion resented it before, public opinion accepts it now, and is happy in it. Why? Was the resentment reasoned out? Was the acceptance reasoned out? No. The instinct that moves to conformity did the work. It is our nature to conform; it is a force which not many can successfully resist. What is its seat? The inborn requirement of self-approval. We all have to bow to that; there are no exceptions. Even the woman who refuses from first to last to wear the hoopskirt comes under that law and is its slave; she could not wear the skirt and have her own approval; and that she *must* have, she cannot help herself. But as a rule our self-approval has its source in but one place and not elsewhere — the approval of other people. A person of vast consequences can introduce any kind of novelty in dress and the general world will presently adopt it — moved to do it, in the first place, by the natural instinct to passively yield to that vague something recognized as authority, and in the second place by the human instinct to train with the multitude and have its approval. An empress introduced the hoopskirt, and we know the result. A nobody introduced the bloomer, and we know the result. If Eve should come again, in her ripe renown, and reintroduce her quaint styles — well, we know what would happen. And we should be cruelly embarrassed, along at first.

10 The hoopskirt runs its course and disappears. Nobody reasons about it. One woman abandons the fashion; her neighbor notices this and follows her lead; this influences the next woman; and so on and so on, and presently the skirt has vanished out of the world, no one knows how nor why, nor cares, for that matter. It will come again, by and by and in due course will go again.

Twenty-five years ago, in England, six or eight wine glasses stood grouped by each person's plate at a dinner party, and they were used, not left idle and empty; to-day there are but three or four in the group, and the average guest sparingly uses about two of them. We have not adopted this new fashion yet, but we shall do it presently. We shall not think it out; we shall merely conform, and let it go at that. We get our notions and habits and opinions from outside influences; we do not have to study them out.

Our table manners, and company manners, and street manners change from time to time, but the changes are not reasoned out; we merely notice and conform. We are creatures of outside influences; as a rule we do not think, we only imitate. We cannot invent standards that will stick; what we mistake for standards are only fashions, and perishable. We may continue to admire them, but we drop the use of them. We notice this in literature. Shakespeare is a standard, and fifty years ago we used to write tragedies which we couldn't tell from — from somebody else's; but we don't do it any more, now. Our prose standard, three quarters of a century ago, was ornate and diffuse; some authority or other changed it in the direction of compactness and simplicity, and conformity followed, without argument. The historical novel starts up suddenly, and sweeps the land. Everybody writes one, and the nation is glad. We had historical novels before; but nobody read them, and the rest of us conformed — without reasoning it out. We are conforming in the other way, now, because it is another case of everybody.

The outside influences are always pouring in upon us, and we are always obeying their orders and accepting their verdicts. The Smiths like the new play; the Joneses go to see it, and they copy the Smith verdict. Morals, religions, politics, get their following from surrounding influences and atmospheres, almost entirely; not from study, not from thinking. A man must and will have his own approval first of all, in each and every moment and circumstance of his life — even if he must repent of a self-approved act the moment after its commission, in order to get his self-approval *again*:

but, speaking in general terms, a man's self-approval in the large concerns of life has its source in the approval of the peoples about him, and not in a searching personal examination of the matter. Mohammedans are Mohammedans because they are born and reared among that sect, not because they have thought it out and can furnish sound reasons for being Mohammedans; we know why Catholics are Catholics; why Presbyterians are Presbyterians; why Baptists are Baptists; why Mormons are Mormons; why thieves are thieves; why monarchists are monarchists; why Republicans are Republicans and Democrats, Democrats. We know it is a matter of association and sympathy, not reasoning and examination; that hardly a man in the world has an opinion upon morals, politics, or religion which he got otherwise than through his associations and sympathies. Broadly speaking, there are none but corn-pone opinions. And broadly speaking, corn-pone stands for self-approval. Self-approval is acquired mainly from the approval of other people. The result is conformity. Sometimes conformity has a sordid business interest — the bread-and-butter interest — but not in most cases, I think. I think that in the majority of cases it is unconscious and not calculated; that it is born of the human being's natural yearning to stand well with his fellows and have their inspiring approval and praise — a yearning which is commonly so strong and so insistent that it cannot be effectually resisted, and must have its way.

A political emergency brings out the corn-pone opinion in fine force in its two chief varieties — the pocketbook variety, which has its origin in self-interest, and the bigger variety, the sentimental variety — the one which can't bear to be outside the pale; can't bear to be in disfavor; can't endure the averted face and the cold shoulder; wants to stand well with his friends, wants to be smiled upon, wants to be welcome, wants to hear the precious words, "*He's* on the right track!" Uttered, perhaps by an ass, but still an ass of high degree, an ass whose approval is gold and diamonds to a smaller ass, and confers glory and honor and happiness and membership in the herd. For these gauds many a man will dump his life-long principles into the street, and his conscience along with them. We have seen it happen. In some millions of instances.

Men think they think upon great political questions, and they do; but they think with their party, not independently; they read its literature, but not that of the other side; they arrive at convictions, but they are drawn from a partial view of the matter in hand and are of no particular value. They swarm with their party, they feel with their party, they are happy in their party's approval; and where the party leads they will follow, whether for right and honor, or through blood and dirt and a mush of mutilated morals.

In our late canvass half of the nation passionately believed that in silver lay salvation, the other half as passionately believed that that way lay destruction. Do you believe that a tenth part of the people, on either side, had any rational excuse for having an opinion about the matter at all? I studied that mighty question to the bottom — came out empty. Half of our people passionately believe in high tariff, the other half believe otherwise. Does this mean study and examination, or only feeling? The latter, I think. I have deeply studied that question, too — and didn't arrive. We all do no end of feeling, and we mistake it for thinking. And out of it we get an aggregation which we consider a boon. Its name is Public Opinion. It is held in reverence. It settles everything. Some think it the Voice of God.

Outlaw

by Jose Antonio Vargas

Jose Antonio Vargas (b. 1981) is founder and CEO of #EmergingUS and Define American. He is a journalist, filmmaker, and immigrant rights activist. "Outlaw" was originally published in The New York Times Magazine *in 2011.*

One August morning nearly two decades ago, my mother woke me and put me in a cab. She handed me a jacket. "*Baka malamig doon*" were among the few words she said. ("It might be cold there.") When I arrived at the Philippines' Ninoy Aquino International Airport with her, my aunt, and a family friend, I was introduced to a man I'd never seen. They told me he was my uncle. He held my hand as I boarded an airplane for the first time. It was 1993, and I was twelve.

My mother wanted to give me a better life, so she sent me thousands of miles away to live with her parents in America — my grandfather (*Lolo* in Tagalog) and grandmother (*Lola*). After I arrived in Mountain View, California, in the San Francisco Bay Area, I entered sixth grade and quickly grew to love my new home, family, and culture. I discovered a passion for language, though it was hard to learn the difference between formal English and American slang. One of my early memories is of a freckled kid in middle school asking me, "What's up?" I replied, "The sky," and he and a couple of other kids laughed. I won the eighth-grade spelling bee by memorizing words I couldn't properly pronounce. (The winning word was *indefatigable*.)

One day when I was sixteen, I rode my bike to the nearby DMV office to get my driver's permit. Some of my friends already had their licenses, so I figured it was time. But when I handed the clerk my green card as proof of U.S. residency, she flipped it around, examining it. "This is fake," she whispered. "Don't come back here again."

Confused and scared, I pedaled home and confronted Lolo. I remember him sitting in the garage, cutting coupons. I dropped my bike and ran over to him, showing him the green card. "*Peke ba ito?*" I asked in Tagalog. ("Is this fake?") My grandparents were naturalized American citizens — he worked as a security guard, she as a food server — and they had begun supporting my mother and me financially when I was three, after my father's wandering eye and inability to properly provide for us led to my parents' separation. Lolo was a proud man, and I saw the shame on his face as he told me he purchased the card, along with other fake documents, for me. "Don't show it to other people," he warned.

I decided then that I could never give anyone reason to doubt 5
I was an American. I convinced myself that if I worked enough, if I achieved enough, I would be rewarded with citizenship. I felt I could earn it.

I've tried. Over the past fourteen years, I've graduated from high school and college and built a career as a journalist, interviewing some of the most famous people in the country. On the surface, I've created a good life. I've lived the American dream.

But I am still an undocumented immigrant. And that means living a different kind of reality. It means going about my day in fear of being found out. It means rarely trusting people, even those closest to me, with who I really am. It means keeping my family photos in a shoebox rather than displaying them on shelves in my home, so friends don't ask about them. It means reluctantly, even painfully, doing things I know are wrong and unlawful. And it has meant relying on a sort of twenty-first-century underground railroad of supporters, people who took an interest in my future and took risks for me.

Last year I read about four students who walked from Miami to Washington to lobby for the DREAM Act, a nearly decade-old immigration bill that would provide a path to legal permanent residency for young people who have been educated in this country. At the risk of deportation — the Obama administration has deported almost 800,000 people in the last two years — they are speaking out. Their courage has inspired me.

There are believed to be eleven million undocumented immigrants in the United States. We're not always who you think we are. Some pick your strawberries or care for your children. Some are in high school or college. And some, it turns out, write news articles you might read. I grew up here. This is my home. Yet even though I think of myself as an American and consider America my country, my country doesn't think of me as one of its own.

10 My first challenge was the language. Though I learned English in the Philippines, I wanted to lose my accent. During high school, I spent hours at a time watching television (especially *Frasier*, *Home Improvement*, and reruns of *The Golden Girls*) and movies (from *Goodfellas* to *Anne of Green Gables*), pausing the VHS to try to copy how various characters enunciated their words. At the local library, I read magazines, books, and newspapers — anything to learn how to write better. Kathy Dewar, my high school English teacher, introduced me to journalism. From the moment I wrote my first article for the student paper, I convinced myself that having my name in print — writing in English, interviewing Americans — validated my presence here.

The debates over "illegal aliens" intensified my anxieties. In 1994, only a year after my flight from the Philippines, Governor Pete Wilson was reelected in part because of his support for Proposition 187, which prohibited undocumented immigrants from attending public school and accessing other services. (A federal court later found the law unconstitutional.) After my encounter at the DMV in 1997, I grew more aware of anti-immigrant sentiments and stereotypes: *they don't want to assimilate;*

they are a drain on society. They're not talking about me, I would tell myself. I have something to contribute.

To do that, I had to work — and for that, I needed a Social Security number. Fortunately, my grandfather had already managed to get one for me. Lolo had always taken care of everyone in the family. He and my grandmother emigrated legally in 1984 from Zambales, a province in the Philippines of rice fields and bamboo houses, following Lolo's sister, who married a Filipino American serving in the American military. She petitioned for her brother and his wife to join her. When they got here, Lolo petitioned for his two children — my mother and her younger brother — to follow them. But instead of mentioning that my mother was a married woman, he listed her as single. Legal residents can't petition for their married children. Besides, Lolo didn't care for my father. He didn't want him coming here, too.

But soon Lolo grew nervous that the immigration authorities reviewing the petition would discover my mother was married, thus derailing not only her chances of coming here but those of my uncle as well. So he withdrew her petition. After my uncle came to America legally in 1991, Lolo tried to get my mother here through a tourist visa, but she wasn't able to obtain one. That's when she decided to send me. My mother told me later that she figured she would follow me soon. She never did.

The "uncle" who brought me here turned out to be a coyote, not a relative, my grandfather later explained. Lolo scraped together enough money — I eventually learned it was $4,500, a huge sum for him — to pay him to smuggle me here under a fake name and fake passport. (I never saw the passport again after the flight and have always assumed that the coyote kept it.) After I arrived in America, Lolo obtained a new fake Filipino passport, in my real name this time, adorned with a fake student visa, in addition to the fraudulent green card.

Using the fake passport, we went to the local Social Security 15
Administration office and applied for a Social Security number

and card. It was, I remember, a quick visit. When the card came in the mail, it had my full, real name, but it also clearly stated: "Valid for work only with INS authorization."

When I began looking for work, a short time after the DMV incident, my grandfather and I took the Social Security card to Kinko's, where he covered the "INS authorization" text with a sliver of white tape. We then made photocopies of the card. At a glance, at least, the copies would look like copies of a regular, unrestricted Social Security card.

Lolo always imagined I would work the kind of low-paying jobs that undocumented people often take. (Once I married an American, he said, I would get my real papers, and everything would be fine.) But even menial jobs require documents, so he and I hoped the doctored card would work for now. The more documents I had, he said, the better.

While in high school, I worked part-time at Subway, then at the front desk of the local YMCA, then at a tennis club, until I landed an unpaid internship at the *Mountain View Voice*, my hometown newspaper. First I brought coffee and helped around the office; eventually I began covering city hall meetings and other assignments for pay.

For more than a decade of getting part-time and full-time jobs, employers have rarely asked to check my original Social Security card. When they did, I showed the photocopied version, which they accepted. Over time, I also began checking the citizenship box on my federal I-9 employment eligibility forms. (Claiming full citizenship was actually easier than declaring permanent resident "green card" status, which would have required me to provide an alien registration number.)

20 This deceit never got easier. The more I did it, the more I felt like an impostor, the more guilt I carried — and the more I worried that I would get caught. But I kept doing it. I needed to live and survive on my own, and I decided this was the way.

Mountain View High School became my second home. I was elected to represent my school at school board meetings, which gave me the chance to meet and befriend Rich Fischer, the superintendent for our school district. I joined the speech and debate team, acted in school plays, and eventually became coeditor of the *Oracle*, the student newspaper. That drew the attention of my principal, Pat Hyland. "You're at school just as much as I am," she told me. Pat and Rich would soon become mentors, and over time, almost surrogate parents for me.

After a choir rehearsal during my junior year, Jill Denny, the choir director, told me she was considering a Japan trip for our singing group. I told her I couldn't afford it, but she said we'd figure out a way. I hesitated, and then decided to tell her the truth. "It's not really the money," I remember saying. "I don't have the right passport." When she assured me we'd get the proper documents, I finally told her. "I can't get the right passport," I said. "I'm not supposed to be here."

She understood. So the choir toured Hawaii instead, with me in tow. (Mrs. Denny and I spoke a couple of months ago, and she told me she hadn't wanted to leave any student behind.)

Later that school year, my history class watched a documentary on Harvey Milk, the openly gay San Francisco city official who was assassinated. This was 1999, just six months after Matthew Shepard's body was found tied to a fence in Wyoming. During the discussion, I raised my hand and said something like: "I'm sorry Harvey Milk got killed for being gay . . . I've been meaning to say this . . . I'm gay."

I hadn't planned on coming out that morning, though I had 25
known that I was gay for several years. With that announcement, I became the only openly gay student at school, and it caused turmoil with my grandparents. Lolo kicked me out of the house for a few weeks. Though we eventually reconciled, I had disappointed him on two fronts. First, as a Catholic, he considered

homosexuality a sin and was embarrassed about having "*ang apo na bakla*" ("a grandson who is gay"). Even worse, I was making matters more difficult for myself, he said. I needed to marry an American woman in order to gain a green card.

Tough as it was, coming out about being gay seemed less daunting than coming out about my legal status. I kept my other secret mostly hidden.

While my classmates awaited their college acceptance letters, I hoped to get a full-time job at the *Mountain View Voice* after graduation. It's not that I didn't want to go to college, but I couldn't apply for state and federal financial aid. Without that, my family couldn't afford to send me.

But when I finally told Pat and Rich about my immigration "problem" — as we called it from then on — they helped me look for a solution. At first, they even wondered if one of them could adopt me and fix the situation that way, but a lawyer Rich consulted told him it wouldn't change my legal status because I was too old. Eventually they connected me to a new scholarship fund for high-potential students who were usually the first in their families to attend college. Most important, the fund was not concerned with immigration status. I was among the first recipients, with the scholarship covering tuition, lodging, books, and other expenses for my studies at San Francisco State University.

As a college freshman, I found a job working part-time at the *San Francisco Chronicle*, where I sorted mail and wrote some freelance articles. My ambition was to get a reporting job, so I embarked on a series of internships. First I landed at the *Philadelphia Daily News*, in the summer of 2001, where I covered a drive-by shooting and the wedding of the 76ers star Allen Iverson. Using those articles, I applied to the *Seattle Times* and got an internship for the following summer.

But then my lack of proper documents became a problem again. The *Times* recruiter, Pat Foote, asked all incoming interns to bring certain paperwork on their first day: a birth certificate, or a passport, or a driver's license plus an original Social Security card. I panicked, thinking my documents wouldn't pass muster. So before starting the job, I called Pat and told her about my legal status. After consulting with management, she called me back with the answer I feared: I couldn't do the internship.

This was devastating. What good was college if I couldn't then pursue the career I wanted? I decided then that if I was to succeed in a profession that is all about truth telling, I couldn't tell the truth about myself.

After this episode, Jim Strand, the venture capitalist who sponsored my scholarship, offered to pay for an immigration lawyer. Rich and I went to meet her in San Francisco's financial district.

I was hopeful. This was in early 2002, shortly after Senators Orrin Hatch, the Utah Republican, and Dick Durbin, the Illinois Democrat, introduced the DREAM Act — Development, Relief, and Education for Alien Minors. It seemed like the legislative version of what I'd told myself: if I work hard and contribute, things will work out.

But the meeting left me crushed. My only solution, the lawyer said, was to go back to the Philippines and accept a ten-year ban
before I could apply to return legally. 35

If Rich was discouraged, he hid it well. "Put this problem on a shelf," he told me. "Compartmentalize it. Keep going."

And I did. For the summer of 2003, I applied for internships across the country. Several newspapers, including the *Wall Street Journal*, the *Boston Globe*, and the *Chicago Tribune*, expressed interest. But when the *Washington Post* offered me a spot, I knew where I would go. And this time, I had no intention of acknowledging my "problem."

The *Post* internship posed a tricky obstacle: it required a driver's license. (After my close call at the California DMV, I'd never gotten one.) So I spent an afternoon at the Mountain View

Public Library, studying various states' requirements. Oregon was among the most welcoming — and it was just a few hours' drive north.

Again, my support network came through. A friend's father lived in Portland, and he allowed me to use his address as proof of residency. Pat, Rich, and Rich's longtime assistant, Mary Moore, sent letters to me at that address. Rich taught me how to do three-point turns in a parking lot, and a friend accompanied me to Portland.

The license meant everything to me — it would let me drive, fly, and work. But my grandparents worried about the Portland trip and the Washington internship. While Lola offered daily prayers so that I would not get caught, Lolo told me that I was dreaming too big, risking too much.

I was determined to pursue my ambitions. I was twenty-two, I told them, responsible for my own actions. But this was different from Lola's driving a confused teenager to Kinko's. I knew what I was doing now, and I knew it wasn't right. But what was I supposed to do?

I was paying state and federal taxes, but I was using an invalid Social Security card and writing false information on my employment forms. But that seemed better than depending on my grandparents or on Pat, Rich, and Jim — or returning to a country I barely remembered. I convinced myself all would be okay if I lived up to the qualities of a "citizen": hard work, self-reliance, love of my country.

At the DMV in Portland, I arrived with my photocopied Social Security card, my college ID, a pay stub from the *San Francisco Chronicle*, and my proof of state residence — the letters to the Portland address that my support network had sent. It worked. My license, issued in 2003, was set to expire eight years later, on my thirtieth birthday, on February 3, 2011. I had eight years to succeed professionally, and to hope that some sort of immigration reform would pass in the meantime and allow me to stay.

It seemed like all the time in the world.

My summer in Washington was exhilarating. I was intimidated to be in a major newsroom but was assigned a mentor — Peter Perl, a veteran magazine writer — to help me navigate it. A few weeks into the internship, he printed out one of my articles, about a guy who recovered a long-lost wallet, circled the first two paragraphs, and left it on my desk. "Great eye for details — awesome!" he wrote. Though I didn't know it then, Peter would become one more member of my network. 45

At the end of the summer, I returned to the *San Francisco Chronicle*. My plan was to finish school — I was now a senior — while I worked for the *Chronicle* as a reporter for the city desk. But when the *Post* beckoned again, offering me a full-time, two-year paid internship that I could start when I graduated in June 2004, it was too tempting to pass up. I moved back to Washington.

About four months into my job as a reporter for the *Post*, I began feeling increasingly paranoid, as if I had "illegal immigrant" tattooed on my forehead — and in Washington, of all places, where the debates over immigration seemed never-ending. I was so eager to prove myself that I feared I was annoying some colleagues and editors — and worried that any one of these professional journalists could discover my secret. The anxiety was nearly paralyzing. I decided I had to tell one of the higher-ups about my situation. I turned to Peter.

By this time, Peter, who still works at the *Post*, had become part of management as the paper's director of newsroom training and professional development. One afternoon in late October, we walked a couple of blocks to Lafayette Square, across from the White House. Over some twenty minutes, sitting on a bench, I told him everything: the Social Security card, the driver's license, Pat and Rich, my family.

Peter was shocked. "I understand you one hundred times better now," he said. He told me that I had done the right thing by telling him, and that it was now our shared problem. He said he didn't want to do anything about it just yet. I had just been hired, he said, and I needed to prove myself. "When you've done enough," he said, "we'll tell Don and Len together." (Don Graham is the chairman of the Washington Post Company; Leonard Downie Jr. was then the paper's executive editor.) A month later, I spent my first Thanksgiving in Washington with Peter and his family.

In the five years that followed, I did my best to "do enough." I was promoted to staff writer, reported on video game culture, wrote a series on Washington's HIV/AIDS epidemic, and covered the role of technology and social media in the 2008 presidential race. I visited the White House, where I interviewed senior aides and covered a state dinner — and gave the Secret Service the Social Security number I obtained with false documents.

I did my best to steer clear of reporting on immigration policy but couldn't always avoid it. On two occasions, I wrote about Hillary Clinton's position on driver's licenses for undocumented immigrants. I also wrote an article about Senator Mel Martinez of Florida, then the chairman of the Republican National Committee, who was defending his party's stance toward Latinos after only one Republican presidential candidate — John McCain, the coauthor of a failed immigration bill — agreed to participate in a debate sponsored by Univision, the Spanish-language network.

It was an odd sort of dance: I was trying to stand out in a highly competitive newsroom, yet I was terrified that if I stood out too much, I'd invite unwanted scrutiny. I tried to compartmentalize my fears, distract myself by reporting on the lives of other people, but there was no escaping the central conflict in my life. Maintaining a deception for so long distorts your sense of self. You start wondering who you've become, and why.

In April 2008, I was part of a *Post* team that won a Pulitzer Prize for the paper's coverage of the Virginia Tech shootings a year earlier. Lolo died a year earlier, so it was Lola who called me the day of the announcement. The first thing she said was, "*Anong mang yari hung malaman nang tao?*"

What will happen if people find out?

I couldn't say anything. After we got off the phone, I rushed to the bathroom on the fourth floor of the newsroom, sat down on the toilet, and cried. 55

In the summer of 2009, without ever having had that follow-up talk with top *Post* management, I left the paper and moved to New York to join the *Huffington Post*. I met Arianna Huffington at a Washington Press Club Foundation dinner I was covering for the *Washington Post* two years earlier, and she later recruited me to join her news site. I wanted to learn more about web publishing, and I thought the new job would provide a useful education.

Still, I was apprehensive about the move: many companies were already using E-Verify, a program set up by the Department of Homeland Security that checks if prospective employees are eligible to work, and I didn't know if my new employer was among them. But I'd been able to get jobs in other newsrooms, I figured, so I filled out the paperwork as usual and succeeded in landing on the payroll.

While I worked at the *Huffington Post*, other opportunities emerged. My HIV/AIDS series became a documentary film called *The Other City*, which opened at the Tribeca Film Festival last year and was broadcast on Showtime. I began writing for magazines and landed a dream assignment: profiling Facebook's Mark Zuckerberg for *The New Yorker*.

The more I achieved, the more scared and depressed I became. I was proud of my work, but there was always a cloud hanging over it, over me. My old eight-year deadline — the expiration of my Oregon driver's license — was approaching.

After slightly less than a year, I decided to leave the *Huffington Post*. In part, this was because I wanted to promote

the documentary and write a book about online culture — or so I told my friends. But the real reason was, after so many years of trying to be a part of the system, of focusing all my energy on my professional life, I learned that no amount of professional success would solve my problem or ease the sense of loss and displacement I felt. I lied to a friend about why I couldn't take a weekend trip to Mexico. Another time I concocted an excuse for why I couldn't go on an all-expenses-paid trip to Switzerland. I have been unwilling, for years, to be in a long-term relationship because I never wanted anyone to get too close and ask too many questions. All the while, Lola's question was stuck in my head:
60 what will happen if people find out?

Early this year, just two weeks before my thirtieth birthday, I won a small reprieve: I obtained a driver's license in the state of Washington. The license is valid until 2016. This offered me five more years of acceptable identification — but also five more years of fear, of lying to people I respect and institutions that trusted me, of running away from who I am.

I'm done running. I'm exhausted. I don't want that life anymore.

So I've decided to come forward, own up to what I've done, and tell my story to the best of my recollection. I've reached out to former bosses and employers and apologized for misleading them — a mix of humiliation and liberation coming with each disclosure. All the people mentioned in this article gave me permission to use their names. I've also talked to family and friends about my situation and am working with legal counsel to review my options. I don't know what the consequences will be of telling my story.

I do know that I am grateful to my grandparents, my Lolo and Lola, for giving me the chance for a better life. I'm also grateful to my other family — the support network I found here in America — for encouraging me to pursue my dreams.

It's been almost eighteen years since I've seen my mother. Early on, I was mad at her for putting me in this position, and then mad at myself for being angry and ungrateful. By the time I got to college, we rarely spoke by phone. It became too painful; after a while it was easier to just send money to help support her and my two half siblings. My sister, almost two years old when I left, is almost twenty now. I've never met my fourteen-year-old brother. I would love to see them.

Not long ago, I called my mother. I wanted to fill the gaps 65
in my memory about that August morning so many years ago. We had never discussed it. Part of me wanted to shove the memory aside, but to write this article and face the facts of my life, I needed more details. Did I cry? Did she? Did we kiss goodbye?

My mother told me I was excited about meeting a stewardess, about getting on a plane. She also reminded me of the one piece of advice she gave me for blending in: if anyone asked why I was coming to America, I should say I was going to Disneyland.

What Is Liberty?

by Woodrow Wilson

Woodrow Wilson (1856–1924) was the twenty-eighth President of the United States, serving from 1913 to 1921. During this time, Wilson led the United States into World War I, claiming that it was America's duty to make the world "safe for democracy." Wilson's presidency also included the emergence of the era of Prohibition and the passage of the Nineteenth Amendment, which gave women the right to vote. Wilson's book, The New Freedom, *was published in 1913. This excerpt comes from Chapter 12, "The Liberation of a People's Vital Energies."*

I have long had an image in my mind of what constitutes liberty. Suppose that I were building a great piece of powerful machinery, and suppose that I should so awkwardly and unskillfully assemble the parts of it that every time one part tried to move it would be interfered with by the others, and the whole thing would buckle up and be checked. Liberty for the several parts would consist in the best possible assembling and adjustment of them all, would it not? If you want the great piston of the engine to run with absolute freedom, give it absolutely perfect alignment and adjustment with the other parts of the machine, so that it is free, not because it is let alone or isolated, but because it has been associated most skillfully and carefully with the other parts of the great structure.

What is liberty? You say of the locomotive that it runs free. What do you mean? You mean that its parts are so assembled and adjusted that friction is reduced to a minimum, and that it has perfect adjustment. We say of a boat skimming the water with light foot, "How free she runs," when we mean, how perfectly she is adjusted to the force of the wind, how perfectly she obeys the great breath out of the heavens that fills her sails. Throw her head up into the wind and see how she will halt and stagger, how every sheet will shiver and her whole frame be shaken, how instantly she is "in irons," in the expressive phrase of the sea. She is free only when you have let her fall off again and have recovered once more her nice adjustment to the forces she must obey and cannot defy.

Human freedom consists in perfect adjustments of human interests and human activities and human energies.

Now, the adjustments necessary between individuals, between individuals and the complex institutions amidst which they live, and between those institutions and the government, are infinitely more intricate today than ever before. No doubt this is a tiresome and roundabout way of saying the thing, yet perhaps it is worthwhile to get somewhat clearly in our mind what makes all the trouble today. Life has become complex; there are many more elements, more parts, to it than ever before. And, therefore, it is harder to keep everything adjusted, — and harder to find out where the trouble lies when the machine gets out of order.

You know that one of the interesting things that Mr. 5
Jefferson said in those early days of simplicity which marked the beginnings of our government was that the best government consisted in as little governing as possible. And there is still a sense in which that is true. It is still intolerable for the government to interfere with our individual activities except where it is necessary to interfere with them in order to free them. But I feel confident that if Jefferson were living in our day he would see what we see: that the individual is caught in a great confused nexus of all sorts of complicated circumstances, and that to let him alone is to leave him helpless as against the obstacles with which he has to contend; and that, therefore, law in our day must come to the assistance of the individual.

It must come to his assistance to see that he gets fair play; that is all, but that is much. Without the watchful interference, the resolute interference, of the government, there can be no fair play between individuals and such powerful institutions as the trusts. Freedom today is something more than being let alone. The program of a government of freedom must in these days be positive, not negative merely.

The Unnatural Distinctions Established in Society

by Mary Wollstonecraft

Mary Wollstonecraft (1759–1797) was an English writer, philosopher, and advocate for women's rights. In 1792 she published her most famous work, A Vindication of the Rights of Woman, *which influenced generations of women's rights advocates. This excerpt comes from Chapter 9, "Of the Pernicious Effects Which Arise from the Unnatural Distinctions Established in Society."*

From the respect paid to property flow, as from a poisoned fountain, most of the evils and vices which render this world such a dreary scene to the contemplative mind. For it is in the most polished society that noisome reptiles and venomous serpents lurk under the rank herbage; and there is voluptuousness pampered by the still sultry air, which relaxes every good disposition before it ripens into virtue.

One class presses on another; for all are aiming to procure respect on account of their property: and property, once gained, will procure the respect due only to talents and virtue. Men neglect the duties incumbent on man, yet are treated like demi-gods; religion is also separated from morality by a ceremonial veil, yet men wonder that the world is almost, literally speaking, a den of sharpers or oppressors.

There is a homely proverb, which speaks a shrewd truth, that whoever the devil finds idle he will employ. And what but habitual idleness can hereditary wealth and titles produce? For man is so constituted that he can only attain a proper use of his faculties by exercising them, and will not exercise them unless necessity, of some kind, first set the wheels in motion. Virtue likewise can only be acquired by the discharge of relative duties; but the importance of these sacred duties will scarcely be felt by the being who is cajoled out of his humanity by the flattery of sycophants. There must be more equality established in society, or morality will never gain ground, and this virtuous equality will not rest firmly even when founded on a rock, if one half of mankind are chained to its bottom by fate, for they will be continually undermining it through ignorance or pride.

It is vain to expect virtue from women till they are, in some degree, independent of men; nay, it is vain to expect that strength of natural affection, which would make them good wives and mothers.

5 Whilst they are absolutely dependent on their husbands they will be cunning, mean, and selfish, and the men who can be gratified by the fawning fondness of spaniel-like affection, have not much delicacy, for love is not to be bought, in any sense of the words, its silken wings are instantly shriveled up when any thing beside a return in kind is sought. Yet whilst wealth enervates men; and women live, as it were, by their personal charms, how can we expect them to discharge those ennobling duties which equally require exertion and self-denial? Hereditary property sophisticates the mind, and the unfortunate victims to it, if I may so express myself, swathed from their birth, seldom exert the locomotive faculty of body or mind; and, thus viewing every thing through one medium, and that a false one, they are unable to discern in what true merit and happiness consist. False, indeed, must be the light when the drapery of situation hides the man, and makes him stalk in masquerade, dragging from one scene of dissipation to another the nerveless limbs that hang with stupid listlessness, and rolling round the vacant eye which plainly tells us that there is no mind at home.

I mean, therefore, to infer that the society is not properly organized which does not compel men and women to discharge their respective duties, by making it the only way to acquire that countenance from their fellow-creatures, which every human being wishes some way to attain. The respect, consequently, which is paid to wealth and mere personal charms, is a true northeast blast, that blights the tender blossoms of affection and virtue. Nature has wisely attached affections to duties, to sweeten toil, and to give that vigor to the exertions of reason which only the heart can give. But, the affection which is put on merely because it is the appropriated insignia of a certain character, when its duties are not fulfilled, is one of the empty compliments which vice and folly are obliged to pay to virtue and the real nature of things.

To illustrate my opinion, I need only observe, that when a woman is admired for her beauty, and suffers herself to be so far intoxicated by the admiration she receives, as to neglect to discharge the indispensable duty of a mother, she sins against herself by neglecting to cultivate an affection that would equally tend to make her useful and happy. True happiness, I mean all the contentment, and virtuous satisfaction, that can be snatched in this imperfect state, must arise from well regulated affections; and an affection includes a duty. Men are not aware of the misery they cause, and the vicious weakness they cherish, by only inciting women to render themselves pleasing; they do not consider that they thus make natural and artificial duties clash, by sacrificing the comfort and respectability of a woman's life to voluptuous notions of beauty, when in nature they all harmonize. . . .

Women are, in common with men, rendered weak and luxurious by the relaxing pleasures which wealth procures; but added to this they are made slaves to their persons, and must render them alluring that man may lend them his reason to guide their tottering steps aright. Or should they be ambitious, they must govern their tyrants by sinister tricks, for without rights there cannot be any incumbent duties. The laws respecting woman, which I mean to discuss in a future part, make an absurd unit of a man and his wife; and then, by the easy transition of only considering him as responsible, she is reduced to a mere cypher.

The being who discharges the duties of its station is independent; and, speaking of women at large, their first duty is to themselves as rational creatures, and the next, in point of importance, as citizens, is that, which includes so many, of a mother. The rank in life which dispenses with their fulfilling this duty, necessarily degrades them by making them mere dolls. Or, should they turn to something more important than merely fitting drapery upon a smooth block, their minds are only occupied by some soft platonic attachment; or, the actual management of an intrigue may keep their thoughts in motion; for when they neglect domestic duties, they have it not in their power to take the field and march and counter-march like soldiers, or wrangle in the senate to keep their faculties from rusting. . . .

10 But, to render her really virtuous and useful, she must not, if she discharge her civil duties, want, individually, the protection of civil laws; she must not be dependent on her husband's bounty for her subsistence during his life, or support after his death — for how can a being be generous who has nothing of its own? or, virtuous, who is not free? The wife, in the present state of things, who is faithful to her husband, and neither suckles nor educates her children, scarcely deserves the name of a wife, and has no right to that of a citizen. But take away natural rights, and there is of course an end of duties. . . .

In the superior ranks of life, every duty is done by deputies, as if duties could ever be waived, and the vain pleasures which consequent idleness forces the rich to pursue, appear so enticing to the next rank, that the numerous scramblers for wealth sacrifice every thing to tread on their heels. The most sacred trusts are then considered as sinecures, because they were procured by interest, and only sought to enable a man to keep good company. Women, in particular, all want to be ladies. Which is simply to have nothing to do, but listlessly to go they scarcely care where, for they cannot tell what.

But what have women to do in society, I may be asked, but to loiter with easy grace? Surely you would not condemn them all to suckle fools and chronicle small beer! No. Women might certainly study the art of healing, and be physicians as well as nurses. And midwifery, decency seems to allot to them, though I am afraid the word midwife, in our dictionaries, will soon give place to accoucheur, and one proof of the former delicacy of the sex be effaced from the language.

They might, also, study politics, and settle their benevolence on the broadest basis; for the reading of history will scarcely be more useful than the perusal of romances, if read as mere biography; if the character of the times, the political improvements, arts, etc. be not observed. In short, if it be not considered as the history of man; and not of particular men, who filled a niche in the temple of fame, and dropped into the black rolling stream of time, that silently sweeps all before it, into the shapeless void called eternity. For shape, can it be called, "that shape hath none?"

Business of various kinds, they might likewise pursue, if they were educated in a more orderly manner, which might save many from common and legal prostitution. Women would not then marry for a support, as men accept of places under government, and neglect the implied duties; nor would an attempt to earn their own subsistence, a most laudable one! Sink them almost to the level of those poor abandoned creatures who live by prostitution. For are not milliners and mantua-makers reckoned the next class? The few employments open to women, so far from being liberal, are menial; and when a superior education enables them to take charge of the education of children as governesses, they are not treated like the tutors of sons, though even clerical tutors are not always treated in a manner calculated to render them respectable in the eyes of their pupils, to say nothing of the private comfort of the individual. But as women educated like gentlewomen, are never designed for the humiliating situation which necessity sometimes forces them to fill; these situations are considered in the light of a degradation; and they know little of the human heart, who need to be told, that nothing so painfully sharpens the sensibility as such a fall in life.

Some of these women might be restrained from marrying by a proper spirit of delicacy, and others may not have had it in their power to escape in this pitiful way from servitude; is not that government then very defective, and very unmindful of the happiness of one half of its members, that does not provide for honest, independent women, by encouraging them to fill respectable stations? But in order to render their private virtue a public benefit, they must have a civil existence in the state, married or single; else we shall continually see some worthy woman, whose sensibility has been rendered painfully acute by undeserved contempt, droop like "the lily broken down by a plow-share."

It is a melancholy truth; yet such is the blessed effect of civilization! the most respectable women are the most oppressed; and, unless they have understandings far superior to the common run of understandings, taking in both sexes, they must, from being treated like contemptible beings, become contemptible. How many women thus waste life away the prey of discontent, who might have practiced as physicians, regulated a farm, managed a shop, and stood erect, supported by their own industry, instead of hanging their heads surcharged with the dew of sensibility, that consumes the beauty to which it at first gave luster; nay, I doubt whether pity and love are so near akin as poets feign, for I have seldom seen much compassion excited by the helplessness of females, unless they were fair; then, perhaps, pity was the soft handmaid of love, or the harbinger of lust.

How much more respectable is the woman who earns her own bread by fulfilling any duty, than the most accomplished beauty! — beauty did I say! — so sensible am I of the beauty of moral loveliness, or the harmonious propriety that attunes the passions of a well-regulated mind, that I blush at making the comparison; yet I sigh to think how few women aim at attaining this respectability by withdrawing from the giddy whirl of pleasure, or the indolent calm that stupefies the good sort of women it sucks in.

Proud of their weakness, however, they must always be protected, guarded from care, and all the rough toils that dignify the mind. If this be the fiat of fate, if they will make themselves insignificant and contemptible, sweetly to waste "life away let them not expect to be valued when their beauty fades, for it is the fate of the fairest flowers to be admired and pulled to pieces by the careless hand that plucked them. In how many ways do I wish, from the purest benevolence, to impress this truth on my sex; yet I fear that they will not listen to a truth that dear bought experience has brought home to many an agitated bosom, nor willingly resign the privileges of rank and sex for the privileges of humanity, to which those have no claim who do not discharge its duties.

Those writers are particularly useful, in my opinion, who make man feel for man, independent of the station he fills, or the drapery of factitious sentiments. I then would fain convince reasonable men of the importance of some of my remarks, and prevail on them to weigh dispassionately the whole tenor of my observations. I appeal to their understandings; and, as a fellow-creature, claim, in the name of my sex, some interest in their hearts. I entreat them to assist to emancipate their companion, to make her a help meet for them!

Would men but generously snap our chains, and be content with rational fellowship instead of slavish obedience, they would find us more observant daughters, more affectionate sisters, more faithful wives, more reasonable mothers — in a word, better citizens. We should then love them with true affection, because we should learn to respect ourselves; and the peace of mind of a worthy man would not be interrupted by the idle vanity of his wife, nor the babes sent to nestle in a strange bosom, having never found a home in their mother's.

Text Acknowledgments

The Bill of Rights
This text comes from the United States Archives (www.archives.gov). This document is in the public domain because it is a work of the United States government.

Clarence Darrow, "Crime and Criminals"
From the 1919 edition of *Crime and Criminals: An Address to the Prisoners in the Chicago County Jail* (Chicago: Charles H. Kerr & Company). This text is in the public domain because it was published before 1923.

Frederick Douglass, "Learning to Read and Write"
From the 1845 edition of *Narrative of the Life of Frederick Douglass, An American Slave* (Boston: The Anti-Slavery Office). This text is in the public domain because it was published before 1923.

Frederick Douglass, "What to the Slave is the Fourth of July?"
From the 1855 edition of *My Bondage and My Freedom* (New York and Auburn: Miller, Orton & Mulligan). This text is in the public domain because it was published before 1923.

W. E. B. DuBois, "Of Our Spiritual Strivings"
From the 1903 edition of *The Souls of Black Folk* (Chicago: A. C. McClurg & Co.). This text is in the public domain because it was published before 1923.

Dwight D. Eisenhower, "Farewell Address"
The transcript of this speech comes from the Dwight D. Eisenhower Presidential Library and Museum (www.eisenhower.archives.gov). The transcript of this speech is in the public domain because it is a work of the United States government.

Ralph Waldo Emerson, "Self-Reliance"
From the 1863 edition of *Essays: First Series* (Boston: Ticknor & Fields). This essay is in the public domain because it was published before 1923.

Benjamin Franklin, "On the Slave-Trade"
From the 1839 edition of *The Life and Miscellaneous Writings of Benjamin Franklin* (Edinburgh: William and Robert Chambers), with spelling and capitalization adapted to follow modern conventions. This essay is in the public domain because it was published before 1923.

Emma Goldman, "Anarchism: What It Really Stands For"
From the 1917 edition of *Anarchism and Other Essays* (New York: Mother Earth Publishing Association). This essay is in the public domain because it was published before 1923.

Florence Hartley, "Politeness"
This essay serves as the introduction to the 1860 edition of *The Ladies' Book of Etiquette and Manual of Politeness* (Boston: G. W. Cottrell). This text is in the public domain because it was published before 1923.

Patrick Henry, "Give Me Liberty, or Give Me Death"
From the 1909 edition of *Eloquent Sons of the South (Vol. 1): A Handbook of Southern Oratory* (Boston: Chapple Publishing Company), pages 4–10, edited by John Temple Graves, Clark Howell, and Walter Williams. This text is in the public domain because it was published before 1923.

Zora Neale Hurston, "How It Feels to Be Colored Me"
This essay was first published in *The World Tomorrow* in May 1928. This essay appears to be in the public domain because it was published between 1923 and 1967, and it appears that the copyright was not renewed. It is reprinted here with permission of the author's estate.

Thomas Jefferson, The Declaration of Independence of the United States of America
This text comes from the United States Archives (www.archives.gov). This document is in the public domain because it is a work of the United States government.

Helen Keller, "Strike Against War"
From the 1967 edition of *Helen Keller: Her Socialist Years* (New York: International Publishers) as transcribed by the Helen Keller Reference Archive (www.marxists.org). The transcript of this speech is in the public domain because it was published before 1923.

John F. Kennedy, "Inaugural Address"
The transcript of the speech comes from the John F. Kennedy Presidential Library and Museum (www.jfklibrary.org). The transcript of this speech is in the public domain because it is a work of the United States government.

Winona LaDuke, "Our Home on Earth"
This essay was published May 16, 2012, in *Commons Magazine* (www.onthecommons.org) and is made available for redistribution by On The Commons through a Creative Commons BY-SA 3.0 license.

Abraham Lincoln, "The Gettysburg Address"
From the 1908 edition of *The Works of Abraham Lincoln (Vol. 5): Speeches and Presidential Addresses, 1859–1865* (New York: The University Society), edited by John H. Clifford and Marion M. Miller. The transcript of this speech is in the public domain because it is a work of the United States government.

Niccolò Machiavelli, "Concerning Cruelty and Mercy, and Whether It Is Better to Be Loved than Feared"
Adapted from W. K. Marriott's 1916 translation of *The Prince* (New York, E.P. Dutton). This text is in the public domain because both it and its translation were published before 1923.

Angela Morales, "The Girls in My Town"
This essay was first published in *Southwest Review*, Vol. 97, Issue 2. From *The Girls in My Town* by Angela Morales. Copyright © 2016. University of New Mexico Press, 2016.

Barack Obama, "Remarks by the President at Howard University Commencement Ceremony"
The transcript of the speech comes from the Office of the White House Press Secretary (www.whitehouse.gov). The transcript of this speech is in the public domain because it is a work of the United States government.

Thomas Paine, "The American Crisis"
From the 1839 edition of *The Complete Works of Thomas Paine, Volume* 1 (Granville, Middletown, NJ: George H. Evans). This essay is in the public domain because it was published before 1923.

Richard Rodriguez, "Does America Still Exist?"
This essay was first published in *Harper's Magazine* in March 1984. Copyright © 1984 Richard Rodriguez. Reprinted by permission of Georges Borchardt, Inc., on behalf of the author.

Franklin Delano Roosevelt, "Four Freedoms"
The transcript of the speech comes from the Franklin Delano Roosevelt Presidential Library and Museum (www.fdrlibrary.marist.edu). The transcript of this speech is in the public domain because it is a work of the United States government.

Jean-Jacques Rousseau, "The Social Contract"
From Book 1 from the 1913 edition of *The Social Contract or Principles of Political Right* (London: J. M. Dent & Sons [Everyman's Library: 660]), translated by G. D. H. Cole. This text is in the public domain because both it and its translation were published before 1923.

Margaret Sanger, "Morality and Birth Control"
The essay was originally published in the Feb–Mar 1918 edition of *Birth Control Review* and is available through the Margaret Sanger Project (www.nyu.edu/projects/sanger). This essay is in the public domain because it was published before 1923.

Elizabeth Cady Stanton, "Declaration of Sentiments and Resolutions"
From the 1887 edition of *History of Women's Suffrage (Vol. 1): 1848–1861* (Rochester, NY: Susan B. Anthony), pages 70–11, edited by Elizabeth Cady Stanton, Susan B. Anthony, and Matilda Joslyn Gage. This text is in the public domain because it was published before 1923.

Elizabeth Cady Stanton, "The Solitude of Self"
The transcript of this speech was published in the January 23, 1892, edition of *The Woman's Journal.* The transcript of this speech is in the public domain because it was published before 1923.

Henry David Thoreau, "Civil Disobedience"
From the 1866 edition of *A Yankee in Canada: with Anti-Slavery and Reform Papers* (Boston: Ticknor and Fields). This essay is in the public domain because it was published before 1923.

Henry David Thoreau, "Simplify, Simplify"
Excepted from the 1854 edition of *Walden; or, Life in the Woods* (Boston: Ticknor and Fields). This text is in the public domain because it was published before 1923.

Alexis de Tocqueville, "The Tyranny of the Majority"
From Chapter 15 of *Democracy in America*, Vol. 1 (New York: J. & H. G. Langley, 1841), translated by Henry Reeve. This text is in the public domain because both it and its translation were published before 1923.

Sojourner Truth, "Ain't I a Woman?"
From Chapter 6 of the 1887 edition of *History of Woman Suffrage, Volume 1,* edited by Elizabeth Cady Stanton, Susan B. Anthony, and Matilda Joslyn Gage (New York: Charles Mann). This text is in the public domain because it was published before 1923.

Mark Twain, "Corn-pone Opinions"
From the 1923 edition of *Europe and Elsewhere* (New York: Harper and Brothers Publishers). This text is in the public domain because it was published before 1923 and more than 70 years after the author's death.

Jose Antonio Vargas, "Outlaw"
This essay was first published in *The New York Times Magazine,* June 26, 2011. Copyright © 2011 Jose Antonio Vargas. Reprinted by permission of the author. Jose Antonio Vargas is founder and CEO of #EmergingUS and Define American. For more info, visit EmergingUS.com and DefineAmerican.com.

Woodrow Wilson, "What Is Liberty?"
From the 1913 edition of *The New Freedom: A Call for the Emancipation of the Generous Energies of a People* (New York and Garden City: Doubleday, Page & Company). This text is in the public domain because it was published before 1923.

Mary Wollstonecraft, "The Unnatural Distinctions Established in Society"
Excerpted from Chapter 9 of the 1833 edition of *A Vindication of the Rights of Woman* (New York: Matsell). This text is in the public domain because it was published before 1923.

CPSIA information can be obtained
at www.ICGtesting.com
Printed in the USA
LVOW03s0403220817
545794LV00003B/3/P